MAN, MILIEU, AND MISSION
IN ARGENTINA

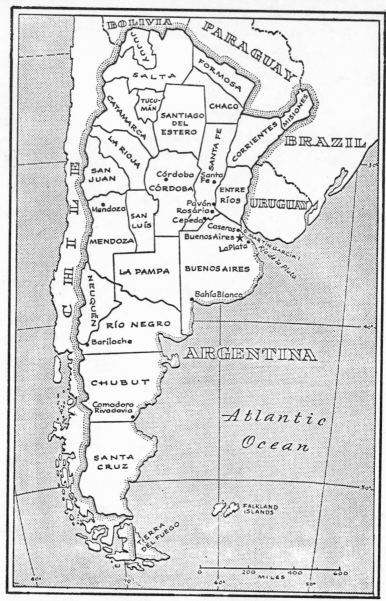

MAP OF ARGENTINA

SOURCE
Arthur P. Whitaker, ARGENTINA, © 1964. Reprinted
by permission of Prentice-Hall, Inc., Englewood
Cliffs, New Jersey

Man, Milieu, and Mission
in Argentina

A Close Look at Church Growth

by

ARNO W. ENNS

WILLIAM B. EERDMANS PUBLISHING COMPANY
GRAND RAPIDS, MICHIGAN

Foreword

One of my primary interests in the work of the Christian Church has been evangelism. For many years I was Executive Secretary of the Methodist Church in Argentina; and during the past twenty-one years, as leader of that Church, I have always stressed the need for presenting Christ to every individual. So when Rev. Enns asked me to write the Foreword to his book, I accepted gladly.

Rev. Enns' study of Argentina, of its people and of the development of the Evangelical Churches there, is a very conscientious and scholarly work, as indicated by the selected bibliography at the end of the book.

Rev. Enns is extremely fair in his analysis of the people and churches of Argentina. The synthesis he presents at the end of each study is especially valuable, for it provides a clear understanding of both the positive and negative aspects of evangelism there. His frank criticisms are always tempered by sympathetic understanding, and he shows not only the shortcomings of each church group but its positive contributions as well. His willingness to search for the reasons behind each situation, negative or positive, helps to prevent misunderstandings of the mission and to promote the maximum growth of each particular church.

The reader will find very useful information about the beginning and development of ten of the main denominations at work in Argentina. Of course much of the data is of relative value and indicates only the general trends of the churches. Then, too, there are other aspects of the work of the churches which do not reveal themselves in numerical growth and strength. Sometimes the smallness of a denomination does not indicate a complete lack of evangelistic zeal; in fact, a small church may make a more substantial contribution to the nation than a much larger one. But signs of stagnation are always evidence of some kind of paralysis in the evangelistic passion or of unresponsiveness to the appeals of the Holy Spirit.

This book is not only an interesting historical study and analysis of the religious situation in Argentina, but a call to serious reflection about the future. There may be other points of view besides those included in this analysis, but those presented here should surely be taken seriously.

This study should be of interest both to nationals and missionaries, both to mission boards and leaders of churches. For this reason it should also be made available in Spanish, so that it may be accessible to the churches in Argentina, and especially to their leaders.

For those in the United States and other English-speaking regions, it indicates clearly what kind of missionaries are necessary to carry out the evangelistic task in such a way as to bring about a more profound knowledge of our Lord Jesus Christ. Not only must they have sound theological knowledge, but they should understand the environment in which they work and be able to accommodate themselves to it. Of course a great deal of sympathy is necessary in order to overcome the natural impulses they may bring with them as a product of the environment in which they grew up and got their training; this means that the new missionaries should come first to learn and afterwards to teach. Moreover, they should be aware that they will not as a rule go out to occupy posts of leadership, but rather secondary places, leaving the leadership in the hands of nationals, even if in some cases they are not as able as the missionaries think they should be.

The author also points out very clearly that we do not need a "theological elite," but a body of Christian workers who center all their work around the person of Jesus Christ. He stresses that above all the churches should stick to the main goal set out by Saint Paul — "to know nothing, except Jesus Christ and him crucified."

Sante Uberto Barbieri

El Palomar, Province of Buenos Aires, Argentina

Contents

Foreword		5
List of Illustrations		9
Abbreviations		10
Introduction		13
1.	The Imprint of Roman Catholicism on Argentina	19
2.	Four Centuries of Socio-Cultural Influences	37
3.	The Argentine Basic Personality	55
4.	Evangelical Beginnings in Argentina	69
5.	The Assemblies of God	76
6.	The Christian and Missionary Alliance	88
7.	The Conservative Baptists	96
8.	The Disciples of Christ	106
9.	The Lutheran Church–Missouri Synod	114
10.	The Mennonite Church	123
11.	The Methodist Church	136

12. The Plymouth Brethren   145

13. The Seventh-Day Adventists   158

14. The Southern Baptists   166

15. Church Growth Trends in Argentina   175

16. Previous Surveys of Evangelical Churches in Argentina   199

17. Factors Affecting Church Growth in Argentina   206

18. What Should Missions and Churches Do Now?   232

    Notes   241

    Bibliography   243

    Index   255

List of Illustrations

1. Map of Argentina   2
2. Growth Graph–Assemblies of God   80
3. Growth Graph–Christian and Missionary Alliance   91
4. Growth Graph–Conservative Baptists   100
5. Growth Graph–Disciples of Christ   109
6. Growth Graph–Lutheran Church–Missouri Synod   117
7. Growth Graph–Mennonite Church   130
8. Growth Graph–Methodist Church   138
9. Growth Graph–Plymouth Brethren   152
10. Growth Graph–Seventh-Day Adventists   162
11. Growth Graph–Southern Baptists   169
12. The Evangelical Church in Argentina–Statistical Summary   178
13. Comparison of Growth Graphs   180
14. Proportionate Size of Churches–Communicant Membership   182
15. Comparison of Growth Rates–Evangelical Communicants
    and National Population   184
16. Comparison of Date of Entrance and Growth Achieved   186
17. Comparative Size–Interdenominational Affiliation   189
18. Comparative Size–Theological and Ecclesiastical
    Identification   190
19. Comparative Size–Mission-Related and Latin American
    Churches   193
20. Comparative Size–Religious Temperament   195

Key to Abbreviations

BFBS	British and Foreign Bible Society
C&MA	Christian and Missionary Alliance
CGRILA	Church Growth Research in Latin America
CB	Conservative Baptist Foreign Mission Society
CN	Church of the Nazarene
DC	Disciples of Christ
IMA	Iglesia Metodista Argentina
LCA	Lutheran Church in America
LCMS	Lutheran Church–Missouri Synod
MBMC	Mennonite Board of Missions and Charities
MC	Methodist Church
MRL	Missionary Research Library
SDA	Seventh-Day Adventists
SBC	Southern Baptist Convention
SK	Svenska Kyrkan
WCH	World Christian Handbook–1968

Acknowledgments

When I started writing this book, my first, I was quite naively unaware of the crucially important role many others would play in its formation. Without their generous help it would never have been written. Their unselfish contribution to the book and to my own personal enrichment will not pass unrecognized. My hope is that those who read these pages will be equally enriched through this secondhand sharing in their generosity.

Ten years in northwestern Argentina have made me the grateful spiritual debtor of many fellow-followers of Christ and His Gospel. Each in his own unique way has helped to broaden my understanding of how the Church grows in Argentina. I wish to express my appreciation to them for this foundational contribution.

No one will read this book without recognizing that the author spent many profitable hours with Dr. Donald A. McGavran. I wish to pay broad and public tribute to the missiological legacy which he has passed on to me. Without his encouragement and guidance this book would never have appeared. Appreciation goes to the other members of the faculty of the School of World Mission and Institute of Church Growth at Fuller Theological Seminary, where this book began as a master's thesis, for many valuable insights and criticisms. I am equally grateful to the Church Growth Research in Latin America (CGRILA) team, with whom I spent many helpful hours comparing observations of the church growth scene in Latin America.

Several board secretaries and mission leaders have had the opportunity to read sections of the manuscript of particular interest to them. They have been helpful with their valuable comments and suggestions. Many with firsthand knowledge of the church scene in Argentina have unselfishly answered my queries and questionnaires.

The editorial help of Mary Gautschi, and her many suggestions for improving the style of the manuscript, is especially appreciated. Finding me rather helpless at this great distance from the center of publication, she walked the second mile and enlisted the unselfish assistance of her husband Ted to prepare my penciled graphs and charts for publication. A very special "thank you" is theirs.

Finally, the entire project would have been impossible had it not been for the countless hours spent in research and writing. This contribution of time has been the gift of the Conservative Baptist Foreign Mission Society and her supporting churches. Throughout I have felt the patient and sympathetic understanding of my fellow missionaries in Argentina.

Arno W. Enns

Tucumán, Argentina

Introduction

The *conquistadores* were slow to discover the potential economic advantages of the fertile pampas. In their passionate drive for gold and conquest, the sons of Columbus found little to attract them to the productive plains of the River Plate region, then filled only with roving bands of hostile Indian tribes. The galleons of the Spanish fleet tirelessly cut their paths through the rough waters of the Atlantic, through the Caribbean, along the shortest routes toward the heart of the Maya, Aztec and Inca empires. From there, their sturdy steeds carried them inland to victory. Their passion was conquest and their reward was gold. They knew what they were after and were beyond fatigue in securing their goal. But there was nothing to satisfy this passionate hunger for gold on the vast pampas. The genuine riches of the Plate region were hidden to eyes long conditioned to following only the glitter of gold.

A similar error is being committed by Evangelical Christian mission in Argentina today. In 1957 Bolivia had more than seven times as many ordained missionaries in proportion to the population as did Argentina. This is not too serious in light of the unusually strong Argentine leadership in the Churches. What is indeed tragic is the fact that both missionary staff and Argentine pastors are largely unaware of where the "gold" lies buried in their own cities and towns. We have comfortably settled for "fool's gold"—little growth—when Spirit-inspired application of growth-inducing principles could lead to the real treasure: grand-scale church expansion. The rich and

13

rewarding experience of generous church growth is readily available
to all who serve Christ in Argentina.

WHY THIS BOOK WAS WRITTEN

The idea for this book grew largely out of my increasing desire to
know the facts contributing to the growth of the Church in
Argentina. What factors had produced the nearly one-quarter million
communicant members of the Evangelical Churches? Why, after
more than a century of Protestant missionary effort, were there not
more?

No in-depth study of these Argentine Churches had been
conducted for twenty-five years. None whatever had been done from
the illuminating perspective of church growth principles. Such an
analysis of a Church so highly gifted with potential was long
overdue. After ten years of missionary service in Argentina, I felt
that I could identify some of the elements that had hampered—or
stimulated—growth. But I realized, too, that there were many less
obvious factors yet to be ferreted out, studied carefully and,
hopefully, shaped into an effective instrument that could be used to
advantage by all who are concerned with the future of the Church in
Argentina. These, then, were the tasks I set out to accomplish.

Argentina is a leader in the areas of leadership potential,
publishing facilities, pastoral training schools and economic resources—all of which enhance the opportunities available to the
Church today. As more realistic and therefore more effective
planning for expansion replaces outmoded, growth-inhibiting methods, the important position of the Argentine Evangelical Church will
be greatly strengthened. It is my sincere hope that this book will
contribute to the attainment of that purpose.

HOW THE SUBJECT HAS BEEN APPROACHED

Milieu and Mission

The basic premise of this book is that the cultural milieu in which
Christian mission takes place affects the patterns by which the
Church grows. No Church grows in a vacuum. Nor does church
growth take place in the artificially ideal conditions which stand
behind some wishful thinking about mission policy. To understand
the real situation we must get at the hard facts involved. Nothing
short of a complete and sympathetic appreciation of the cultural
climate will furnish an adequate and solid base for that mission

policy which aims to achieve rapid church expansion. This relationship between the cultural milieu and Christian mission is confirmed by several observers. Ignacio Vergara, S. J., who has spent years seeking to understand the Chilean Pentecostal movement, holds this position. He attributes the growth of this movement to the fact that they have worked out a cordial adaptation of their church forms to the idiosyncrasies of the ordinary people. In short, they grow because they fit.

The Premise Applied

The present study of Evangelical mission in Argentina is handled in three parts. Part I is divided into three chapters. The first two chapters develop the historical background of the Argentine personality profile which follows in Chapter III. Both the religious and the general socio-cultural influences are explained. The interdisciplinary nature of the approach and the concept of *basic personality* are treated as a part of the third chapter.

Against this background material ten denominational profiles are sketched. These ten brief profiles of mission organizations working in Argentina form the greater part of Part II. In addition a brief introductory chapter concerning mission occupation prior to 1900 is included. As a conclusion to this section, a chapter of statistical comparisons is presented. These provide the reader with a quick review of the numerical strength of the Evangelical Church in Argentina today. The denominational profiles themselves have not been written with a view to presenting a full history of each Church. Only enough historical material is presented to capture the flavor of the movement and to draw out the outstanding characteristics of each Church. Throughout the book, "church" is used in reference to a single congregation or as an adjective, whereas "Church" refers both to a denomination and to the universal Church.

Part III presents the conclusions of this church growth study. This is first accomplished against the background of previous surveys of the Argentine Church scene. Their conclusions and suggestions are analyzed in the light of subsequent developments in Argentina. The intention here is to demonstrate the need for analysis on the basis of church growth principles essential to a genuinely maturing and growing Church. Chapter XVII and XVIII form the heart of the conclusions as they present the factors, discovered or confirmed through this study, which affect church growth in Argentina.

Because of the racial and religious similarities which exist between the different areas of Latin America, these factors have a broader application. Any mission working in Latin America would be rewarded by a wise and selective application of these factors to their own scene. The final chapter, "What Should Missions and Churches Do Now?", develops practical suggestions and identifies several detractors which must be eliminated if greater church growth is to be achieved.

Part I

BACKGROUND OF ARGENTINE
CHURCH GROWTH

CHAPTER 1

The Imprint of Roman Catholicism
on Argentina

A. COLONIAL CATHOLICISM

The Evangelical Church of Argentina has not grown in a vacuum. The soil in which the Churches planted the seed of the Gospel of Christ was already sustaining a vast religious establishment. It was the product of four centuries of passionate Roman Catholic religious fervor and dedication. Spain not only occupied the land and subjugated the Indians, but through the instrumentality of thousands of priests (the vast majority of whom right up to the beginning of independence were peninsular Spaniards) deeply engraved the marks of medieval Catholicism on the Argentine mentality. Both the European settler and the subservient Indian in varying degrees reflected this image. After the restless and uncertain period of revolutionary movements, Roman Catholicism, now somewhat changed in the new situation, continued to exert a dominating religious influence over the newly independent Argentines. Both the successes and the failures of this continuing Catholic dominance exert strong influences on the growth of the Evangelical Churches.

1. Catholicism of the Conquistadores

The Catholicism which the *conquistadores* brought to the shores of the Americas was the product of centuries of formation. This observation is borne out by the almost fruitless attempt to ascertain whether Roman Catholicism is the product of the Latin mind and way of life, or if the Latin way of life and mode of thinking is the

19

mold into which primitive Christianity was poured and then solidified into what we know as the Roman Catholic Church. The problem of the origin of the combination of factors reflected in the process of formation of modern Catholicism probably will never be solved to the complete satisfaction of all. Some valuable observations, however, have been made concerning its development.

Spain of the late fifteenth and early sixteenth centuries stood in sharp contrast to the Catholic nations of the rest of Europe. She was experiencing a spirit of renovation, born of the growing sense of empire which resulted from the Spanish conquests, both abroad and against the Moors on Spanish soil itself. Furthermore, the imaginative organizing skill of Cardinal Jiménez de Cisneros (1436-1517), expressed through the Inquisition (created in Spain by royal edict in 1477), became a dominating influence for reform. The same year that Columbus landed on the western shores of the Atlantic, the last kingdom of the Moors (Granada) fell to the armies of Queen Isabella of Castile. Spain was living her *siglo de oro* (Golden Century). The Society of Jesus, founded by Ignatius Loyola in 1534, became the chief instrument in carrying resurgent Spanish religious zeal around the world. The New World, including Argentina, was just another world to conquer for Christ and the Crown. This was the religious force which shaped the world where Evangelical Christians centuries later proclaim the Christ who reshapes men in His own likeness.

The men who discovered the New World were the sons of this New Spain. Clissold (1965:52) quotes Columbus' words to the queen on witnessing the fall of Granada: "I watched the Moorish king come out to the city gates and kiss your royal hands." Clissold then proceeds to relate this Spanish victory to the victories on the horizon of the New World:

> The two great enterprises of *Reconquista* and *Conquista* were indeed intimately related. The New World was won by men whose beliefs and outlook had been forged in the epic achievement of Spain's Middle Age. The mentality of the first European settlers was thus compounded of medieval no less than renaissance traits which left their impress on the life of the colonial period (1965:53).

The settlers and clergy who came to the Americas were drunk with the heady wines of victory and bent on continuing similar and greater exploits for the Crown, no less than for themselves individually.

Such conditions were inevitably to affect greatly the development of Roman Catholicism in Argentina as well as in the entire New World. The crusading zeal of the Spanish priests led to the forceful conversion of the Indians. At least it can be said that the vast majority were baptized with no understanding of what their new faith meant beyond the very evident satisfaction of the missionaries. In most cases they continued in their pagan religious practices, especially as it concerned private family beliefs. There were voices raised in protest at the ill treatment and forceful conversion of the Indians. Bartolome de las Casas, Bishop of Chiapas in Mexico, became their champion as he persuaded the Crown to accept more peaceful means for the conversion of the Indians. But it is quite evident that even in the mind of de las Casas, Christianization was confused and equated with the pacification and Hispanicization of the hostile Indians.

2. Development of Christo-paganism

Such methods of superficial conversion led to the development of syncretistic manifestations in the Roman Catholicism of Latin America. Nida (1961a:1) calls this phenomenon "Christo-paganism" and describes it as an amalgam of Christian and pagan beliefs and practices. In another article, he points out that the Jesuit system of accommodation began centuries earlier in 601 with the instructions of Pope Gregory VII to priests attempting to convert the Britons. Quoting Peter Duignan, Nida says:

> We must refrain from destroying the temples of the idols. It is necessary only to destroy the idols, and to sprinkle holy water in these same temples, to build ourselves altars and place holy relics therein. If the construction of these temples is solid, good and useful, they will pass from the cult of demons to the service of the true God; because it will come to pass that the nation, seeing the continued existence of its old places of devotion, will be disposed, by a sort of habit to go there to adore the true God.
>
> It is said that the men of this nation are accustomed to sacrificing oxen. It is necessary that this custom be converted into a Christian rite. On the day of the dedication of the temples thus changed into churches, and similarly for the festivals of the saints, whose relics will be placed there, you should allow them, as in the past, to build structures of foliage around the same churches. They shall bring to the churches

their animals and kill them, no longer as offerings to the devil, but for Christian banquets in name and honor of God, to whom, after satiating themselves, they will give thanks. Only thus, by preserving for men some of the worldly joys, will you lead them more easily to relish the joys of the spirit (1959:111, 112).

With this principle as a guide, the current Christo-pagan manifestations found in northern Argentina are no surprise. The popular "saints" such as Juana Figueroa, Bazán Frías and Santo González, before whom hundreds of devotees burn their candles every Monday in hope of their intervention in some desperate personal or family problem, are contemporary evidence of this syncretistic tendency. Although repudiated by the hierarchy, in the popular mind this is a meaningful expression of their religion.

Another influence which contributed to the development of these syncretistic tendencies among the *mestizo* population was the mixed marriages. The early *conquistadores* took Indian women and fathered large families. The traditional Iberian separation of religion and life took a surprising turn under these circumstances. The men in most Latin cultures had always maintained strict control of the authority patterns in the family, whereas the women took the leadership in religious matters, especially in the training of the children. The Indian women were ill-equipped to teach their children the religion of the fathers. The result was a minimal Catholicism with strong syncretistic tendencies which, with subsequent generations, was somewhat attenuated by faithful catechists. But the seeds of modern Christo-paganism were already sown in the soul of the *gaucho*. This tendency toward syncretism, evident since the early colonial period, was further aggravated by the revolutionary tensions of the independence period and the consequent shortage of clergy. Today syncretistic manifestations are largely limited to marginal areas of minimal Roman Catholic Christianization. The exceptions to this are the ancient syncretistic accretions which Catholicism adopted from early Roman pagan religions. Missionaries will be well advised to distinguish between the Catholicism which is the result of this New World syncretism and the Catholicism of modern Rome. Such a clear understanding of this feature of Catholicism will greatly influence the effectiveness of the missionary in producing and stimulating church growth.[1]

3. Jesuit Settlements

In contrast to these corrupting tendencies, the Jesuits realized noble efforts to propagate their religious zeal. The *reducciones* (reservations or settlements of converted Indians), of which about thirty existed with a population of at least 100,000 Guaraní Indians, are the classic example. These were located in Paraguay and extended both north and south into Brazil and Argentina. An "empire within an empire" was built around these farming and manufacturing communities organized and managed by the followers of Loyola. As their power grew here and throughout the Spanish Empire, Charles III of Spain became wary of their intentions and banished them from Spain and all her dominions in 1767. This action left the Church weak at a time when Catholicism in the New World was about to undergo the strains of new and powerful ideas represented in the Enlightenment and manifested in the movements toward the independence of her former colonies.

4. Spanish Clerical Dominance

The unfavorable consequences of an earlier practice of Spain was to make itself felt acutely with approaching independence. The clergy were very slow to train Indian or creole (Spaniards born in America) priests to aid them in the Christianization of the indigenous peoples. This erroneous procedure grew out of their mistaken zeal to purge the Church of every infidel. Tibesar comments:

> For the inquisition in colonial Latin America was the keeper of *hispanidad*. By law, no post in the Spanish empire from town crier to viceroy could be occupied by anyone but a *cristiano viejo*. A *cristiano viejo* was a Spanish Catholic who for four generations had no Mohammedan, Jew or Indian in his ancestry, nor one condemned by the Inquisition. The Inquisition was the keeper of the genealogies. And so Philip II in his junta of 1568, impelled largely by European circumstances, had not only given his definitely Hispanic cast to the church of the Indies but by 1570 and 1571 had set the tribunal of the Inquisition to guard the door of *hispanidad*, so that, even though in matters of faith the Indian was partially

exempt from the tribunal, he could not escape its genealogies. No applicant for any office in Spanish America (Portuguese America, too, from 1580–1640) could avoid the preliminary *interrogatorio,* which included his status as a *cristiano viejo* (1966:416, 417).

This situation largely continued into the eighteenth century with. little change, when the Crown began to press for the ordination of the Indians. But the supply of native priests in Argentina and Latin America in general was never sufficient. Even today, at least 25 per cent of the diocesan clergy in Argentina are of foreign origin (Alonso 1964:184,208).

Herring summarizes the situation of the church just before independence:

> The Church remained largely Spanish to the end of the colonial period. In religious as in civil control, the kings theoretically limited appointments to those born in Spain; but there were exceptions. Some creoles were named to bishoprics after the middle of the seventeenth century, but the most and best appointments were to the Spanish-born. Slowly the priesthood was opened to the creole, and then to a few *mestizos.* Some Indian converts were given limited appoint- ments as missionaries on the frontier. The exceptions were unimportant. The Church remained a thoroughly Spanish institution in days when the great majority of the people she served were thinking of themselves as Americans (1961:186).

5. A Neglected Opportunity?

The Latin American independence revolutions followed closely on the heels of the establishment of the first Protestant missionary societies at the close of the eighteenth century. Few besides the British and Foreign Bible Society were alert to the significance of this event. It remains somewhat unclear as to whether Thomson's pleas for missionary occupation were simply naive optimism, or if they represented a genuine evangelistic opportunity. It must be admitted that the revolution did set in motion a process of liberalizing tendencies which eventually produced today's unparal- leled opportunities. One still wonders if this early period might have been one of the Evangelical Church's greatest missed opportunities for a vast people's movement to Christ in Latin America. It has taken the Anglican Church almost a century and a half to recognize the paganism and the missionary opportunity which exist in Latin America. What is tragic in the face of today's burgeoning potential for church growth is the fact that large segments of the Evangelical Church are interpreting evangelism as social involvement and revolution. At the same time, those involved in social reform are a rapidly shrinking minority of the Evangelical movement. This statistical fact will greatly and quickly attenuate their influence in bringing about the genuine, spiritually oriented social change which is so desperately needed. The growing political and social influence of Chile's "Third Force" Churches is a case in point. Will another opportunity for church growth be missed where a result of evangelism is mistaken for evangelism itself?

B. CATHOLICISM AND THE NEW REPUBLIC

This explicit identification of the religion of the colonies with Spain produced a severe crisis for the Church during the period of growing independence. In a bull of 1473, Pope Sixtus IV gave Ferdinand and Isabella the right to make ecclesiastical appointments as well as to receive all tithes in the colonies, in return for their promise to support the Church there. This was known as the right of patronage, or *patronato,* and the Spanish sovereigns guarded it jealously.

1. Patronage Backfires

With the rejection of Spain by the founders of the Argentine nation, the higher clergy, who were almost all loyal to Spain, found themselves to be *personae non gratae.* In 1812, when the politically unacceptable Spanish Bishop of Buenos Aires died, he was practically a prisoner (Considine 1964:164). The suspension of relations with Spain and consequently with the Holy See greatly affected the powers and maneuverability of the Church. For close to a quarter of a century Argentina was without a bishop (Ryan 1932:50), and the priesthood was threatened with extinction. Not until 1834 was a bishop appointed to Argentina by the Holy See which, with this gesture, began to recognize the new nation as completely independent of Spain. The right of patronage was disregarded even though it was still claimed by the new government.

Although there was this reaction against the higher foreign clergy, more than half the delegates to the Congress of Tucumán were priests and religious, but their loyalties were firmly aligned on the side of the new nation. The Congress of 1816 voted to establish relations with Rome, largely through the influence of the priests who were present. But despite this strong religious influence in the founding of the nation, secularizing tendencies inspired by the French Enlightenment began to be felt.

This process of secularization was encouraged by the brilliant Rivadavia in advocating the formation of a national Church in 1824. Some monasteries were closed, and charitable institutions were transferred from the care of the Sisters of Charity to that of La Sociedad de Beneficencia. Interpreting the actions of Rivadavia, Rómulo Cabría comments:

> Neither Rivadavia nor the clerics who assisted him in his reforms were Masons, nor was the reform, even in its advanced stages, other than the consequences of a clear regalism, executed imprudently, with a well-defined object and a clear orientation. . . . In no case was the reform a Voltarian campaign against the Church (Mecham 1966:228).

During the government of the *caudillo* Rosas, some of the privileges of the Church were restored, including the recognition of the first bishop since independence and the return of the Jesuits. His cordial relations with the Church were ended when he sought to use her to further his own purposes. It was Rosas who asserted the right of the *patronato* which the young nation considered her own now that Spain no longer exerted influence in Argentina. Mecham summarizes the situation in the words of Ingenieros:

> Rosas began by assisting ecclesiastical interests and ended by persecuting the clergy. But Bishop Medrano, it appears, was a willing, abject supporter of Rosas; he was a sort of mayor-domo (steward) to a feudal lord. "In the persons of Rosas and Medrano," says Ingenieros, "was realized the union of throne and altar" (1966:232).

2. Liberalizing Influence

A reaction came in 1853 and in the person of Alberdi. In his *Bases and Suggestions for the Political Organization of the Argentine Republic,* the framers of the Argentine constitution found their guide for the relationship between Church and State. It was the clear thinking of Alberdi who, while he felt that the Church should be supported, also advocated the doctrine of religious tolerance under the motto "Religious liberty is the means of populating the country." The legal way was paved for the increasing waves of Evangelical missionaries and Protestant immigrants. This was the period when the missions were authorized to conduct worship services in Spanish (1867) and the growing tide of immigrants included German Lutherans, Welsh Protestants and Waldensians from Italy. The constitution of 1853 provides for financial support of the Catholic Church by the State, the exercise of ecclesiastical patronage in some appointments, presidents and vice-presidents who are Roman Catholics, and for governmental scrutiny of all papal documents. This is essentially the situation today as far as the constitutional expression of the relation between the Church and the State is concerned. The practical outworkings of this have fluctuated, however, depending on whether the government happened to be of liberal or conservative tendency, and also for reasons of political expediency. Mecham states:

> The support of the cult is regarded as an obligation based upon the enjoyment of patronage. The government is required to make annual appropriations for the hierarchy, cathedral chapters, seminaries and Indian missions. The subvention is not large. The lower clergy of parochial churches and charitable institutions receive no aid from the State, but depend on fees and contributions of the faithful. Only the priests attached to cathedrals are paid salaries, and consequently are regarded as government employees.
>
> Thus, although Argentina is a Catholic country and the Catholic Church is a State establishment, one encounters there lay primary education, civil marriage, and purely municipal cemeteries (1966:244, 246, 247).

3. Catholicism since Perón

In recent years, although the Roman Catholic Church has enjoyed her traditional position of power and privilege, there have been temporary gains and setbacks, largely attributable to political winds. Perón assiduously cultivated a cordial relationship with the Church, especially in making religious instruction in the schools compulsory (1943), and consequently won the overwhelming support of the clergy in the elections of 1946. A few years later, seeing the Church as a threat to his absolutism, he decided to eliminate her opposition, especially by reducing her influence in the labor unions which he considered his own and by legalizing divorce and prostitution. This action precipitated the opposition, and Perón's government was overthrown in less than a year after these actions had been taken (Pendle 1963a:120,121).

With the modern day *caudillo,* plus the authorization to establish Catholic universities qualified to grant degrees and professional titles on a par with the secular state universities, the post-Perón Church has regained all that she lost during the days of conflict. The hierarchy was hopeful that greater advantages could be pressed in the period of relief after Perón, but these were not forthcoming except for this precedent-shattering law "placing Catholic universities on the same legal footing as state universities" (D'Antonio 1964:84,85). Among the other special desires of the hierarchy is the signing of a concordat with Rome, but this seems unlikely unless the present military government, which is extremely sympathetic to the Church, should move in this direction. Estrada, former Argentine minister to the Holy See, in arguing for a concordat gives his considered reasons why he feels Catholicism is the proper religion of Argentina:

> The present nature of the relations between the Argentine government and the church does not derive, then, from a mechanical decision of a legislator, nor is it the causal result of a mere coincidence of judicial traditions inherited from the Spanish political and social regime, but rather the inescapable consequence of our own mode of national being. This does not mean that being Argentine need be identified with being Catholic. It would be absurd to deny the existence of non-Catholic Argentines, and unjust to make them inferior Argentines. But, beyond any individual consideration, we are forced to recognize the deep-rooted permanence of Catholicism in the habits, ways and social and political customs, shared in even by persons who are outside the Church (1963:55, 56).

Even in this impassioned pro-Catholic reasoning, it is clearly evident that the idea of a pluralistic society is unavoidable in Argentina. Present-day Evangelicals enjoy the fullest liberty in the free exercise of their religious faith. The political climate in this freedom-loving country is not an obstacle to vigorous evangelistic activity. There is no legal barrier to dynamic church growth.

C. CATHOLICISM IN A REVOLUTIONARY AGE

The Roman Catholic Church in Argentina is both responding to a social revolution which is shaping the New Latin America and at the same time experiencing violent revolutionary pressures within her traditional and antiquated ecclesiastical structures. These are revolutionary times, and not even Rome can maintain herself aloof from this mounting demand for changed social conditions. Without, the masses cry for justice and a fair share of this world's wealth. Within the Church, the clergy, influenced both by a profound biblical rediscovery and a revolution-inspired desire for greater liberty, are demanding *aggiornamento*. Pressures are building up daily, and the Church is seeking to accommodate her internal structure and her position in the world to the demands of this revolutionary age. Guidelines and inspiration for this updating and reshaping came from the decisions of Vatican Council II and the refreshing spirit of John XXIII.

The Roman Church is torn by violent tensions between the conservatives, who would seek to maintain the status quo, and the progressives, who are passionately driving forward to forge a new image of the Church consonant with the spirit and demands of modern times. Some of the latter are ready to give away much of the Church's extensive land holdings to the poor farmers and even to permit the priests to marry. The focal point of the struggle between progressives and conservatives in Argentina has been the Archbishopric of Mendoza, and centers around the application of the dictums which came out of Vatican Council II. Richard O'Mara (1966:612) feels that this dispute between conservatives and progressives has expressed itself nowhere else as acutely as it has in Argentina. Twenty-seven young progressives known as the "rebel priests" have gone on strike protesting the appointment of a conservative auxiliary bishop by their conservative archbishop, Alfonso M. Buteler. Reflecting the divergent viewpoints, one priest has commented: "We have one Church and two mentalities."

A similar struggle between reformers and traditionalists broke out earlier with bomb-like force in what is considered Argentina's most Catholic city, Córdoba. Here the dispute centered around this new revolutionary mentality which was made manifest in freedom of thought and expression, in the urgent need for renovation, and in work toward a Church which would be more "evangelical and poorer." Approximately thirty priests were involved in this kind of revolutionary thinking and the three leaders were censured by the bishop. One of the priests commented:

> The Capitalists of Latin America want to use the Church to stop social reforms and appeal to an anti-communism founded on a false defense of religious values.
>
> There is a new air in the Church that is coming out of the Vatican Ecumenical Council, but it is still not breathed among us (*Gaceta* 1964:1).

Priests such as these take courage and gain confidence to speak in ways contrary to the tenor of the pronouncements of their own bishops by reading the writings of other Latin American bishops. Probably the most progressive of these is the late Bishop of Talca in Chile, Manuel Larrain Errazuriz, President of the Latin American Bishops Council, who wrote in a pastoral as early as 1944:

> The Church, through her pontiffs, demands a deep social reform, and for an obvious reason: because present organization, in many of its aspects is far from being Christian. There are, in the present organization of the world, a great number of mistakes and injustices that a Roman Catholic must never accept. In the field of principle, Christian ideas on ownership and work have been forgotten and an ancient pagan concept has been substituted for them. In the field of economy, there is poor distribution of wealth, a fact that has established misery as a normal product of modern society, and has created in the social field the conflict of classes, rather than the Christian concept of cooperation and harmony. In a word: social order requires thoroughgoing reform and it is the Catholic's duty to fight for it (Considine 1964:45).

The conservative wing of the Church is sympathetic with the present military government of General Onganía, a faithful practicing Catholic who has surrounded himself with active Catholics as ministers. His campaign against the autonomy of the leftist-dominated universities during the winter of 1966 received the praise of the conservative clerics, but the progressives accused him of being dominated by the "pre-conciliar Catholics" (O'Mara 1966:613). At the same time, attempts are being made to disassociate the Church from the new government (*Time* 1966:28), reflecting the tensions within the Church and the customary Catholic shrewdness in not placing all the eggs in the same basket.

1. Shortage of Priests

Revolutionary tensions are having their adverse effects on the supply of priests. As noted above, Argentina's shortage of priests dates from the days of independence, but modern tensions continue to erode the supply and aggravate the problem. Although this shortage exists, with one priest to every 4,300 Catholics, according to Alonso (1964:217) she still has a lower ratio than the South American average of one to every 5,000. Only Colombia, Ecuador, Chile and Uruguay have a more favorable proportion of priest to people.

Other problems affect the number of priests also. The number of postulants in one of the seminaries in Buenos Aires dropped from sixty in 1945 to only ten in 1966. Furthermore, during the past decade, between 180 and 200 Argentine priests (between 4 and 5 per cent of the total) asked to be returned to lay status. One priest who became a Protestant said: "I couldn't renounce my priestly vocation, nor my vocation for marriage" (*Primera Plana* 1966:40). Principal reasons given for such defections are the desire to marry and the search for a greater liberty. This latter reason can be traced to the revolutionary spirit which has invaded the Church.

2. Radicals Among the Religious

There are radicals among the priests who seek rapid and revolutionary social change and feel that much of the foreign ecclesiastical aid to Latin America is only a cover-up for an attempt of the conservative hierarchy to maintain the traditional social and ecclesiastical structures intact. One of these is Ivan Illich, who has spent six years training North American priests to serve in Latin America. Illich comments:

> The U.S. Church must face the painful side of generosity: the burden that a life gratuitously offered imposes on the recipient. The men who go to Latin America must humbly accept the possibility that they are useless or even harmful, although they give all they have. They must accept the fact that a limping ecclesiastical assistance program uses them as palliatives to ease the pain of a cancerous structure, the only

hope that the prescription will give the organism enough time and rest to initiate a spontaneous healing. Much more probably, the pharmacist's pill will both stop the patient from seeking a surgeon's advice and addict him to the drug.

We must acknowledge that missionaries can be pawns in a world ideological struggle and that it is blasphemous to use the gospel to prop up any social or political system (1967:90).

Such comments certainly ought to help us capture the tone of Catholicism in Latin America today. There are dynamic proponents of this orientation in Argentina and this attitude is becoming evident to the man on the street through the Council-inspired innovations in daily religious practices and worship patterns. In the town of San Isidro in the province of Buenos Aires, all fees for the sacraments have been abolished. In the northern part of the country, experiments are being conducted using authorized laymen to conduct worship where there is no priest available to celebrate mass. The biblical renewal affecting Catholicism internationally has had a profound effect in Argentina through the translation of the Scriptures into modern-day Spanish by Monsignor John Straubinger. Recently the mass has been set to Argentine folk music, and the Bible has been translated into the *gaucho* language and expressions of Martín Fierro. In the northern province of Tucumán, in early 1968, the Catholic hierarchy sided with the demonstrating workers of one of the sugar mills against the provincial authorities. The provincial government arrested a priest under the pretext that his active support of the workers was an improper extension of the intentions of this new mood in Catholicism.

D. RELIGIOUS MOTIVATIONS OF CATHOLICISM

The picture of modern Catholicism in Argentina would not be complete with just this description of the trend of thought among the priests and the hierarchy and the tensions and problems affecting the ecclesiastical structures. What is the religious index among Catholics at the popular level?

The primary indicator of the degree of religious fervor is the percentage of members attending mass. According to Pin (1963:14,15) attendance in the small urban areas of Argentina runs the highest, with 13 per cent, whereas in the more difficult workers' parishes in the large urban centers the percentage is as low as 2.3 per cent. This is considerably lower than the Latin American average of between 17 and 18 per cent. The percentage of those who confess and receive the sacrament is, of course, much lower. These workers' parishes surrounding the heart of the cities represent the greatest opportunity for evangelism. This observation is confirmed by what has happened in the growing cities of Latin America, from Mexico to Chile. The vast bulk of rapidly expanding churches in Latin America are in these neighborhoods.

What are the religious motivations behind a people who practice such minimal attendance at the central ritual of a religion whose effectiveness for the individual is based on the regular participation in the sacraments? Pin (1963:29ff) suggests four basic motivations. Missionaries throughout Latin America would do well to understand fully what this discerning observer has to say about the underlying causes of religious practices there.[2] They are summarized here to capture their principal meaning.

1. Fulfillment of Natural Needs

First, there is the desire that religious practice or devotion secure a fulfillment of the natural needs of the person or his loved ones. Such needs include a desire for health, economic success, success in a love affair or protection from some cosmic evil. This type of religious motivation is not primarily, if at all, oriented to the supplicant's moral life. Generally there is a complete separation of religious practice and morals in the mind of the faithful who practice their religion with such motives. People use their religion to get what they want. There is no sense of belonging to a religious community in this outlook which views the ecclesiastical establishment as the depository of sacred things and powers to be manipulated for specific solutions of natural needs. Pin feels that this type of aspiration on the part of the people is the open way for the people to enter the Protestant Churches or, even more likely, spiritism. In fact, the Pentecostal emphasis on healing has found its corollary in this craving to have natural needs satisfied through religious practice.

2. Identification with Social Group

Pin calls the above religious expression "popular" Catholicism in contrast to "cultural" Catholicism, which is defined as the need of the individual to identify himself with his social group in its prescribed religious practices. This second religious motivation is based on the person's acceptance of the cultural pattern bestowed upon him at birth, with no attempt made to discover the deeper religious meaning of the label he carries. This is the religion of the group to which the individual belongs, and any departure would be interpreted as a rejection of his cultural heritage. Evangelical converts from among this group are generally social outcasts. Adherents of this viewpoint feel that the Church is somewhat subservient to the culture and is its public servant. Zealous priests who have attempted to refine the belief system and practices of these people are often labeled Protestants or communists. There is a tendency to view all problems of Latin American Catholicism as exterior; e.g., Protestantism, spiritism, communism, secularism.

Traditionally, this group within Catholicism has been difficult to penetrate with the Gospel on a broad scale, and continues to be highly resistant. Exceptions have come from among those who through their anti-clericalism have sought salvation outside the Roman Catholic Church. Such anti-clericalism is greatly affected by the public image the Church projects among the people. The reaction against the Church immediately following the fall of Perón and the positive results of the image resulting from Vatican Council II are opposite cases in point. This segment generally does not represent a high potential for church growth. In the light of today's revolutionary situation of rapid social change, Pin feels that this kind of Catholicism is in real danger of being unable to survive.

3. Pursuit of Mystical Transformation

The third religious motivation is the pursuit of salvation through an interior and mystical transformation. Religion is characterized by prayer, reception of the sacraments, and an effort to conform daily life and behavior to the norms imposed by religion. There are two expressions of this type of devotion: the individual religious exercises with a view to eternal salvation, and the communal expression leading to internal spiritual transformation. The first is characterized by an obsession with mortal sin and the sacramental "mechanisms" available to alleviate its eternal consequences. Regretfully, such a religious orientation too frequently has little to do with genuine change of life. Pin believes that the social disorganization and normlessness of Latin (and more particularly of Latin American) culture can be attributed to this religious motive. The second type, on the other hand, provides a real hope for profound spiritual transformation. Its feature of communal life attacks the very nerve center of human failure and sin—egocentricity. Small Catholic Action groups are oriented largely around this type of communal religious experience. Pin feels that this expression of Catholicism, although but an infinitesimal minority, is that which can produce a "communal spirituality of spiritual transformation." This type of genuine fellowship has been the Evangelicals' chief contribution in Argentina as well as throughout Latin America and is one of the keys to effective church planting.

4. Attachment to the Religious Group

The final religious motivation suggested by Pin is attachment to the religious group.

> They baptize their children, attend Sunday mass, confess, not to escape bad luck, nor because of fidelity to the cultural norms of the nation or people, nor—at least not directly—to free themselves from hell, but because they feel themselves to be members of a community of believers and desire to conform their behavior to the demands of this community (Pin 1963:41).

This type of religious motivation is particularly strong where the Church is a minority. Where the Church has been in the majority, this function of belonging has been performed by the microstructure of the family, the plantations or the small communities. These smaller cultural units no longer group the people, and the Church finds her people grouped by others, even by competing institutions. Among the causes for this breakdown of traditional structures are the demographic changes (urbanization and the population explosion), immigration, and the shortage of priests. Pin urges the Church to seek ways to integrate these families and individuals in a true microstructure of her own.

Here, again, the Evangelicals find a broad opportunity for church growth. It is no accident that the fastest growing Evangelical Churches in Latin America are those located in the new shanty towns which are springing up around the cities. This uprooted mass of new urban humanity is blindly and unknowingly seeking for new structures around which to orient their lives, in the absence of the securities which formerly grouped them in the smaller communities.

The former stable institutions such as the family, the Church, the large farms (*estancias* and *haciendas*) which gave meaning to life are disintegrating under the new and relentless pressures of the city. The victim is the individual who is looking for a new purpose and meaning in life. This uprooted individual is open to the Gospel in a way that would never have been possible in the tradition-bound society from which he came. Coupled with this is the fact that until only recently the Roman Catholic Church has been clumsy and slow to respond to this new situation. The mushrooming Churches of Brazil, Mexico and Chile are eloquent proof of the continuing ripeness and responsiveness of these masses.

Behind and pervading the entire religious temperament of Argentina and Latin America, especially on the part of the men, the prevailing attitude is one of indifference. Summarizing the religious attitudes of the faithful, as distinguished from the clergy, the statement of Childs assesses the religious temperament of Latin America as indifference:

> What really impresses one about the whole situation in Latin America is ... the appalling extent and degree of religious indifference. This is really the religious problem of Latin America. The Roman Church has not coped and seemingly cannot cope with it. The people of Latin America are not only losing faith in the Roman Church, but are losing faith in religion generally (1955:17).

Even after Vatican Council II much of this same attitude and temperament continues in Argentina.

This is the religious situation of the people among which the Evangelical Church in Argentina is growing. Indifference dominates the lives of most of Argentina's nominal Catholics. The message of the Gospel has a unique contribution to make in this situation. Who can meet these felt needs of Argentina's millions better than Christ? Who can weld their hearts and spirits together in community and fellowship more harmoniously than the Holy Spirit? Who can give them eternal salvation and produce their spiritual transformation but the God of the Scriptures?

CHAPTER 2

Four Centuries of Socio-Cultural Influences

A. EARLY ETHNIC CONTRIBUTIONS

The shaping of the Argentine personality had its beginning in medieval Spain, the Spain of Miguel Cervantes de Saavedra's immortal characters, Don Quixote and Sancho Panza. Cervantes, undoubtedly the greatest literary genius in the Spanish language, captured the archetype of the Spanish race at the time of Spain's greatest glory. The symbol does not stand alone, but is always accompanied in his noble exploits by his inseparable companion, Sancho. Quixote is a man of ideas, visions and dreams. Idealistic, he rides forth on his steed, in shining armor, to right the wrongs of this world and to liberate its captives. With utter disregard for his personal welfare, he launches out in pursuit of a cause which would do honor to the glory of the knightly past. Such total abandonment to a self-sacrificing cause is made possible by the ever-present Sancho Panza, the complement of Spanish personality. Sancho is down-to-earth, realistic and even materialistic. He remembers that man does not live by ideals alone, and by his generous support preserves the dignity of his master, Quixote. Mackay, commenting on the conquests of the Americas, concludes:

> The founding and administrating of the Iberian empire in America, up to the War of Independence, is a historical commentary on the exploits of the famous characters of

37

Cervantes. In this living commentary the Quixotic strain appears at its best and the Sancho Panzian at its worst, till Don Quixote finally dies and is survived by Sancho and his progeny (1935:17).

1. The Spaniard

The Spaniard, shaped in Europe under the pressures and tensions of the Middle Ages, preserved his distinctive characteristics in the Americas. He has left his unmistakable imprint indelibly stamped on the Argentine *basic personality*, [1] even though indigenous and subsequent immigratory influences have been strong. During the centuries of the development of the Argentine basic personality, each new racial and cultural contact contributed its distinctive hue to this Spanish sketch, resulting in a painting uniquely Argentine. The Argentine basic personality in many respects is similar to that of their Latin American neighbors, largely because of a broad convergence of cultural factors. To consider the Argentine typically Latin American, however, is to commit the fallacy of oversimplification and superficial judgment.

The fundamental ingredient of this Spanish contribution is the *dignidad de la persona* (or the dignity of the person, although the English word "dignity" does not fully capture the complete nuance of meaning in Spanish), or what Madriaga (Rycroft 1958:44) calls *el honor.* Broadly understood, the Spaniard sought to preserve the integrity of his individual person through passionate involvement in all that he put his hand to. Quixote is the archetype of this passion. Logical results of this passionate emphasis of the person and his honor are the personalism, individualism and humanism so common to the Spanish American and manifested in the Latin American liberal, and particularly in the *caudillo.* The Latin masses enthusiastically follow the dictator who passionately projects his *dignidad* and *honor.* The opposition to the dictator polarizes in the opponent's nonconformity based on the same motive, *el honor,* even if he must stand alone against the strong man. But he stands alone passionately and with dignity. This characteristic feature of the Spanish personality has made its influence felt in the matter of how Argentines become Evangelical Christians. Many, for fear of social censure eventuating in the tarnishing of their *dignidad,* find it difficult to continue in their decision to follow Christ. The mechanisms of public disapproval employed to discourage the religious deviant are particularly effective in reinforcing this innate drive to preserve *el honor.*

2. The Indian

When the Spaniard reached the Americas he found the Indians of the pampas not so highly developed in material and social culture as their distant cousins of the Andean highland. Under the continual onslaughts of the Spanish *hidalgos,* the innate Indian personality characteristic akin to Oriental fatalism manifested itself in passivity. The Spanish took his gold and his lands and the Indian retreated, but not without first resisting. He was nevertheless finally defeated and absorbed. The Indian suffered his greatest humiliation, before this passionate desire of the *conquistador* for personal fulfillment, when the Spanish colonist took the Indian women for his own. Colonial conditions were such that few Spanish women came to the colonies during the early periods. Miscegenation of the Indian and the Spaniard brought negative repercussions to both, but the Indian suffered the most. In retaliation and in imitation of the exploitation of the Spaniard, they captured many of the European women from the colonial settlements. The *cautivas* (white women captured by the Indians) and the *indigenas* (Indian women taken by the Spaniards) became the mothers of the emerging *gauchos* who dominated the plains and valleys of Argentina until around 1850, thirty-five years after the independence of the nation under the Southern Cross.

3. The Gaucho

The *gaucho* greatly influenced the destiny of Argentina, and still does, through his nostalgic appeal for everything distinctively Argentine. Born on the endless pampas, and alone, the *gaucho* never became accustomed to living under authority. Due to his excessive independence and fierce disregard for all authority, he was dominated only by the *caudillo,* who later came to control the Argentine political scene. José Hernández during the last third of the nineteenth century immortalized the individualistic *gaucho* spirit in his epic poem, *Martín Fierro.* In the poem, Martín Fierro expresses the heart of the *gaucho* in these few words:

> It is my pride that I live as free
> As the bird in the sky ... (Pendle 1961:33).

B. THE WAVE OF IMMIGRANTS

1. Foreign Invasion

The personality of the Argentine nation, both that of the *gaucho* who dominated the plains and the pre-independence European settlers who controlled the cities, was subjected to the acculturative influences of a veritable invasion of "foreigners." In 1852 Argentina had an estimated population of 800,000, composed of 7,000 white foreigners, 15,000 white Argentines, 553,000 *mestizos* (mixed Indian and white), 100,000 Indians, 15,000 negros and 110,000 mulattos. By 1914 the population had multiplied tenfold, whereas the number of white foreigners increased 339 times to 2,360,000 (Ingenieros 1918:510).

Eighty per cent of the immigrants during the latter half of the nineteenth century were Spanish or Italians, with the remainder composed of Russians, Polish, Germans, British, French, Portuguese, Uruguayans, Brazilians, Armenians, Lebanese, Turks and many others. Among them were several hundred Welsh Protestants who settled in Patagonia in 1864. This area was thought to be uninviting and uninhabitable for economic exploitation until this hardy band of pioneers, by rugged determination and strong religious faith, carved out a home in this bleak wilderness. In recent years there have been large numbers of Bolivians, Chileans and Paraguayans who have crossed their borders seeking better living conditions in Argentina. The significance of these immigrations for church growth has been largely overlooked by the established missions. The growth of the Pentecostal movement among the recent arrivals from Chile since the 1940's is patent evidence of this potential. Mission executives would be well advised, when formulating their policy decisions, to consider this sociological phenomenon, which is freighted with evangelistic promise. Ignorance of the sociological dimensions of how people come to Christ (whether it be an absence of intuitive perception or a deliberate neglect of a systematic understanding of these dimensions) will most certainly diminish its effectiveness.

During the peak period of the world's overseas migrations from 1821 to 1932, Argentina absorbed 6,405,000 immigrants and ranked second only to the United States in total immigrants. However, in 1914 the proportion of foreign residents in Argentina was 30.3 per cent, more than twice the proportion ever reached in the United

States (14.4 per cent in 1890 and 1910). This figure has consistently remained twice the proportion of foreign residents in the United States. In 1950 the proportions were 15.7 per cent in Argentina and 6.7 per cent in the United States (Whitaker 1964:55,56). This wave of immigrants, which began around the middle of the last century and lasted almost one hundred years in varying degrees of intensity, coincided during most of this period with Argentina's governments of political liberalism and strong anti-clericalism, and was directly responsible for the early penetration of the Gospel in Argentina. The first decades of this period saw the increase of immigrant Churches and the inauguration of worship in the Spanish language.

The immigrants found life easier in the cities, a factor which contributed to the disproportionate centralization of the masses in Buenos Aires and surrounding cities, and further compounded the neglect of rural development, the great source of Argentina's riches. Internal migration and urbanization also contribute to a high degree of concentration around the large and growing urban centers. This trend has accelerated until today almost one-third of Argentina's total population lives within fifty miles of the city of Buenos Aires. Other cities are experiencing similar rapid growth.

So great was the influence of these foreign elements that the Argentine Socialist Party when first organized used Italian, French, Spanish and German in their meetings and their committees were called "internationals" (Pendle 1961:67). The foreign communities tended to maintain their own customs and language. Third generation Anglo-Argentines who have never visited England still speak of "being out here" and "going back home."

2. Social Disorientation

What have been the psychological and social consequences of this foreign invasion of Argentina? Argentina found itself incapable of absorbing and shaping this veritable army of people who came in search of a land of promise. Mafud in his significant book astutely analyzes the plight of his country:

> Argentina does not have spiritual continuity. Her soul has been constituted by ruptures. After the Indians were exterminated, a rupture and an unfilled vacuum were left. Then the act was repeated with the *gaucho*. He was excluded from the Argen-

tine process and thrown out on the pampa. Later, the immigrant came and it was hoped the two vacuums would be filled; that left by the Indian, and by the *gaucho*. We weren't an Indian country because we didn't like the Indian we had exterminated. And we didn't want to be a *gaucho* country either, because we had evicted him and thrown him out on the plains. Later, by irony and a paradox, we couldn't be a European country either. Thus we remain projected as an incomplete country (1965:157).

Mafud discusses (1965:93,94,368) the acculturating influences of this immigrant wave that threatened to overcome everything distinctively Argentine. He feels that these continual pressures brought to bear on this young country, which had not come to its own consensus before the tide of immigration began to rise, have been an unsettling influence. In his earlier book, *El Desarraigo Argentino* (1959), he sees the country as "uprooted" and consequently suffering from a lack of necessary integrating social influences. He believes the Argentine to be incapable of full social realization and thus without a sense of belonging. The "cult of friendship" which he finds among groups of men is interpreted by Mafud as a compensation for this lack of social fulfillment on a larger scale. The Gospel addresses itself to this problem and through the new community of redeemed men in Christ meets the need of the uprooted Argentine masses.

This inability to arrive at a spirit of community is also projected into the national political sphere, as reflected in the exaggerated number of political parties. One Argentine author has called his country, "the country that is seeking itself." The loneliness and disillusionment of the Argentine is reflected in this popular tango:

> Brother, what things
> there are in life!
> I didn't love her
> when I met her,
> until one night
> she said to me determined:
> *I'm very tired*
> of it all, and went away . . . .

The processes operative in Argentina's national development have resulted in social dislocation. This in turn has led to a disproportionate emphasis of the early Spanish characteristic of individualism. Summarizing, Mafud says:

> Taking her most outstanding characteristics, we can say that the *inhibition against a social togetherness* is the distinctive content of the basic Argentine personality. . . . For this reason he lives without a social background. The Argentine, unmistakably, lives in his country in a world view [shaped by] immigrants—a stranger and marginal man—with a complete loss of ties to the social structure of his society (1965:372,373).

C. THE LITERARY CONTRIBUTION

The outstanding literary giants of the Argentine Republic have left their verbal impact on this progressively developing national consensus. Among the more significant contributors have been Sarmiento, Alberdi, Hernández, Rojas, Rodó and Güiraldes.

1. Debasing of the Gaucho

Sarmiento (1811-1888), in exile during the dictatorship of Rosas (1835-1852) and with an abundance of time to think about the problems of his country, arrived at what he felt was the solution to her political instability and slow economic progress. His principal literary contribution came in 1845 in the *Life of Facundo, or Civilization and Barbarism* in which he recounted the life of Don Facundo Quiroga, who ruled the area of present-day La Rioja as the *caudillo* of a marauding band of *gauchos*. Sarmiento was inclined to idealize the progress of the European countries and the United States and to blame all of Argentina's problems on the crude and barbarous *gaucho*. He felt that Argentina's problems could be solved by imitating and bringing in European peoples to displace the *gaucho*. As the *gaucho* had made the Indian the scapegoat of all his problems, Sarmiento made the *gaucho* the scapegoat of the emerging nation's problems (Mafud 1959:69). Sarmiento, on writing to Mitre, the president, expressed his feelings about the *gaucho*:

> Try not to economize *gaucho* blood. This is the fertilizer that is useful to the country. Blood is the only thing they have that is human.

Alberdi confirmed Sarmiento's views on immigration:

> Don't fear that our nationality will be compromised by the

accumulation of foreigners nor that our national distinctives disappear .... Great amounts of foreign blood have flowed in the defence of American independence (Dickmann 1946:74).

2. Glorification of the Gaucho

A reaction was in the making and came in the writings of José Hernández (1834-1886), who wrote the epic poem *Martín Fierro*, immortalizing the life of the *gaucho*. Even today, the Argentine who wishes to please his international visitor with a special gift presents to him an expensively leather-bound copy of this poem. Hernández presented the *gaucho* life of Martín Fierro as a noble and free existence untrammeled by the trappings of civilization. Clissold remarks:

> Hernández was concerned with correcting the false picture of the *gaucho* as presented by the political pamphleteers. So well did he succeed, and so thoroughly did he steep himself in the authentic *gaucho* spirit, that the epic adventures of his Martín Fierro not only fixed the image of the *gaucho* in the imagination of his literate compatriots for all time, but speedily took a commanding place in the folklore of the *gauchos* themselves (1965:95).

Years later, as the immigrating waves and supporting Argentine politicians continued to impose Europeanism, another work which was destined to share Martín Fierro's place as the outstanding epic of the *gauchos* was written in 1926 by Ricardo Güiraldes (1886-1927), entitled *Don Segundo Sombra*. Pendle provides us with a résumé of this masterpiece whose central figure reflects the image of the immortal Don Quixote:

> This was the story of a boy named Fabio who, as a protégé of an old *gaucho*, Don Segundo Sombra, roamed the pampa, breaking in horses and driving cattle from place to place. One day Fabio inherits an *estancia;* but he did not wish to be a landowner, and at night he continued to sleep on the ground in the open air, refusing to live indoors. For a short while Don Segundo stayed with him, helping him to run his estate; but the old *gaucho* could not for long tolerate being tied to the ranch, in spite of his affection for the boy. And so at the end of the book we see Don Segundo going away on his horse,

cantering towards the horizon to live again the rough and
lonely life to which he and his ancestors had been accustomed
(1961:173,174).

The profound appeal of this story to the Argentine reveals his
ambivalent desires to reaffirm what is distinctively Argentine, but his
inability to leave the comforts brought him by the modern
European-influenced city.

3. Idealism Enthroned

Ricardo Rojas (1882-1957) and the Uruguayan Enrique Rodó
(1871-1917) turned the arguments of Sarmiento and his supporters
around on them. They argued that the modern city, which was a
reflection of the Colossus of the North (the United States) and
Europe, was the uncivilized world. They eloquently presented their
case that the materialism of the so-called "civilized" countries was in
reality barbarism. In contrast, the lesser developed Latin nations
were shown to be characterized by idealism, the mark of true
civilization. One of the most significant books ever written in Latin
America was Rodó's *Ariel*, in 1900. Although written by a
Uruguayan, this work had profound effects on Argentine thinking at
the turn of the century. In *Ariel* Rodó implied that North America
reflected the Caliban-materialism and absence of culture and
refinement of Shakespeare's *Tempest*, while the Latin American
reflected the Ariel-idealism and high cultural values. *Ariel* achieved
immediate and immense popularity in Latin America and became
the watershed of the Latin intellectual's attitude toward the United
States (Clissold 1965:107). Clissold concludes:

> For educated Latin Americans, in the words of one of their
> writers who had misgivings about its ultimate effect, Rodó's
> myth provided the "justification of their racial characteristics,
> the compensation for their practical backwardness, the claim
> to spiritual superiority over the Titan of the North"
> (1965:108).

Sarmiento, who was branded as the worst slanderer (Tamagno
1963:307) of his country, was discerning enough to see that his
early analysis of her problems and his oversimplified solution of
Europeanization might prove to be a nightmare. In his later writing
Sarmiento says of Buenos Aires:

The most industrious and progressive of its 400,000 strangers here who . . . remain unchanged in their roles as instruments, makers, builders . . . . We shall build, if we have not already built, a tower of Babel in America, its workmen speaking all tongues, not blending them together. . . . One does not construct a homeland without patriotism . . . nor does one build . . . a city without citizens (Whitaker 1964:57).

Although not totally correct, the remarks were penetratingly prophetic of the cause of a large part of Argentina's lack of complete consensus and social integration. Today Argentines are divided in their opinions about Sarmiento and his influence. He continues to be highly praised and, at the same time, severely criticized.

D. THE STRUGGLE FOR A NATIONAL CONSCIOUSNESS

1. Swinging Pendulum

The racial and ideological tensions have also been expressed in the political arena. Argentina has fluctuated between self-assertion of her distinctive and American personality as a nation, and imitative adoption of everything European. Samuel Ramos (1963:93-100) analyzes one of Mexico's chief problems as being this same ambivalent fluctuation between the values and viewpoints of the New World and the Old. The many times that political opinion has swung abruptly between these two poles have inscribed their mark on the emerging nation's collective personality. The failure to assert her distinctively Argentine characteristics has left the nation in a no-man's-land, and extremely self-conscious, even with a degree of self-contempt because she is not the great nation she knows her natural and human conditions have promised her to become.

When we look back over the development of the nation, we see the pendulum swing between the Europists and the nationalists. First Rivadavia sought solutions in a sharp increase of foreign investment and immigration. Rosas' reaffirmation of the *caudillo* and *gaucho* spirit was in brusk reaction to the Europeanizing and civilizing influences of Rivadavia. The Rosas years were the heyday of the *gaucho caudillo*. It was an assertion of the Argentine way of life.

During the years from 1853 to 1916, years of stable governments represented first by Mitre and Sarmiento, there was a resurgence of

European influence in finance, immigration and transportation development. These years marked the period of greatest economic progress, as materialism asserted itself in ever-increasing measure. Argentine opinions are sharply divided in their interpretation of these years. Saravia, registering these reactions, comments:

> This age, which was the golden age of Argentine liberalism, has elicited disparate judgments. It represents for some, the finest example of the patriotism, culture and intelligence of the generation that made it possible; for others, it is a reproachful surrender and submission to foreign domination (1959:55).

The immigrants, ironically enough, proved to be the element out of which the Radicals under Irigoyen forged their party of the moderate left and the next reaction against European influences, which culminated in the nationalizing of all natural resources.

When the military intervened for the first time in modern Argentine politics, it was in support of a move by the conservative oligarchy which again sought solutions from overseas. The economic and moral consequences of the Roca-Runciman Treaty, signed in 1933 with Britain, constituted an insult to Argentina's national pride and prepared the terrain for the next violent nationalistic reaction. In 1943 the military intervened, but this time on the side of nationalistic interests in the person and government of Perón. Although a reaffirmation of the Argentine way, the Perón administration lacked the idealism of Rodó's *Ariel*. During both the earlier Irigoyen government and that of Perón, nationalism reached the extreme of genuine xenophobia.

The overthrow of the Perón regime brought on a period of national confusion and conflict. The nation finds it almost impossible to know itself, as the many competing factions seek to assert their particular interpretation of what the nation should be. It remains to be seen whether the present *de facto* government of President Onganía will devise solutions uniquely Argentine or resort to a policy of imitation.

2. City and Nation Conflict

Another struggle inherent to the Argentine problem is the conflict between the "city and the nation." This is another expression of the problems which grew out of the settlement of hordes of immigrants in the greater Buenos Aires metropolitan area. Almost one-third of Argentina's population lives in the city and province of Buenos Aires. When the nation's railroads were built by British companies and finance, they contributed further to the tendency toward centralization which had its beginning in the agitations of the colonial *porteños* (port people) for the creation of the Viceroyalty of the River Plate. Pendle states:

> Opposition between the capital city and the provinces was a characteristic of the life of most of the newly formed Spanish American republics. In Argentina, indeed, this was the central theme in the country's early history (1963b:133,134).

The struggle became known as the fight between the *Unitarios* (unitarians) and the *Federales* (federals), the terms expressing opposite views of political reality and organization. The *Unitarios* generally reflected the Europeanizing tendency, while the *Federales* were the champions of the *gauchos*. The difference of political opinion centered on the view each held regarding centralization of authority in the burgeoning nation. *Unitarios* were strong advocates of centralization, or in other words, they favored the dominance of the city (Buenos Aires) over the nation. On the other hand, the *Federales* urged a generous degree of decentralization in deference to the regional *caudillos* and their freedom-loving *gauchos*.

Strangely enough, when Rosas, a *Federal,* gained control during a period covering two decades under the scarlet banners of the *Federales,* he soon imposed a more rigid unitarian centralization than that espoused by the *Unitarios.* Through the successive administrations of Mitre, Sarmiento and others, the unitarian principle of government was confirmed, and the provinces of the nation largely remained mere satellites of the port city. This dependence is reflected in the national government's authority to intervene in the three branches of any provincial government when, at the president's discretion, it is felt that the local processes of government have failed to function properly.

3. Democracy Latin Style

Latin Americans generally are still struggling to attain democracy as known by North Americans. Rycroft (1958:60-62) in a discussion of the work of the Colombian writer Michelson explains the Calvinistic concepts of government which have been written into the constitutions of the Latin American nations. These principles include government by the people and free examination, which is diametrically opposed to traditional Roman Catholicism. Consequently, although the nations of Spanish America have brilliantly written lofty democratic principles into their constitutions, the people, for centuries conditioned by the atmosphere of a totalitarian Church, are unprepared for an understanding of and meaningful participation in the democratic processes of their countries. It will be fascinating to watch the developments of democratic institutions in Latin America during the next half-century as free inquiry makes its impact on the Roman Catholic Church. The growing Evangelical community will also have its impact on political developments. Already in Chile the Evangelical voting block is jealously cultivated by the politicians.

E. PRESSURES OF THE SOCIAL REVOLUTION

1. Changes of Governing Elite

The recent decades have witnessed an inexorable and relentless build-up of revolutionary pressures in Latin America. This is but a beginning of what the world will observe in the coming years as the masses, more and more acutely aware that they need not silently resign themselves to their traditional level of subsistence living, throw off their chains and enter into the dignity of genuine human existence. The revolutions of independence in Latin American countries were not genuine changes of governmental institutions, but the exchange of the colonial Spanish ruling elite for an indigenous creole elite who preserved the semi-feudal structures of government and society. The South American colonies threw off the chains of European domination, but the revolution of broad participation in the governmental and economic life of the nation by the average citizen was not included. A governing elite continued to control (frequently by limited democratic processes) the destinies of the people.

Argentina and her Ibero-American neighbors were the products of medieval Roman Catholic Spain, and not of Puritans from England who cherished the principles of human dignity and of representative government as expressed in the Magna Carta. Revolutions which followed the wars of independence have in almost every instance been mere changes of political power, with the exception of the revolutions in Mexico (1910), Bolivia (1952) and Cuba (1960), which represented definite divergences from former political structures and ideologies.

2. Incorporation of the Proletariat

The current build-up of revolutionary pressures is not oriented in its goals toward a simple switch of political factions, but rather seeks a drastic and far-reaching restructuring of basic political, economic and social institutions. The proponents of such radical changes can be divided into two types: those who advocate violent methods (who themselves range from militant communists to revolutionary church leaders, both Protestant and Catholic), and those who urge peaceful and orderly means of transition. It remains to be seen which of these procedures becomes the dominating characteristic of the inevitable revolution of the not too distant future.

There are current tensions peculiar to Argentina as she searches for her place in this revolutionary age. Chief among them is the political destiny of Perón's shirtless ones who were "politicized" by their champion and *caudillo* (Potenze 1966:662). The slogan of the peronists was "Perón cumple (fulfills or keeps his promises) y Evita dignifica" (gives dignity). The masses who were seeking political and economic gains found their "savior" in Perón, who kept his word to them, and found that Evita, his wife, gave them a new dignity. Since then, although their *lider* is gone, the shirtless ones are always present to haunt and remind, even though the former opposition parties might wish the problem would vanish. The present Christian Democratic Party president of Chile, Eduardo Frei Montalva, expresses the plight of this segment of society throughout Latin America in these words:

> There is no doubt that a great deal of what is happening in Latin America is implied in the process described by Arnold Toynbee, who maintains that one factor involved in the collapse of civilization is the presence in it of an internal proletariat, a group that is in a society but not of society. Certainly there is a proletariat within our societies that is not a part of them. This is noticeable throughout our lands. Whoever has experienced life in the Latin American countries can readily observe at every moment the horizontal divide that separates those who belong to society from those who are

alien. At any moment of our national existence we can show
that the reactions of this alienated proletariat are quite
different from those of the men who rule the community. This
proletariat is completely foreign to, completely beyond the
sphere of influence of the ideas and feelings that move the
community (Pike 1964:217).

This is in large part the sector of the community to whom Perón
appealed, and from whom he received the broadest support for his
popular dictatorship. Even today, if there were a fully free election
allowing the supporters of Perón to vote as they wished, they could
marshal more votes than any other single party. The repeated denial
of active participation as a political party to this segment of society
has produced resentment among the masses and increased the
revolutionary tensions. The constructive incorporation into full and
productive political activity of these masses remains the current
government's greatest challenge, although there are some indications
that this may be achieved.

3. Students and Intellectuals React

Other manifestations of these pressures are the student revolts
against the intervention of the universities (DeHainaut 1967:40-43).
In 1918 the Reform movement in Latin American universities began
in Córdoba (Argentina). It advocated the tripartite government of
the university, consisting of members of the faculty, the alumni and
the students. The present government has reversed this trend in the
interest of a university under the rigid control and direction of the
State. Tensions are high as the students shout, " ¡Libros sí, botas
no!" (Books yes, boots no!) (*Newsweek* 1966:49).

Argentina also suffers from economic stagnation and a "brain
drain." Argentina's educational system is advanced and capable of
producing the highest type of professional men, among them a
Nobel prize winner. Frustrated by the political instability of their
own country and infatuated with the promise of material abundance
in the United States, some of Argentina's best young minds have left
their country's problems behind. The situation they leave is one of
economic stagnation. Since World War II, Argentina's per capita
economic growth has increased only 1 to 1.5 per cent per year (*U.S.
News and World Report* 1966:59). Mexico's 3 per cent is nearer

normal. And inflation continues rampant with a continually devalu-
ating peso.

Herbert L. Mathews assesses the revolutionary significance of
present events in Latin America:

> Latin America is in the process of upheaval. It is one of the
> most dramatic and explosive movements in all history. An
> industrial revolution, urbanization, the growth of a middle
> class, a population explosion unequaled anywhere in the
> World, a political ferment that is introducing all the revolu-
> tionary doctrines of democracy, a social revolution in which
> the masses who accepted ignorance, poverty and disease as the
> natural course of events—are now demanding and beginning to
> get equality of opportunity, education, health, and a higher
> standard of living—all these and other dynamic forces are
> creating a situation comparable in its way, and in the impact it
> is going to have on the Western World, to the European
> Renaissance (Toynbee 1962:205).

Toynbee (1962:181-205) with his characteristically penetrating
insight analyzes the causes behind this mounting revolutionary
tension. He points out four areas of pressure which are the chief
contributing factors in this build-up. The first is the breakdown of
the traditional structures of Latin American society, reflected
principally in the growing size and influence of the middle sectors of
society. With this new ingredient the semi-feudal structures of
society are crumbling, and the previously entrenched power groups
are being forced to make adjustments and concessions. Next he
mentions the Hispanic economic feudalism reflected in the *latifundia*
(literally in Latin—broad farms). The large land holdings dating from
colonial and early post-colonial times have concentrated the land in
the hands of a few large *latifundarios*. This system is supported by
antiquated legal and taxation systems. He observes that the
intellectuals were permitted to write the constitutions in the foreign
idiom inspired by the North American and French revolutions so
long as they left the land and the power in the hands of the
latifundistas. With industrialization, less labor is needed, driving
hordes of migrants to the exploding cities in search of a better than
subsistence-level life. This uprooted peasantry is undergoing the
severe strains of rapid social change in the burgeoning urban centers.

Thus the urban population of Argentina continues to increase. In

1950 it stood at 64 per cent of the total population. By 1960 it had increased to 68 per cent. It is estimated that by 1975 it will stand at 71 per cent (Rycroft 1961:14,15). Toynbee provides us with the pathetic picture of the psychological overtones of the situation of the peasant who moves from the static-rural situation to the fluid-urban world.

> In these unhappy circumstances the peasant who migrates to the city is likely to lose most of his customary psychological and spiritual supports without having been able to wean himself from feeling the need for them. A President Cárdenes is, no doubt, a more disinterested and benevolent 'protector of the poor' than the local *hacendado* whom the revolutionary President has justly evicted. But the *hacendado* was accessible, whereas the President is remote. The peasant engulfed in the city may find the political party or trade union less remote than the President; these new secular organizations may prove, in fact, to be as demanding as the Church used to be. But the relatively prosaic institutions can hardly fill the place that the Church used to occupy in the peasant's imagination and affection. In his urban exile—and it is exile, even if it has been voluntary—the peasant is being offered a stone in place of bread. His psychological plight is a painful one (1962: 199,200).

The third factor he mentions is inflation, which is wreaking havoc on this displaced peasantry.

> It robs those classes that are condemned to live on a fixed income for the benefit of those that are not, and this inevitably makes the victims feel that they are cheated—as indeed they are (Toynbee 1962:204).

Finally, he points to the fluctuation of world prices of primary products, upon which the Latin American nations depend for income, as another contributing factor to revolutionary tensions.

This combination of socio-cultural factors has produced a situation which must be understood by every person involved in the extension of the Gospel in Argentina and all of Latin America. This is the crucible in which the growing Evangelical Church is being forged. Our responsibility to God, the supporting constituency (in the case of the missionaries), and the masses without Christ must be interpreted in the light of these circumstances. An enlightened understanding of today's "fullness of time" is essential if we are to achieve the accelerated church growth we are seeing in many quarters of Latin America. There is no legitimate excuse to plan for or to expect anything but the best quantitative and qualitative results such as are being seen in other areas of Latin America.

CHAPTER 3

The Argentine Basic Personality

A. PRELIMINARY CONSIDERATIONS:
CONCEPTS AND MEANINGS

During the past several decades observers of the Latin American church growth scene have repeatedly mentioned an interesting and thought-provoking phenomenon. The unusually rapid growth of the Pentecostal Churches in Latin America, in contrast to that of the Churches affiliated with the historic mission organizations, has demanded the repeated attention of the best of the interpreters of Evangelical developments in that part of the world. These observers have all coincided in one feature of their evaluations. All have emphasized what might be called the appropriateness or congeniality of this movement of the Latin culture and temperament. Pentecostalism seems to fit the Latin spirit. More penetrating observers have found other non-Pentecostal Churches which have made equally cordial adjustments to the Latin temperament, although on a far more limited scale.

1. Church Growth and the Cultural Milieu

This leads to the observation that church growth takes place in a cultural milieu. An understanding of this body of surrounding influences and circumstances is necessary to a productive and meaningful interpretation of church growth dynamics. It is the purpose of this chapter to point up the correlation between these cultural factors and church growth. Previous chapters have presented the various facets of Argentina's historical development. These different currents and tendencies have had a strong influence on the people of Argentina. A common expectation and outlook on life have developed. A second purpose of this chapter will be to draw out this configuration of factors which together form the Argentine character.

This interesting study of the relationship between cultural factors and the character of a nation has received the attention of several writers. A pioneer in this field in Latin America was Samuel Ramos. In his *Profile of Man and Culture in Mexico* (1963) Ramos described the cultural influences which have formed the Mexican national character. In 1961 Tomás Roberto Fillol, in his *Social Factors in Economic Development, The Argentine Case,* developed the Argentine national character and demonstrated how this affects the economic development of the country. There is a similar correlation between the Argentine national character and church growth dynamics.

2. Basic Personality Type

Anthropologists and psychologists were the pioneers in this field of national character studies, although sociologists have also made significant contributions. The interdisciplinary nature of these investigations is derived from the necessity of employing explanatory concepts from more than one discipline. This need for cooperation between disciplines was recognized by Ralph Linton (1945:4) and Florence R. Kluckhohn (1954:343). Through the writings of these two anthropologists and those of Abram Kardiner (1939:133; 1945a:107-122), a psychologist, basic concepts were developed. Linton's introduction to Kardiner's book, *The Psychological Frontiers of Society,* contains a historical résumé of the development of these concepts and a definition of *basic personality type.* He states that:

> The *basic personality type* for any society is that personality configuration which is shared by the bulk of the society's members as a result of the early experiences which they have in common. It does not correspond to the total personality of the individual but rather to the projective system or, in different phraseology, the value attitude systems which are

basic to the individual's personality configuration. Thus the same basic personality type may be reflected in many different forms of behavior and may enter into many different total personality configurations (1945b:viii).

The concept of basic personality type has become a useful tool in studying the influences of culture on the personality and in determining those personality traits most commonly shared by a group of people. DuBois (1960:xx-xxiii) discusses the further developments of these concepts and the limitations to which these investigations are subjected. Perhaps the most significant amplification of Kardiner's and Linton's view was the study by Florence Kluckhohn (1954) in which she developed the concept of *value orientation profiles*. She devised categories by which to determine the *dominant* and *variant value orientations* of a culture, and suggested that it is a combination of these values or outlooks on certain basic areas of human relationships and beliefs which determines the basic personality. Her observation regarding the necessary presence of variants (1954:352) confirms this writer's intention that the basic personality characteristics of the Argentine as presented in this chapter not be interpreted as a description of any single Argentine, nor of the nation as a whole. Ethnic and class divergencies are present and form the basis of several of our observations and conclusions. The value of these concepts is that they furnish a tool, or categories, by which the complexity of data which enters into our consideration when we attempt to determine the basic personality type can be classified. An area for stimulating research would be the investigation of how people adopt variant value orientations within the culture. This would shed considerable light on the subject of how people become Christians.

The application of these concepts to the study of complex societies has met with more difficulties than when used by anthropologists to study primitive society. Linton, in his evaluation of Kardiner's concept of basic personality structure, states:

"Western Society" is not a single culture but a conglomeration of cultures in which the socio-economic order has gone through a host of vicissitudes. The number of factors which must be brought into correlation is much greater than any we have encountered in primitive society (1945:121).

In the light of this, the most promising avenue open to us for application to church growth research is the "intuitive and highly interpretative level" which Du Bois (1960:xxi) mentions. Although less than ideal, this is the only approach which is available, short of extensive field research. This has been the approach of two Argentine sociologists, José Manuel Saravia and Julio Mafud, who are our principal sources for data on the Argentine basic personality. These two authors in large part furnish us with an interpretative picture similar to Ramos' (1963) analysis of Mexico, which has had considerable influence in this field.

3. Meaning for Church Growth

What meaning do these concepts have for church growth? As observed above, the development of the Evangelical Churches in Latin America has not occurred in a vacuum. Further, there is abundant evidence to support the conclusion that accelerated growth has occurred where the presentation and institutionalization of the Gospel has been congenial and appropriate to the cultural setting. The description and understanding of the basic personality type can aid us in achieving a greater degree of congeniality and appropriateness. The more we can make the forms and expressions of the unchangeable Gospel fit, the greater degree of church growth can be expected.

This is true in three distinct areas of missionary endeavor. A clear understanding of the relationship between the basic personality and church growth principles will affect the communication of the Gospel, the development of church structures and finally the nature of church-mission relationships. The methods and emphases with which the Christian message is communicated will affect the nature and extent of the decision people make to follow Christ. A clear grasp of the basic personality can help the missionary and missionary-trained leadership assure that people make *whole decisions*—"whole" in the sense that the complete Gospel is appropriated by the entire person. Truncated Christian decision adversely affects both the quality and the quantity of church growth. The target people must be understood by both foreign and indigenous church leadership to assure whole decisions.

Insights regarding the basic personality also influence the development of cordial church structures. The arbitrary imposition of foreign forms has done more to frustrate church growth than any other single factor. This was particularly true during the early years of missionary penetration and influence. However, at no period of church development where missionary influence or international ecclesiastical aid continues to be offered or requested is it too late to adapt methodologies and policies to the national characteristics of the host culture. Wise adjustments will lead both mission and Church to the adoption of congenial structures. These in turn will provide broader "bridges of God" from the host culture into the new community and back into the surrounding world in authentic Christian witness and service. The absence of congenial structures in the emerging Churches hinders growth far more than most of us care to admit. The more rapid growth of certain Churches in Brazil, Chile and Mexico is evidence of this fact. All "foreign" influence cannot be eliminated, nor would this be desirable, since the work of Christ throughout the world and in distinct cultures is analogous to the work of the Spirit in any one country or culture. It is the small and subtle differences, however, which prove to be either our undoing or the secret of accelerated church growth.

Finally, the clear understanding of the basic personality of the people to whom the mission addresses itself concerns the relationship between the emerging Church and the mission organization. Breakdowns and tensions in this crucial area of missionary concern have all too frequently been the primary cause of arrested growth of the Churches. A sympathetic understanding of the culture of the target people and a sincere desire to adjust to the forms and structures encountered there will eventuate in mutually responsible relationships. Such relationships concern both the mission and the Church. The mission organization, both collectively and individually, will be greatly aided in serving and ministering among the sister churches. This would result in responsible missionary vocation (I Corinthians 9:19-23). The Church, on the other hand, will respond to this alerted and sensitive approach of the mission with maturing reactions. Progressively the new community will assume increasing responsibility. This is responsible church growth (I Thessalonians 1:6-10).

The conclusion of the matter is this: The more complete our understanding of the basic personality and how it affects church growth, combined with a cordial and spiritually oriented application of these insights, the greater will be the result, both quantitatively and qualitatively.

B. UNDERSTANDING THE ARGENTINE BASIC PERSONALITY

1. An Important Clarification

The previous chapters have described the religious, ethnic, literary, demographic, political and revolutionary factors which have been influential in the formation of the Argentine nation. The pressures and tensions resulting from various combinations of these influences have produced the Argentine basic personality. The components which we shall describe are the dominant value orientation (Kluckhohn 1954). The sum of these components does not describe any single Argentine; nor do these features fully describe the entire Argentine nation. They are those characteristics which are most commonly shared by the Argentine. Isolated homogeneous units within the Argentine society and those marginal to it, such as certain immigrant groups and indigenous Indian tribes, are not included and would be better described by Kluckhohn's concept of variant value orientation. Furthermore, the following does not claim to be an exhaustive treatment, but rather a selection of those features which are particularly pertinent to an understanding of church growth dynamics in Argentina.

The basis of our observations on the features which comprise the Argentine basic personality is the analysis of the Argentine sociologist José Manuel Saravia. Saravia's (1959) book, *Argentina 1959, Un Estudio Sociológico,* describes the typical Argentine in his social, economic and political environment. His insights into the salient features of his countryman's basic personality are penetrating and well substantiated with historical and psychological reasonings. His conclusions are summarized in six characteristics, of which we will develop four that have particular bearing on church growth. Other Argentine observers such as Mafud (1959, 1965) and Fillol (1961) confirm his conclusions.

2. Moralism

Saravia calls his first characteristic *moralism.* He explains this as the tendency to canonize a particular position, be it political or intellectual, and then hold tenaciously to the viewpoint with rigid intransigence. All actions are judged according to certain moral precepts. The centuries of inculcation of the Ten Commandments and other moral precepts by zealous Roman Catholic catechists has reinforced this tendency to absolutize. The accepted method of enforcing superficial conformity to the "rules" is to make the deviator from the generally accepted pattern of behavior an object of gossip. Such rigidity results in daily conflicts between the conduct of the average Argentine and the values which he holds. The Argentine has an innate sense of justice and cringes at the sight of the perpetration of some small injustice. But if he himself can arrange some favor or privilege through the good offices of a friend, he will quickly take advantage of the situation. Moralism also tends to place the Argentine in a position of rejecting the pragmatic, as such solutions would be a betrayal of his high idealism, or moralism. Yet, the Argentine finds himself constantly compromising these religiously indoctrinated standards and ideals. He is powerless to check his moral lapses. This is particularly true of the man who has lost contact with the Roman Catholic Church and has found no faith to take its place. The resulting conflict between his ideals and his conduct produces a guilt which is sublimated in a variety of ways. This situation provides one of the Church's greatest opportunities, as well as obligations, for the mediation of the forgiveness of Christ and for genuine Christian evangelism. An understanding of the nature of the guilt borne by the average Argentine and how to effectively communicate the forgiving grace of Christ is essential to church growth.

3. Individualism

Saravia next mentions a characteristic which springs from the Hispanic heritage of the Argentine. It is the *individualism* which plays such an important role in the Argentine's view of himself. He shares this characteristic with other Latin Americans in so far as they participate in the same Hispanic culture. Whyte and Holmberg describe the features of this individualism thus:

> In Latin America it is more than the doctrine that the individual, and not society, is of paramount importance in human life. Personalism goes even deeper than this. Not man in the abstract, but man in the concrete, becomes the center of the universe. And the concrete man in the center of the universe is the person himself (1956:3).

Saravia (1959:145,146) describes this individualism further and spells out the consequences. He feels that the individual Argentine so strongly believes in his own position that he demands special treatment for his particular case. Many times he will blatantly proceed to act upon these convictions with almost total disregard for others. This can have adverse social consequences and often leads to social isolation. Saravia believes that this glorification of the individual and his rights tends to thwart the "formation of voluntary organizations, and where [these] institutions exercise a certain authority over individual desires ... sects and tendencies toward anarchy easily develop." H.A. Murena (quoted in Fillol) summarizes:

> There is no community in Argentina. We do not form a body, though we may form a conglomeration. . . . It is not an organism of which all feel themselves a part. Each organ believes itself the whole, and functions as if it were more important than the whole (1961:22).

The meaning of this personality characteristic for church growth is obvious. Especially where the churches are new is it difficult to form a sense of community. However, Churches which have met this deficiency in the Argentine personality configuration with the fellowship of the new Christian community have seen genuine growth. On the other hand, this same characteristic is sometimes the source of growth when the individualism is expressed in a spiritually sensitive leader. This type of leader gathers about him people who admire him and sense themselves complete when following him. Many of the Pentecostal leaders function in this pattern, which is not unlike the methods of the political *caudillo*.

4. Formalism

Formalism is the next characteristic Saravia sees in the Argentine basic personality. By formalism he means the hierarchical ordering of interpersonal relationships. This concerns the traditional norms which determine the nature of the relationships which subsist between persons, especially with regard to the different age sets. These standards regulate the actions and behavior of men in their relationships to others. There are vast unwritten regulations of interpersonal protocol which must be observed if life is to be lived harmoniously. He detects a slight erosion of the rigidity of these norms in recent years among the youth, but there is no significant departure from the general continuing application of these rules. Men demand to be treated with the deference which they feel is due them according to their personal concept of their own abilities and qualities. Saravia (1959:149) states that:

> The tremendous zeal with which this pretension is usually defended, is a clear indication of a psychologically compulsive attitude, which originates in the absence of a confidence and security experienced by the person in question with respect to the legitimacy of the hierarchy and treatment that he demands.

He illustrates this attitude by what he calls the cult of old age. He says:

> The average Argentine professes an almost sacred respect for those who in the course of a long life have accumulated "experience". . . . Youth finds itself in a position of inferiority with respect to old age, and his youth at times the obstacle to occupy positions or assume responsibilities for which, objectively, he is well trained.

When such formal concepts and rules govern the relationships between age groups, the patterns and dynamics of leadership are particularly affected. This is especially true in growing churches where people are being incorporated rapidly from the world. The traditional pattern of leadership in Evangelical Churches, where the new leadership is largely from among the younger set, is placed under severe strain. The normal and natural leaders from among the older men are too frequently overlooked in favor of the young men. This tends to isolate the churches from the surrounding culture. A balance between the two leadership sets must be provided in order to assure continued and dynamic church growth. Our methods of training leadership are particularly in need of extensive modification.

5. Nationalism

Finally, Saravia discusses Argentine *nationalism*. He describes it as traditional patriotism which manifests itself in loyalty to the national institutions and way of life. They are proud to be Argentines and proud of the glories of their national history. However, this simple, almost naive patriotism is modified by several factors. First, he mentions the large quantity of foreigners who live in Argentina and maintain their sympathy ties with their native country. This loyalty is transmitted from father to son for several generations. Secondly, among Argentines generally there is a strong feeling that in recent years they have been frustrated in their aspirations to progress. A certain degree of resentment has developed against their own country because it hasn't been generous to them. Nationalism is further tempered by an often naive acceptance of things foreign. Finally, he suggests that the Argentine sees a sharp discrepancy between what is verbally professed as the ideals of the nation and the behavior of many of its private citizens, public officials and institutions. This has produced strong sentiments of disillusionment and a self-debasing of the Argentine character.

These tempering factors also have produced certain defense mechanisms which reveal the overt characteristics of the Argentine personality. There are two of these psychological mechanisms. First Saravia mentions the strong tendency to rationalization manifested in the remark, "This country has an extremely promising future." This attitude derives from those days when the country promised to surpass most in the world in its development, and refuses to die before the real situation of today. The other mechanism has produced a psychologically compulsive pride. This is accompanied by a strong conviction that the problems which Argentina is suffering are not of her own making, but produced by forces outside herself. The natural and obvious outworking of these feelings is a hyper-nationalism, which has become the tool of the politicians, including communistic forces.

Nationalism undoubtedly is an obstacle to paternalistic missions. It does not follow, however, that it is necessarily antagonistic to church growth. The intimate ties between strong nationalistic feelings and the growth of Christianity can be amply illustrated from history. This is true both on a national scale (exemplified by the rapid expansion of the Church in Indonesia today) and on the denominational level. The latter is illustrated by the rapid growth of those national Churches which now have no ties (and in most cases, never sustained such ties) with foreign mission organizations. The Iglesia Metodista Pentecostal in Chile, which experienced phenomenal growth under nationalistic inspiration, follows this pattern (Kessler 1967:309). The nationalism we speak of is not "negative nationalism" (Kessler 1967:309), but rather an accommodation of the Gospel which is both harmonious with the host culture and leadership and at the same time consonant with biblical Christianity. This is a nationalism which the mission and the missionary will find themselves vigorously supporting, and in which they will find their supporting efforts abundantly rewarded.

6. *Poverty of Integration*

Making concluding remarks, Saravia considers these national personality characteristics as a whole and asserts that their chief feature is a "poverty of integration." This is seen in the difficulty with which the Argentine enters into social relationships. He does not possess a universally normative system of values and symbols by which to interpret his social relationships with others. This inability to socialize manifests itself in ambivalent reactions. Saravia comments:

> When the integration of the value system is poor, as happens to be the case in Argentina; when the persons see themselves confronted with norms that are frequently contradictory, when society accentuates the importance of certain values that later are systematically violated without the transgression being accompanied by the corresponding condemnation; when the norms or values are ambiguous, it is to be expected that social relations will give birth to a multitude of ambivalent sentiments (1959:166).

Among these ambivalent reactions are the intransigent fighting spirit of the Argentine; the religious fanaticism and violent anticlericalism; the pro-union and anti-union sentiment; the multiplicity of parties, social and political; the propensity toward drastic power-imposed solutions, and impatience toward the person who dares to contradict.

Saravia concludes in his final paragraph of this treatment:

> The conclusion of all this is clear. The soul of our people is sick. To not attend to her cure at this time, can condemn us to the atrophy of our desires to live, and consequently, to an irremissible decadence (1959:168).

The dominant religious influence in Argentine history has been unable to mitigate significantly the tragic consequences of this combination of component factors which contribute to the formation of the Argentine basic personality. In fact, statistics indicate that the body of practicing Catholics is so small that they could have little constructive moral influence. The Church remains powerful in

Argentine political, social and economic affairs, but apparently powerless to bring eternal meaning into the life of the average Argentine who has lost meaningful contact with her institutions. It remains doubtful that an institution which has lost its constructive influences over the masses can lead them into meaningful existence. The unchristianized masses of Argentina and all of Latin America, as the Anglican Church recognized at Lambeth in 1958, are the legitimate concern of all Christian missionary activity.

This situation spells out opportunity for the emerging and rapidly growing Evangelical Church of Argentina. The message of reconciliation and forgiveness in the Gospel of Christ needs to be broadly and imaginatively interpreted and communicated to Argentina, individually and collectively. The forgiveness which Christ alone offers can quench the guilt complex which wrecks havoc with the Argentine personality. Furthermore, only the fellowship which is born of true Christian forgiveness and reconciliation can produce the pleasant fruit of community so desperately needed in Argentina. This is the message that must be heard in Argentina and now is the hour of opportunity. How will Christians in Argentina and the rest of the world respond in this crucial hour?

Part II

THE ARGENTINE
EVANGELICAL CHURCH

CHAPTER 4

Evangelical Beginnings in Argentina

A. EARLY CONTINENTAL PENETRATION

With the single exception of the work of the Moravians in Dutch Guiana, the first permanent missionary effort in Latin America was begun in Argentina. The Moravians, who arrived in 1738, were explicitly forbidden by the colonial authorities to make contacts with the Indians during the early years and worked chiefly among the Dutch settlers. The Huguenot settlement at Río de Janeiro (1555) and the Dutch Protestant colony around Bahía and Pernambuco had long passed into oblivion, subjected to extinction by the political tensions and religious mood prevailing in Latin America at that time. Portugal ruled the eastern part of South America and the Roman Catholic religion was dominant (H. Brown 1901: 177-181).

The Puritans also manifested interest in reaching the people of South America. Cotton Mather studiously applied himself to the learning of the Spanish language. He prepared a system of the *Christian Religion* in 1699 and published it with a tract called *La Religión Pura* (Mather 1901:285,296). With Judge Samuel Sewall, who promoted the publication of the Valera Bible around 1700, he hopefully watched for favorable changes in the political atmosphere of Latin America to introduce their "literary missionaries" (Whitaker 1942:54,55). We do not know for certain if any of this literature ever reached the River Plate area or, for that matter, any of the other countries of Latin America.

With this early interest in the publication of the Scriptures, it is significant that the first Evangelical entrance into Argentina was by an agent of the British and Foreign Bible Society. David Creighton, under the armed protection of the British occupation forces, distributed copies of the Protestant version of the Bible in 1806, in the Spanish Viceroyalty of the River Plate, four years before the first cry of independence of the Argentine nation.

The first missionary efforts in Argentina centered around the diffusion of the Scriptures. Invited by the *cabildo* of the city of Buenos Aires (the incipient independence government of Argentina), James Thomson, a Baptist, arrived in Buenos Aires on October 6, 1818, just two years after the Declaration of Independence of the Tucumán Congress. The newly independent nation, seeking to educate her citizens, heard of the Lancastrian system of education in England and invited Thomson to organize these schools in Buenos Aires. He arrived as the agent of both the English and Foreign School Society and the British and Foreign Bible Society, with a shipment of four hundred Spanish New Testaments. By 1820, after several delays caused by political instability, a school was established and one hundred Argentine boys were learning to read and write, using specially printed selections from the New Testament as their text. Thomson left Argentina in May, 1821, leaving his schools in the care of a sympathetic Roman Catholic priest (Thomson 1827:1-7). There were soon more than one hundred schools with five thousand pupils (H. Brown 1901:180). These schools received strong support from an early Argentine liberal, Bernardino Rivadavia, who as Minister of Government and Foreign Affairs drew heavily on the Lancastrian school leader's ideas for his educational system (Herring 1961:623).

To follow the thrilling adventures of Thomson through the western republics of Latin America is an unforgettable experience. His letters abundantly reflect the enthusiasm of one who found before himself an unparalleled opportunity for the extension of the Gospel of Christ. Writing from Lima on November 9, 1822, he reports:

> A man begins to see the absurdity of the Catholic system, and from his infancy all that is religion with him has been connected with it. In giving up this system, he gives up with religion itself, as considering popery and it the same thing.

> From these circumstances I conceive this to be the most favorable time for labouring in this field, by introducing the Scriptures, and by every other means which prudence may dictate. Prejudice is growing less every day, and this is the result of the revolution (1827:55,56).

Thomson continues:

> What an immeasurable field is South America; and how white it is to harvest. . . . I do think that since the world began, there never was so fine a field for the exercise of benevolence in all parts.

> I think a door has been opened here which will never be shut, but which will, I trust, from one year to another, open wider and wider, until it become, in the Apostle's language, "great and effectual." Should I say, there are no adversaries, and that all goes on prosperously, without any difficulty or discouragement from any quarter. . . . It is surely a gratifying sight to see darkness fleeing away, and the light of heaven breaking forth (1827:37,50).

So convincing was Thomson in his letters to the British and Foreign Bible Society that they decided in 1824 to print an extravagant 15,000 copies of the Spanish Bible (BFBS 1825:liii,liv). It appears that Browning's (1928:49) later critical judgment of Thomson's estimate of the opportunity was unwarranted. The immediate entrance of the Methodists and Presbyterians is evidence that Thomson's judgment was correct. It was most certainly more true during the years of his residence than later on when the doors closed temporarily. Yet even as late as 1847, Thomson was still urging the formation of "The Southern Colombian Philanthropic Society," whose aim, among other things, would be missionary through the "influence of religious principle" (Thomson 1847:387f.). When opportunities open for the Church, she must occupy immediately, even if drastic temporary redeployment of personnel is indicated.

Will the Lord of the Church someday charge His servants with this early opportunity which was largely neglected for many years? Similar opportunities call for the Church's response from all parts of the world. The Church must retool to be aware of and alert to each moving of His Spirit whether it be in Africa, Asia, Latin America or the islands of the sea. Indonesia presents such an opportunity now, as does all of Latin America. James Thomson would indeed rejoice at the sight today of countless thousands fleeing the darkness to turn to the light of the Son of God.

B. CHURCH-SPONSORED OCCUPATION

The years immediately following the work of Thomson saw the entrance of the first church-sponsored missionaries. This first effort was attempted by the Board of Foreign Missions of the Presbyterian Church in the United States. John Brigham and Theophilus Pravin arrived in Buenos Aires in 1823 and found unparalleled opportunities in the field of education. After teaching in the University of Buenos Aires and later beginning a girls school and another for boys, Pravin left Argentina and Brigham set out for the republics on the Pacific shore of South America (Browning 1928:52; H. Brown 1901:183,184). No tangible results remained of this first attempt.

In 1824, during the government of Rivadavia, the Anglicans and members of the Church of Scotland were given formal permission to conduct worship services in their own language. At this time Mr. Pravin estimated the "number of Protestant foreigners" at not less than three thousand (*Missionary Herald* 1824:375). They would largely have been members of these churches.

During the next decade the Methodist Episcopal Board entered Argentina. Justin Spaulding and in 1836 John Dempster began their short-lived residence in Buenos Aires. It lasted until 1841. After a lapse of two years, and beginning with the year 1843, the Methodists have maintained the longest continuous witness for Christ in Argentina (Browning 1928:53). Their present (1965) small membership (7,382), in comparison to other missions who entered more than half a century later (e.g., the Southern Baptists, the Plymouth Brethren and the Seventh-Day Adventists), is a poignant reminder that mere length of witness is not the most important factor in missions. Its quality, redemptive passion, and outcome in ongoing and reproductive churches are of much greater significance.

Argentine Evangelicals are justly proud to count among their gallant sons of the faith who gave their lives for the extension of the Gospel, one who walked the cold, bleak shores of Patagonia in a frustrated attempt to win the Indians of that region. After several unsuccessful attempts to begin work among the Indians of Chile and Bolivia, Captain Allan Gardiner organized an expedition which was to become the precursor of the South American Missionary Society. Gardiner, with six companions, was the victim of faulty planning. When promised relief supplies failed to arrive during the dark antarctic winter of 1851, all seven died. Gardiner with his dying words urged that the mission to the Fuegians not be abandoned. Undaunted by the tragedy, supporters of the mission organized another ill-fated expedition which met with death at the hands of savage Indians in 1859, save the cook, who had remained on board ship. Similar zeal inspires their mid-twentieth-century disciples in the Chaco forests of northern Argentina among the Mataco and Toba Indian tribes (Daniels 1916:118, Browning 1928:50,51).

1. Protestant Immigrants

The first of several immigrant groups from Europe arrived and began the worship of their God in this hostile environment in 1843. These German Lutherans were soon related to the Prussian State Church. Today their descendants form part of the German Evangelical Church of the River Plate. The Waldensians, spiritual descendants of the French merchant of Lyon, Peter Waldo, arrived in Uruguay from Italy in 1856, but in 1859 crossed the River Plate to establish colonies in Argentina. To the south, in the Chubut Valley, a group of Welsh Protestants settled in 1864, bringing with them their own pastor. By 1897 this community of valiant colonists had grown to 2,372 members (*Hispanic American Historical Review* 1954:482).[1] During subsequent decades other immigrants from Europe arrived and continued to practice their faith. Among them were Danish and Swedish Lutherans, Russian and French Baptists, Armenian Congregationalists, Mennonites and Dutch Reformed from South Africa.

The possibilities for effective missionary action represented by these immigrant congregations were in large part neglected by the mother Churches. At best there was only a holding action which in many instances was wholly ineffective. It is a sad story of too little, too late. By way of contrast, the Missouri Synod Lutherans who actively sought converts to Christ showed remarkable growth, much of it from among scarcely pastored Lutheran families.

2. American Bible Society

In 1864 the American Bible Society entered Argentina and established their first permanent agency, with Andrew Milne as executive secretary. Milne will probably be best remembered for his influence in the life of the untiring and persevering Bible colporteur, Francisco Penzotti, whose imprisonment in Peru brought about conditions favorable to the amendment of the Peruvian constitution in favor of religious liberty (Daniels 1916:222). The colporteurs of the Bible societies have been singularly influential in the establishment of churches throughout the length and breadth of Argentina.

3. First Spanish Services

Argentine presidents of the post-Rosas era were especially cordial to Protestants, undoubtedly feeling that much of the progress of North America and Europe was the fruit of a Protestant heritage. Legislation favorable to the expansion of the Gospel in Argentina through the granting of permission to preach in the Spanish language was enacted during the government of the great Argentine president, Bartolomé Mitre (1862-1868). Services in the Spanish language were prohibited until the year 1867, when the Rev. John F. Thomson, a Methodist missionary, preached the first sermon in an Evangelical church in the national language (Glover 1960:375). However, the real missionary opportunity provided by the liberal tendencies set in motion by the overthrow of Rosas in 1852 was not fully appreciated and acted upon for nearly fifty years. President Roca in 1884 praised Protestant missionaries for their evident contribution to the progress of the Argentine republic.

Another president, the great educator Sarmiento, commissioned a Methodist missionary to send teachers to Argentina. Sarmiento, while serving as Argentine ambassador to Washington, had learned to admire greatly the North American educational system and asked for teachers to set up normal schools throughout the republic. Seventy-five teachers came who, according to Tamagno (1963:310ff.), were almost all active Protestants. Strong reaction to the "heretical" teachers on the part of fanatical women who refused to send their daughters to the new schools did not greatly diminish the overall salutary effect of these teachers. Argentina soon had more highly effective teachers than the other Latin American nations. This in part accounts for the high rate of literacy (above 90 per cent) today.

The request of the Argentine government for teachers through the instrumentality of Evangelical missionaries is sign enough that an open door to missionary occupation was before the Churches in North America and Europe. Yet the opportunity for the entrance of additional Evangelical Missions was almost completely neglected for nearly a quarter of a century.

4. Expanding Evangelical Occupation

Shortly before the turn of the century Evangelical forces in Argentina were strengthened by the arrival of the first missionaries of the Plymouth Brethren (1882), the Salvation Army (1889), the Christian and Missionary Alliance (1895), the South American Evangelical Mission (1895), the South American Missionary Society (1898), and the Regions Beyond Mission (1899). The Seventh-Day Adventists entered Argentina in 1894 (Dennis 1911:96).

After almost a hundred years of, first sporadic, and then concentrated Evangelical effort, William Payne (1904:6), an early Plymouth Brethren pioneer, reports that the total attendance at Spanish services in all of Argentina in the year 1904 was only one thousand eight hundred and fifty-nine. Undoubtedly he was unaware of the Welsh community in the south, but even when the Welsh Protestants in Patagonia are included, the small size of the Evangelical community is evidence that today's optimum conditions for evangelism did not exist at that time. After delays, the missions began to occupy the territory which in the following years was to prove highly responsive. Some of the missions responded to the opportunity. Others, occupied with issues and methodologies of little relevance in Argentina, missed the growth that was possible. It is the purpose of the following chapters to analyze the methods and emphases which the different missions employed at various stages in the development of the Evangelical Churches. While some were achieving accelerated rates of growth, others persisted with practices which proved to be stagnant and unproductive. Several of the profiles will amply demonstrate that generous church growth is possible when opportunities are met by proper conditions, both spiritual and methodological. Others tell the tragic story of those who persist with unproductive policies and emphases while, at the same time, they are witnessing spectacular church growth all around. God desires that His Church grow and that all those involved be rewarded with abundant life.

CHAPTER 5

The Assemblies of God

A. PENTECOSTAL FIRES ON THE PAMPAS

The Pentecostal fires that first fell on the plains of Kansas in 1901 and subsequently spread rapidly into international proportions from the Los Angeles Azusa Street meeting (Bloch-Hoell 1964:18ff.) soon reached Argentina. The year 1909 seems to have been the year of first contact with the Pentecostal message. This was the year that the Italian missionary from Chicago, Louis Francescon, and his companion felt constrained to carry this message of salvation to fellow Italians who were immigrating to Argentina from Italy by the tens of thousands. Their ministry met with limited success and severe opposition, including imprisonment. Francescon's successful ministry in Brazil was in direct contrast to his efforts in Buenos Aires, and today the Congregação Cristã in that country numbers almost 300,000 (Read 1965:22,29). Conn (1959:157) reports that a "Mother Kelty" and her daughter went from New Castle, Pennsylvania, that same year as independent faith missionaries, but remained in Argentina for less than two years.

These temporary efforts were followed in this year (1909) by the first permanent Pentecostal witness in Argentina, begun through the dedicated independent efforts of Miss Alice C. Woods in the settlement of 25 de Mayo on the *pampas* of the province of Buenos Aires. Miss Wood in 1914 became affiliated with the Assemblies of God of Springfield, Missouri, and continued her faithful ministry in

Argentina for fifty years, without furlough, until her death in 1960 at the age of 90, shortly after her return to the United States. The first church continues today under the leadership of national pastors trained in the Bible Institute in Buenos Aires.

From these simple beginnings, the work of the Assemblies of God grew very slowly, in sharp contrast to the rapid growth of the Plymouth Brethren. The missionary force was augmented in 1921 by Canadian Assemblies of God missionaries, but not until 1943 were other missionaries sent from the United States, and their term of service was short-lived. This was true of subsequent arrivals, also, whose ministry lasted for only a brief period. In 1951 there were nine missionaries on the field and only 174 active adult church members. Since 1914 the Church had experienced almost no growth. A rather discouraging picture, but not to the body of faithful missionaries who trusted God for greater growth. Spectacular increases were not far off.

1. Tommy Hicks Arrives

The year 1954 was to mark a very significant departure from this pattern of slow growth. This unusual event drew the editorial attention of the liberal Protestant journal, *Christian Century* (1954:814,815). The vision and organizing drive behind the fifty-two days of the Tommy Hicks meetings were largely the sacrificial work of the missionaries of the Assemblies of God who longed for a break in this pattern of nongrowth. These meetings represent the greatest single Protestant evangelistic effort in Argentina, drawing, according to Buenos Aires newspaper reports, 200,000 on the final night. The aggregate attendance for the two-month campaign in the stadiums of the Atlanta and Huracán football teams was near two million, according to Louis Stokes (1967), chairman of the organizing committee. The sale of Bibles and Scripture portions was so phenomenal that it was necessary to have additional supplies shipped in by air. An Argentine writer reports the sale of 22,018 Bibles, 25,912 New Testaments and 1,100 gospels (Acenelli 1954:97). Hicks claims that President Perón attended at least one meeting (Merritt 1967:2).

The campaign was a typical Pentecostal evangelistic effort, with their traditionally strong emphasis on "divine healing." Many claims of healing were both asserted and contested by the press as well as by noncooperating and even hostile Evangelicals. The effect on the

Evangelical community in general was immense, but not without severe negative reactions. Denominations were divided in their support of the campaign.

Permission for meetings of this kind and magnitude (Hicks insisted on renting a stadium with a capacity of at least 25,000, in opposition to the committee's careful calculation that a place one-tenth the size would be more than adequate) was difficult to secure. It was finally granted personally by the President of the Nation, Juan Domingo Perón, under very unusual circumstances. Miller (1964:33-35) enthusiastically reports the alleged miraculous healing of both a presidential guard and of the President himself. Hicks denies any knowledge of praying for Perón's healing, but he stands by the claim of the healing of the presidential guard (Merritt 1967:2). Full permission for the meetings was granted and radio and press coverage was secured. A great breakthrough for the Evangelical work in Argentina had been achieved. Perón's relations with the Roman Catholic Church at the time were far from being cordial, and that certainly became a decisive factor in his favorable decision. (This same breakdown in relations led to his overthrow in 1955.) Undoubtedly the atmosphere of political and religious tension prevailing at the time and the increasing self-identity of the masses provided by the charismatic leadership of Perón and his recently deceased wife were factors which entered into the picture. The least sign of a favorable attitude on the part of the President could tip the balance of any enterprise which might capture the imagination of the masses toward success. It was these circumstances which provided the Assemblies of God and other cooperating Churches with this unparalleled opportunity in Argentine Evangelical history. Hicks himself says that the meetings "came about" as a result of a meeting with Perón (Merritt 1967:1).

An organizing committee set up for a return campaign in November of 1954 reflected the divisiveness of the healing issue among the denominations. However, a broad but selective committee was set up to organize this second effort. According to *Christian Century's* (1954:815) observer the composition of the sponsoring group for this second campaign included Pentecostal, Assemblies of God, and Christian and Missionary Alliance churches, four each; Baptist and Brethren, three each; Methodists, two, and Mennonites, one. It is significant that the largest Pentecostal Churches did not find it convenient to cooperate. According to Montgomery (1956:158) the plans for this second campaign miscarried and only three meetings were held. The police closed down the campaign ostensibly to investigate the charge that Hicks practiced medicine illegally. The real reason, Montgomery adds, was the fact that because of unstable political conditions no large gatherings were permitted.

2. Sharp Break in Growth Curve

The Assemblies of God as well as other Churches benefited greatly. Louis Stokes reports that they were able to establish many new churches immediately. The largest church before the campaign had a seating capacity of only 150, and special halls had to be rented to accommodate the new converts. Five new churches were begun in the year 1955 alone. Enrollment in the Bible Institute, which had always stood at about twelve to fifteen students, in two years jumped to between forty and fifty. These young men were to be the future leaders of the continually growing movement. Our graph (Figure No. 2) records this sharp increase in church membership between 1951 and 1956, a direct result of the campaign. An intangible but nonetheless solid result of the campaign was a new spirit of faith and spiritual optimism which pervaded the entire Evangelical community, even beyond the limit of the officially cooperating body of churches. Humble and fearful Christians were made aware of their latent potential which could be released in saving power through the exercise of faith. Among the population in general, the prestige and appreciation of the Evangelical Churches increased noticeably.

The Assemblies of God have continued to grow at a phenomenal rate, but not without slight reverses. The graph indicates a plateau in the growth curve between 1958 and 1961. Apparently internal dissension was the principal cause of this leveling off. Several of the younger men were discouraged from making an evangelistic tour of Patagonia. Feeling led of God, they left the Assemblies and became identified with a new movement, an indigenous Pentecostal Church known as the Movimiento Cristiano y Misionero, whose membership today is about 3,000.

The final upsurge of growth, which began in 1961 and has continued unabated to the present, has generated sufficient heat to counteract the cooling off produced by the cold Patagonian winds. During this period the Billy Graham campaign (1964) was organized under general Evangelical auspices. This campaign, although nowhere

Figure No.2

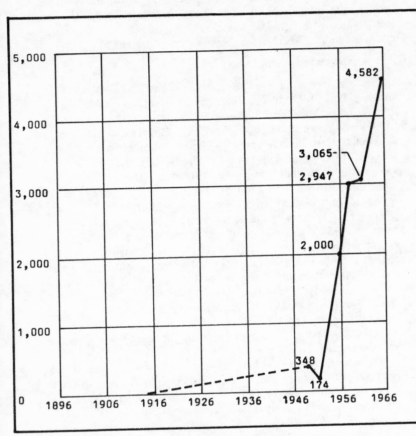

ASSEMBLIES OF GOD

COMMUNICANT MEMBERS

DATE OF ENTRANCE — 1914

SOURCES

1949 GRUBB   1949:304
1951 HODGES,m.   1967
1956 HODGES,s.   1956
1958 WINEHOUSE   1959:223
1961 HODGES,m.   1967
1966 HODGES,m.   1967

near the proportions of the Hicks effort (only 10 days as compared to 52, and 60,000 as compared to 200,000 highest attendance), undoubtedly provided positive influences which have affected the accelerated growth rate of the Assemblies of God churches. Another cause, and probably of greater import, is the steady growth in the Bible Institute, which continues to produce graduates inspired with a passion to win men and to start new Pentecostal churches. Since its inception in 1946 the school has graduated 140 students, 90 of which continue active in the ministry (Nichol 1966:164).

These factors combined have produced a greatly accelerated growth rate among the Assemblies of God churches that shows little signs of slacking off. After a drop from 348 in 1949 to 174 in 1951, the total baptized membership grew to 2,000 in 1956. The impact of the Tommy Hicks meetings is reflected in this sharp increase. Although the rate of growth was not quite as accelerated between 1956 and 1966, the membership grew from 2,000 to 4,582. The evangelistic impact was being utilized to good advantage and consolidated the churches. That healthy church growth was taking place is reflected in the increased numbers of students in the Bible Institute. The pattern of stagnation among the Assemblies of God had been broken. Today, as a direct result of the continuing impact of the Hicks campaign, 78.5 per cent of the Assemblies of God churches are within the province of Buenos Aires, and there is a growing interest in reaching out into the twelve provinces which remain unoccupied (Asambleas de Dios 1966a).

Around 1950 the Assemblies of God of Canada and their fraternal counterpart from the United States joined hands with their Argentine brethren to form the National Union of the Assemblies of God in Argentina. The main purpose in the formation of the organization was to facilitate representation before the Argentine authorities who at that time were making considerable demands on the Evangelical Churches in general. The superintendent since early 1966 has been an Argentine. The improvement of the churches' financial condition and the increase in membership during this period augur well for the future (Hodges 1967).

3. Other Pentecostal Bodies

Several of the larger bodies of Pentecostal Churches in Argentina remained outside this National Union of the Assemblies of God. One of the larger Churches which did not become part of the Union is the Church of God of Cleveland, Tennessee. Conn (1959:155-162) reports that their first contacts with Argentina go back to 1918, although their great growth was achieved when Missionary J. H. Ingram joined forces with a converted Italian immigrant, Marcos Mazzucco, in 1943. Mazzucco's church, which numbered 430 at that time, today has over 3,000 members. The most significant growth experienced by this group is in the Chaco in northern Argentina. Upon retiring in 1945, John R. Lagar turned over the work he had carried on among the Toba Indians to the Church of God in Buenos Aires. At a formal meeting in 1946, 3,800 Indians were received into the Church of God. Hargrave (1967) states that there were as many as 9,000 Toba Christians affiliated with the Church of God. Subsequent developments, however, have reduced this number to 1,000 or less. (These developments are treated in Chapter X.) In this same area there is a Bulgarian congregation of approximately 300 members which operates its own Bible institute (Nida 1961b:97).

Another Pentecostal Church in Argentina is the Chilean Pentecostal, whose crusading zeal has crossed the Andes to reverse the pattern of conquest followed by the great Argentine Liberator, San Martín. Their activities are limited largely to fellow countrymen who have immigrated to Argentina for greater economic opportunity. No accurate figure of their number exists, but conservative estimates place their strength at about 10,000. Another immigrant Church has developed among the hundreds of thousands of Italians who have come to Argentina. Even when their congregations became generously sprinkled with Spanish-speaking Argentines, they continued to sing in Italian—a custom which has been dropped only in very recent years. The mystique of the Pentecostal experience was stronger than national ties and language. The fact that this could happen is evidence of the power of this experience.

B. ANALYSIS OF THE PENTECOSTAL MOVEMENT

In addition to the Chilean and Italian Pentecostals, the Church Growth Research in Latin America team has identified approximately thirty-five different bodies in the Pentecostal family of churches. The CGRILA team, after dozens of interviews with the leaders and many visits to their churches, estimates total Pentecostal strength in Argentina at 98,472 baptized members. This represents a 556 per cent increase since 1943, or 119 per cent per decade, or 8.15 per cent per year. The following table presents a breakdown of the membership of the Pentecostal Churches.

PENTECOSTAL CHURCHES
Communicant Members—1967

Church	Communi- cants	Source[1]
Asamblea Cristiana (Italian)	22,000	1
Asamblea Cristiana Cultural	2,000	1
Assemblies of God—Canada	4,500	1
Assemblies of God—U.S.A.	4,582	5
Church of God—Cleveland, Tennessee	9,680	4
Church of God Prophecy	196	4
Emmanuel Holiness Church	68	4
English Pentecostals	350	1
Four Square Gospel	587	1
Iglesia Evangélica Pentecostal (Chilean)	5,000	1
Iglesia Unida Evangélica (Toba)	3,000	3
Independent Churches (20 groups)	20,000	1
Movimiento Cristiano y Misionero	3,000	1
Norske Pinsevenners Ytremisjon (Norwegian)	3,009	4
Svenske Fria Missionen (Swedish)	20,000	2
Toba Churches (diverse affiliation)	500	3
TOTAL	98,472	

The numerical increase of the combined Pentecostal Churches is far greater than the combined increase of all the other denominations together. Browning in a comment that appears to be directed at these Churches says:

> Others are not only weak in numbers and resources, but represent exotic tendencies which confuse the mind of the people whom they are striving to serve, and hold up to public scorn the manifold divisions of Protestantism (1928:55).

That is the only mention of the Pentecostal work in this comprehensive early survey. The first mention of these Churches in the statistical surveys is made in the 1949 edition of the World Christian Handbook (Grubb 1949:304), but the 1949 total membership figure of 3,610 would have to be modified considerably because the Mazzucco Church (which is not listed) had at least 500 members and the Toba Indian work (also not listed) included 3,800 more. Merle Davis' estimate of 15,000 in 1943 appears to be accurate. Davis

---

[1] Sources: 1. CGRILA estimate; 2. Forsberg 1967; 3. Buckwalter 1967; 4. WCH 1967; 5. Graph in profile.

(1943:101,102) was the first to recognize the rising importance of this "third force" in Argentina. My own investigation and research have led to the conclusion that a more realistic estimate for 1949 would be near 24,500. DuPlessis (1958:201) states that by 1958 there were about 50,000 members in their Argentine Churches.

1. A Continental Comparison

When the strength of the Pentecostal Churches in Argentina is compared with the strength of the Pentecostal Churches of Chile and Brazil, it is seen that they stand in third place both numerically and percentagewise. The following table provides a comparison of the total Evangelical Church communicant membership and the communicant membership of the Pentecostal Churches in the three countries:

Total Population

	Total Population	Communicants	%	Pentecostals	%
Argentina	22,691,000	233,055	1.0	98,472	42.7
					(Enns—See p. 178)
Brazil	82,696,000	2,592,000	3.1	1,689,000	65.1
					(Read 1965:217)
Chile	8,738,000	620,000	7.1	496,000	80
					(Kessler 1967:322)

The interesting conclusion here is that the Pentecostal phenomenon in Argentina has not manifested the same dynamic as has been present in the other two countries. The reasons for this are not understood and constitute an area for further investigation.

2. Questions Other Evangelicals Ask

The vitality and broad outreach of the Pentecostal Churches in ever enlarging circles of active evangelism promises increasing church growth not only in Argentina, but throughout Latin America. Other Evangelical Churches cannot close their eyes to these developments which in the past fifty years have produced a movement which at an increasing rate is outstripping other Evangelical efforts. The secret to such growth must be understood. Yet there are, at the same time, several questions these Churches would like their Pentecostal brethren to answer.

1. To what extent has this rapid expansion contributed to even a minimal understanding of Christian truth on the part of the average Pentecostal church member?

2. To what extent has their conviction that they alone possess the "full gospel" led them to practice proselytism among their

sister Evangelical Churches in their drive to win "converts"? The basic consideration here is not how much the Pentecostal Churches have grown at the expense of others, for this figure would almost certainly prove to be a most insignificant portion of total Pentecostal membership. The key consideration is just how much the growth pattern of the other Churches has been affected, both by actual membership transfers and, what is far more important, by defensive attitudes which have developed to contain the leakage.

3. Finally, to what extent has Pentecostal growth been the result of an unbalanced presentation of biblical truth? This question relates to the first, but should be handled separately.

Frank discussion of these questions could lead all concerned to a fuller understanding of each other and, hopefully, would eventuate in greater growth for the entire Evangelical Church. Most of the other Evangelical Churches are anxious to know the secret of Pentecostal growth, but these perplexing questions cloud the issues. It becomes difficult to achieve a sympathetic understanding of the principles which govern the dynamic of their movement because of these emotional overtones.

3. Features of Pentecostalism in Argentina

It would be a difficult task to analyze and evaluate the distinctive characteristics of each of the almost 35 different Pentecostal movements in Argentina. Therefore I have chosen to discuss those traits which I believe to be true distinctives of the Assemblies of God. A careful study of these features of the Assemblies' churches will help us understand the dynamic of this representative Pentecostal group.

First, they have sought to give the Holy Spirit free rein in their personal and church life. In most evaluations of the Pentecostal phenomenon this factor is ignored or treated with an attitude bordering on the negative. Their experience of the Holy Spirit, in spite of the excesses and abuses which have undoubtedly occurred, is probably the key factor in their rapid growth. This is not the moment to sift the true from the false or the good from the bad, but only to emphasize that it is their *belief* in the presence and power of the Holy Spirit in their lives which drives them on to new spiritual conquests.

Next, it is this writer's persuasion that they have succeeded in "deintellectualizing" the Gospel for the new convert. The experience of the new Christian is not only the increased knowledge and understanding of the biblical message, but a dynamic fellowship with God and with his fellow man through forgiveness in Christ. This has resulted in a worship pattern in their meetings (although at times totally unintelligible and even blasphemous to some Evangelicals) by which they experience the immediacy of God in corporate worship. The Gospel becomes an experience, and not exclusively the acquisition of knowledge.

Thirdly, the Pentecostal message includes the active participation of all the members of the fellowship in the activities of worship and witness. All are expected and helped to be active in their Christian life in some concrete manner. Even the singing, shouting and "dancing" in the meetings provide each person with an opportunity for strong emotional involvement. This participation is sometimes too exclusively limited to the formal institutions and activities of the church and too far divorced from daily living. Many criticize them for an alleged low ethical content in their daily practice of the Christian faith.

Fourth, but certainly not less important than the previous two, is the pattern of leadership employed in the churches. Generally the established leadership of a church is composed of the natural adult leaders who have been converted. They, with the pastor, supervise the life of the growing congregation. The young men, or what we choose to call the emerging leadership, are directed out toward the unbelieving community. The natural and almost inherent tendency of rebellion in the youth is directed, not in competition against the established leadership of the elders, but in revolutionary rebellion against the sinful world. This practice has achieved a great degree of harmony and stimulated an accelerated growth rate. Nida has some interesting insights into this aspect of church growth (McGavran 1965:189).

Not to be overlooked, but mentioned only briefly, are several other characteristics. Among these is their expectancy to see God work in spectacular ways. They live in a day of miracles and great faith, when divine intervention is seen and experienced in the most mundane happening. This is the atmosphere of faith which produces continued church growth. Another feature is the mother church system, with a whole cluster of satellite congregations organically related to her. The tithes of the members are further evidence of the high degree of involvement of each new Christian.

4. *Keys to Accelerated Growth*

What might this growing Church do to improve its position, both numerically and qualitatively? It is difficult to make suggestions where such accelerated growth is being achieved. However, there are two areas where, if correct action is taken, even greater growth can be expected in the future.

The Assemblies of God in Argentina would do well to develop training techniques which would reach more deeply into the grass roots of the movement. Much of the leadership of these churches has not been formerly trained in the Bible Institute program. The creation of a concentrated training program through an extension of the Institute out into the churches would greatly improve the general level of knowledge of the Christian faith and at the same time measurably increase the level of leadership locally. This would make the already involved lay leadership doubly effective. To achieve this purpose, this extension program can be no amplified correspondence course, but a serious effort to bring the entire Institute program of learning to the local level.

Secondly, these churches must avoid the common fascination with entire geographic coverage and occupation. There is a too frequent tendency to attempt to have a church in every provincial capital and call this effective evangelism. This has been the practice of many missions, frequently with less than the desired results. The Assemblies of God would do well to concentrate where at present they are achieving good growth. They seem to have discovered such an area around Buenos Aires. Arbitrary occupation of the entire country might not produce the growth expected. The urban masses are responding at present, and this ought to be the area of emphasis. There are other exploding urban areas which could be occupied in other parts of the country, but every provincial capital does not always represent a responsive situation. Divine guidance here will surely lead these growing churches on into ever-expanding horizons. Other denominations located in provincial capitals which are not responding might consider moving into the larger, highly receptive urban area.

CHAPTER 6

The Christian and Missionary Alliance

A. FROM GUALIGUAYCHU TO TOMMY HICKS

The first efforts of the Christian and Missionary Alliance in the River Plate country began in 1897 with a limited missionary force. Within six years (1903) a church was established in the capital city of the province of Buenos Aires, La Plata. Another church was begun in the town of Gualiguaychú in the province of Entre Rios. A third church, begun some 180 miles south of Buenos Aires in the town of Azul, is the oldest church of the Alliance. The other two churches were turned over to the Baptists (Glover 1960:276, R. Clark 1938:48). By 1925 there were eighteen missionaries actively engaged in the extension of the Gospel. This was the greatest number of Alliance missionaries to occupy the Argentine field at any one time. The demand for workers on other fields and the depression of the 1930's depleted the force.

Clark (1938:48-51) describes the six districts or circuits which comprised the Alliance responsibility in the province of Buenos Aires. They were centered in the towns of Azul, Olavarría, Saladillo, Carhue (Adolfo Alsina), Puán and Nueve de Julio. In Azul the Alliance in 1923 erected a building for their Bible institute, which was the predecessor of the Buenos Aires Bible Institute, founded in 1946. Outside the limits of the capital province the only town occupied which saw the growth of an active church was the *pampa* town of General Pico. During this period there was strong emphasis on the indigenous principles of self-support and self-government motivated by scriptural principles and an increasing spirit of nationalism (C&MA 1964:124). Despite these changing emphases the period 1919 to 1929 saw most of the towns of Alliance responsibility occupied and churches established, the majority of which continue to this day and form the backbone of the movement. It was during this period in the development of the work that almost complete independence of the Argentine Church was achieved. An Argentine was elected superintendent in 1929, and the missionary passed to an honorary and advisory capacity (Clark 1938:53).

1. Dissension and Decimation

Political conditions in Argentina, and the Depression, in addition to internal dissension within the Church, brought the Alliance work to a standstill in the early 1930's. According to King (1967) the dissension centered around varying views on the Holy Spirit's work in the believer held by the missionaries. Strong opinions produced tensions first between the missionaries but quickly infected the young Church as well. This adverse missionary influence produced tragic consequences. These were the result of strife and pessimism which overcame the spiritual resources the young Church was able to muster on her own. Discord within the churches took its toll in workers who reverted to the world or became associated with other missions. These tensions and consequent fluctuations in membership are not reflected in our statistical graph. This is due in part to the fact that by 1938 the movement had recovered and had recouped its losses (Clark 1938:54,55). After the visit of the foreign secretary, A. C. Snead, in 1937, the missionaries and churches began an aggressive program of evangelism which created a spirit of optimism throughout the field.

In 1943, when Merle Davis wrote his survey of work in Argentina, there was only one missionary in Argentina, working with a small band of dedicated and faithful pastors and lay workers. The churches out in the province of Buenos Aires had been decimated by the removal of many members to the cities. In one large provincial city church, one-half of its eighty members left for the city of Buenos Aires, and the following year 38 more left (Davis 1943:96). The missionary felt that the Argentine pastors could ably handle the responsibilities of leadership in the churches and began a program of extensive tent evangelism. This evangelism was directed toward the winning of the "respectable" and "substantial" people of the community. This emphasis was tragic in the light of the fact that the more responsive segment of society are the poorer masses. Possibly this was not understood at the time, but other Churches capitalized on this phenomenon and grew well during this same period.

2. Institute Becomes Central

When the people continued to move to the cities, it was felt that the center of the Alliance work should be moved to the capital. This was indeed a wise decision. The location of the new Bible Institute in the Belgrano district of the capital city, however, reflects the incorrect emphasis on the higher segments of society. This Bible Institute program, begun in 1946, became the nerve and energy center of the Christian and Missionary Alliance movement in Argentina and remains so today. From its classrooms and halls a steady flow of consecrated and dedicated young men have gone out to pastor the churches. In recent years the enrollment has consisted of about 35 to 40 students in the full course, with additional students taking the night course. The Bible Institute, as well as missionary residences, is housed in what is probably the finest building occupied by an Evangelical group in Argentina. The Institute's position today is quite dominant among the Alliance churches. It continues to be the key to expansion in the thinking of the missionaries. And yet, after more than twenty years of this emphasis, the earlier pattern of slow growth has not been appreciably altered. Expansion has occurred only when aggressive evangelistic efforts have been undertaken either by the national Church or the missionaries. However, this growth (particularly in the light of subsequent losses) is not equal to the optimum conditions of responsiveness which are seen in the successes of the Assemblies of God churches.

3. Fresh Breezes

With the Pentecostal Churches, the Alliance churches benefited from the electric impact of the Tommy Hicks meetings in 1954. The pattern of stagnation seemed to have been broken, as it had been among the other sponsoring Churches, but this has not proved to be the case. They, with the Assemblies of God, were among the chief sponsors of the effort, which proved to be such a surprising success.

Figure No.3

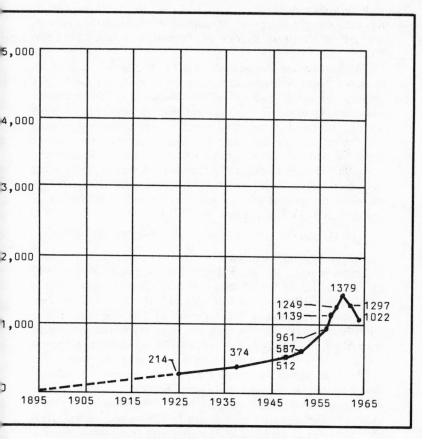

CHRISTIAN AND MISSIONARY ALLIANCE

COMMUNICANT MEMBERS
DATE OF ENTRANCE - 1895

SOURCES

1925 BEACH   1925:119
1938 PARKER   1938:82
1949 GRUBB   1949:304
1952 GRUBB   1952:216
1957-1964   C&MA YEARBOOK

Consequently, they benefited significantly. Mr. Voth (1967), an Alliance missionary in Argentina, reports that three new churches with an aggregate membership of 150 were the direct outcome of this astonishingly successful campaign. The results of the campaign account for the sharp increase in membership between 1952 and 1957.

The momentum thus gained, plus the vision and drive of an increased North American missionary force, translated itself into a growing missionary and evangelistic emphasis by the Argentine churches themselves. This year-to-year push culminated in 1960 in a net increase for the year of 82 members, more than any previous year except that of the Hicks campaign. The five new churches organized that year alone represented an increase of 134 members, more than enough to offset the losses in other areas of the work. The board representative reported: "During the year 1960, we have witnessed the greatest advance and development in the history of our work in Argentina" (C&MA 1961:131).

B. ANALYSIS OF THE ALLIANCE CHURCH IN ARGENTINA

This year (1960) culminated a period of eleven years of steady and rapid growth. The graph (Figure No. 3) indicates that in 1949 the membership of the Alliance churches, after fifty-four years of missionary occupation, stood at only 513. By 1960 total membership was 1,379, showing a net growth of 168 per cent. This is respectable growth for this span of eleven years. The momentum generated through the new spirit released by the Hicks campaign was probably the predominant reason for this period of expansion.

The major part of the growth that year and the years immediately preceding was in the new missionary territory taken on by the Alliance churches in the northern part of Argentina. This area is located in the Argentine province of Corrientes and reaches across the international border into Uruguay, and from the Uruguayan town of Rivera across another international border into Brazil. Much of this thrust was the direct result of the consecrated driving zeal and early success of the first Argentine missionary sent into the area. The year 1965 saw the city of Asunción, Paraguay, entered under this same missionary dynamic.

The strange and enigmatic turn of events since 1960 has resulted in the loss of almost 50 per cent of the gain made since 1949. The only direct comment that can be gleaned from the annual reports from the field is this statement, which seems to be a thin justification of what happened. "This year (1961) our work has been the consolidation of what has been the big missionary push of 1959-1960 so that next year we can lengthen the cords again" (C&MA 1962:135). While subsequent reports mention the continued sacrificial giving and growing interest in the missionary vision of the maturing Argentine Church, an accompanying upsurge in the curve of membership is missing. The net increase between 1949 and 1964 was 509, or 99 per cent. King (1967) gives two reasons for this decline. First, he mentions that each pastor "renovated" his church membership list. All inactive members were removed. This pruning was so deep that the average of 95 baptisms per year did not even maintain the same level of membership. Furthermore, he explains that the exodus from the provincial churches to the larger urban areas continued. Many Christians from the Alliance churches, once in the new environment, found it easier to attend non-Alliance churches nearer their homes. This latter reason is a two-edged sword and could just as well have benefited the Alliance churches, had they been alert to the opportunity represented by people moving into the area of their churches from the other denominations. As for the first reason, it has been observed that the fastest growing Churches in Latin America experience the greatest leakage. Their key to growth is the aggressive evangelism which always exceeds the rate of leakage.

In 1964 the Christian and Missionary Alliance of Argentina had twenty-three organized churches and seventeen unorganized churches. These were located along almost the entire length of the republic, longitudinally directly north and south of Buenos Aires in a line that roughly follows the eastern boundary of the nation. A straight line drawn from the northernmost church (Asunción, Paraguay) to the southernmost (Comodoro Rividavia) falls to the west of the entire Alliance field, with the single exception of the church in General Pico in the province of La Pampa.

Among the salient features of the Alliance work in Argentina has been, first, the strong emphasis on self-support and self-government. After an abortive attempt at total independence in the 1930's, the mission has proceeded toward this goal more cautiously. Many of the churches are entirely self-supporting and their number is increasing. There is an indigenous church organization served by Argentine personnel and guided by an Argentine committee. The caliber of leadership is generally average, but in a few instances it is outstanding. Foreign influences and ideas tend to dominate (especially through the effective Bible Institute program) and frustrate the initiative of genuinely Argentine trends in the Church.

A second characteristic of this Church is the especially strong dedication to missions. The opening of new fields largely through exclusive Argentine support and sponsorship has been indicative of the quality of enthusiasm and vision which pervades some of the churches. Of particular import has been the effective communication to the sending Argentine churches of the nature of the task in these new fields and the need for further expansion. This effort on the part of a Church with an aggregate membership of less than 1,000 in 1957 is worthy of further study. Had it not been for these very successful thrusts to the north, the Alliance work would have suffered even greater reverses.

A further feature of this movement has been their concentration on intensive training. The Bible Institute of Buenos Aires, which has operated since 1946, continues to be the nerve center of the work. The fact that more graduates leave the Institute each year than there are churches to absorb them is healthy, but in so far as it reflects a tendency to plant new churches too slowly, it is cause for alarm and calls for a serious reconsideration of the entire educational program. This strong emphasis on the training of professionals, however, has led to a concomitant neglect of lay leadership and the overdevelopment of the specialized clergy. This characteristic should be compared with the Pentecostal emphasis on lay leadership. It is the effective use of lay leaders which has proved to be the key to the expansion of the Church throughout Latin America, not the paid clergy, important and crucial as their work has been. Speaking of evangelistic preaching, one of the early missionaries says: "We do not entrust this to laymen, although laymen and women work helpfully in the meeting" (Davis 1943:97). This seems to be the continued emphasis among their churches. An effective training of laymen in full pastoral responsibility might have averted the severe slump experienced in 1961 and subsequent years.

Another feature of this Church has been the overbalanced missionary influence. This stemmed partially from the days when the missionary force was reduced to just one, and the mission subsidies were paid through him. This created a tendency toward missionary dominance. A similar pattern seems to have developed in Chile, although the missionary force there was never reduced to that extent (Kessler 1967:246-255). The authority of the mission organization frustrated the natural growth of a vigorous national church government for many years. The cautious attitude that grew out of the failure of the first attempt at self-government in the early 1930's might also have contributed to this tendency toward dominance. Although there has been no violent reaction against this strong influence, it has contributed to the failure of the Argentine leadership to find more cordial forms of church life and expansion. This leadership needs to be encouraged to discover ways that will lead this Church into a new era of growth. The unusually strong influence of the Institute will need to be self-curbed and redirected so that it will make a positive contribution to this process of discovery.

One very positive contribution of the Institute would be a training program which reaches the laymen in their churches (thus avoiding removal to the Institute for study) and inspires them to more active and responsible participation in all phases of pastoral and missionary ministry. This would aid the present churches greatly in establishing new churches near their own base of strength, rather than concentrating their missionary vision on broad and distant geographic expansion. Many of their churches in the city areas are sitting on a gold mine of responsive peoples. This training of another body of leaders would do more than any other single factor to break the status quo and introduce new currents of thought and life into this Church.

CHAPTER 7

The Conservative Baptists

A. IN SEARCH OF NEW FRONTIERS

The Conservative Baptists were invited to enter Argentina in 1946 by both the Christian and Missionary Alliance and the Federation of Evangelical Churches of the River Plate. During the early years the arriving Conservative Baptist missionaries cooperated with the Alliance (who had sponsored their entry into the country) and worked with them in their training program at the Bible Institute of Buenos Aires. During this period, a hall was rented and a store-front church was begun in one of the *barrios* of the capital city. There was early response to the evangelistic efforts of the ministry of the missionaries, and a small church was soon functioning. From the beginning, the arrangement with the Alliance was considered temporary and transitional. The missionaries had a burning desire to reach out into virgin, unexplored territories, even though these were hard to find. They felt that there was a disproportionate concentration of missionaries in the capital city, and the challenge of the primitive North prevailed.

In November of 1947, the two missionaries then in residence initiated an exploratory survey trip through the northern part of Argentina. The trip through the provinces of La Rioja, Catamarca, Tucumán, Salta, Jujuy, Chaco and Corrientes brought them in contact with the area which was to become their field of operation. Through the years their field of influence has been extended from their original base in Jujuy (1948) into Salta (1950) and Tucumán (1956).

The decision to enter the northwestern corner of the country was largely based on conversations with the last active resident missionaries of the San Pedro Mission to the Indians, Mr. and Mrs. Thomas Easdale. They were ready for retirement, but still active and effective in the latter years of their sixth decade. The specific goal of this mission, begun through the efforts of John Linton in 1900, was to reach the members of the Chiriguano Indian tribe, a subtribe of the Tupi-Guaraní group, who during the Portuguese conquest of Brazil migrated from Paraguay westward across the Gran Chaco to the foothills of the Andes. From this new home these tropical-forest-village people made forays against the Inca empire (Steward 1959:114,289). The ministry of the San Pedro Mission among these primitives extended from San Pedro in the Argentine province of Jujuy to the Bolivian town of Santa Cruz and involved rugged journeys of close to 500 miles on muleback (Payne 1904). The two most active centers of their ministry were located in San Antonio de Parapetí in Bolivia, and Cherenta, a village on the La Esperanza sugar plantation near San Pedro.

In 1916, the *World Statistics of Christian Missions* (Beach 1916:72) listed this mission and indicated a body of communicants numbering 225. In 1915, the dispensary at San Pedro administered 2,000 treatments to the Indians. In 1947, when Conservative Baptist missionaries Greenman and Little interviewed Mr. Easdale, they were informed that the Bolivian part of the work had been turned over to the Canadian Evangelical Union of South America. The Argentine half, which became the Conservative Baptist's responsibility, numbered about 225 in 1946.

Little did the early missionaries realize the significance of the complex racial composition of the area which had become their opportunity for occupation and witness. The San Pedro Mission to the Indians concentrated its efforts chiefly among the Chiriguanos. But as demands for cheap labor for the sugar harvests increased, so did the immigration of other racial groupings. Principally, it was the Bolivians from the highlands who migrated annually to the sugar cane fields of northern Argentina and returned to their homes in Bolivia for the summer months. The adventures and hardships of these destitute Indian laborers constitute a sorrowful story far exceeding *Grapes of Wrath* in its pathos, tragedy and death. Through the years, more and more of the Bolivians found it advantageous to remain in Argentina permanently, as here their living conditions improved measurably. Others not associated with the harvests also found their economic opportunities improved in Argentina and migrated permanently to their new home. The provinces of Jujuy and Salta have rapidly growing Bolivian minorities, which are not altogether assimilated culturally and socially into Argentine life.

The early residents of northern Argentina are the native inhabitants, the result of centuries of miscegenation between the Indian and the European colonist.[1] Among these *mestizos* are a special mountain people, protected in their high mountain valley redoubts and isolated by almost impassable trails over passes of 15,000-feet elevation,[2] whose lives have been little affected by recent European cultural patterns. Finally, there are the continual streams of recent European immigrants who filter through the cities in the South into the primitive and provincial North of the Argentine nation. These four racial groupings, the Chiriguano, the Bolivian immigrant of Quechua background, the *mestizo* and the people of European background form the heterogeneous racial complex of these three northwestern provinces. A clear understanding of these divisions and their meaning for church growth is essential to the most productive work in this area.

B. CONSERVATIVE BAPTIST CHURCHES TAKE ROOT

Beginning in San Pedro, the missionaries sought to establish churches among the *mestizo* and Bolivian populations, with some success. Great emphasis was placed on tent evangelism, and churches multiplied. By 1950 there were 23 preaching points which were contacted regularly, and small churches developed under the solicitous care of the missionary force of six men and five women. That same year the work was extended to the city of Salta and the first Bible Institute was begun. The Institute was later abandoned, when it was felt that individual training on the man-to-man level would better meet the needs of the type of leadership envisioned by the missionaries. This decision contributed greatly to the early and wise emphasis on complete lay participation in the ministry of the church. During these years the missionaries traveled extensively, evangelizing and establishing small nuclei of Christians who, as able, and following very simple forms, continued to worship together under the guidance of their own emerging leadership.

By 1956 the missionary force had grown and the number of communicants had increased to 699, from 365 in 1951, representing an increase of 334 members in five years (Figure No. 4). This healthy rate of growth slowed considerably during the next five years even though the missionary force continued to grow and the two remaining provincial capitals were occupied. A surge in growth as might have been expected in the cities was not forthcoming. This strange and enigmatic turn of events in the light of the accelerated growth rates in the cities of Latin America was perplexing and confusing. The city of Tucumán after ten years of occupation (1956 to 1966) had about 55 baptized members in two churches. Jujuy after ten years had approximately 50 members and Salta, occupied since 1950, had only 75 members.

What happened to the good growth pattern of this young Church when it began to work in the larger urban centers? Contrary to the experience of rapidly growing missions which were getting their best growth in the areas surrounding the cities, this young mission found its experience to follow an opposite pattern. Apparently the earlier missionaries sought a work among more primitive peoples, found them to be responsive to the message of Christ, and churches were established. The later arrivals felt that a work should be carried on among the higher class Argentines instead of the Bolivian immigrants, to provide a stronger leadership element. Consequently, they turned to the cities, aiming to win these higher classes. The irony of the matter is that, although concentrating on one element (usually the person of more recent European origin), they found that the converts largely came from among the *mestizo* and Bolivian segments. One wonders if there would not have been far greater growth if they had concentrated on these more responsive peoples. The experience of many missions throughout Latin America says that this church indeed missed an opportunity for great growth. This can still be corrected as the growing suburban areas continue to receive the displaced masses

Figure No.4

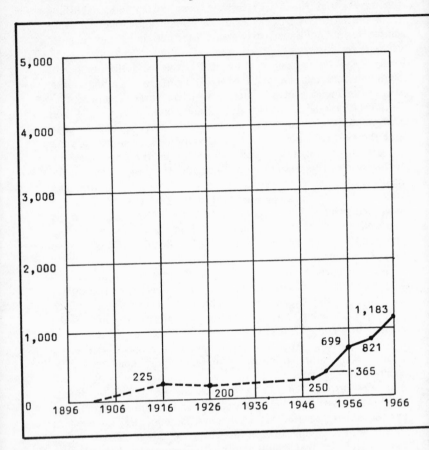

CONSERVATIVE BAPTISTS

(SAN PEDRO MISSION TO THE INDIANS, 1900–1948)
COMMUNICANT MEMBERS
DATE OF ENTRANCE — 1946

SOURCES

1916	BEACH	1916:72
1925	BEACH	1925:119
1948	GREENMAN	1967
1951	GREENMAN	1967
1956	ENNS	1961
1961	ENNS	1961
1966	CB	1966

from the rural areas and villages. This is the Conservative Baptist's highest potential area for growth.

1. A Highly Responsive Field

In sharp contrast to this slower growth pattern, the hill country of the Quebrada of Humahuaca in the province of Jujuy has been characterized by a high degree of responsiveness. First permanent missionary occupation of the area came in late 1954, and two years later there were 56 baptized members. By 1961 this number had increased to 149. This high degree of responsiveness has continued to the present time at almost the same rate and seems destined to continue. Today there are 252 communicants in eleven small mountain churches. The missionary in this area has received letters inviting him to visit community after community, from groups of people ready to follow the Evangelical faith. The following is a typical illustration of this desire for something new among this isolated people:

> In the name of our Lord Jesus Christ, we who sign below are happy to invite you, manifesting that on this date, we have had our first meeting in the house of Señor Anastacio Reynaga with the plan of beginning and continuing to practice your evangelical religion. We have the great hope of carrying out continually that which we have started.
>
> And so we are waiting for your visit in this locality on the date that has been set, in the Grace of God. Amen.

The 34 signers of this letter had already met to study the Bible and had each destroyed the images in his home. The mother church in Humahuaca shares the burden with the missionary for these smaller congregations. The rate of growth in this segment of the field from 1956 to 1966 was 350 per cent, considerably higher than the 69 per cent for the entire field and the rate of 47 per cent in the cities (1961-1966). It has been observed that in this section of the Conservative Baptist field the Roman Catholic communities were infrequently visited by the priests. Many of the people felt that the priests made their occasional visits only when it was financially advantageous to do so. Such attitudes undoubtedly affected the responsiveness of these peoples to the Gospel, especially since in their new faith they became the "priests" who led in worship.

2. Development of Broad Leadership

Educational efforts have been tailored to meet the needs of the natural leaders which emerged in each of the local churches. Following a pattern of church life which emphasizes the leadership of the Spirit-gifted leaders in each congregation, a system of plurality of elders has developed. Although the program was very elementary and minimal to begin with, through the years some of the more gifted men have proved themselves to be unusually good leaders and in some cases extraordinarily effective preachers. To meet the needs of these active leaders, a Mobile Bible Institute has been organized to provide systematic training for these men in their own churches. These are intensive short-term institutes with night classes so that the working man can attend. Several years of such training have demonstrated its effectiveness and it has been enthusiastically received by these lay leaders. During the second year there were 180 students enrolled for the two-week course, and by the fourth year over 300.

Because of the growing need for further training of both the established leaders and the younger emerging leaders, a full term Bible Institute, also with night classes, was begun in 1965. This institution is administrated by a board of Argentine church leaders and North American missionaries. Twelve students were in attendance at the conclusion of the second year of classes, and the first five were graduated in November, 1967. Two have entered into fulltime ministries and the others continue as more effective lay leaders in their churches. Among the most capable and responsible students are three older men with families to support who, had classes been held during the day, could never have taken advantage of this opportunity to prepare themselves for Christian service. One of the factors which contributed to the decision to conduct a more formalized training program without a de-emphasis of the man-to-man training was the alarming discovery that between 1956 and 1961, 80 per cent of those baptized had not continued in active church membership.

3. Unrealized Potential

This mission shows considerable strength, although there are reasons to believe that the greatest potential is not being realized. By and large, growth has been in direct proportion to the increase in the number of foreign missionaries. No solid indigenous break such as the Plymouth Brethren experienced in Palo a Pique in the Chaco East of Orán has happened. (See p. 151.) This breakthrough indicates that the potential exists, even with very limited missionary participation, but the dynamic has still not found full release through their Argentine brethren. The day these Argentine Christians, along with their missionaries, find ways to release the latent spiritual powers available to them, the growing potential of this area will be reaped. Great caution must be exercised to avoid the danger of the missionary organization becoming dominant in church life in such a way that it frustrates genuine Argentine initiative as it emerges.

4. Principal Features of Conservative Baptist Missionary Effort

What have been the characteristic features of the work of the Conservative Baptists whose churches, although very young, show reasonably good growth? Probably the most outstanding feature is the extensive evangelistic itineration, which is always seeking to establish new churches. This was particularly characteristic of the early years. There seems to be some indication that this evangelistic passion is diminishing as the missionaries find themselves involved in a changing ministry. The growing training program cannot be abandoned. It would, however, be advisable to combine it with continuing vigorous evangelistic outreach. Involvement in elaboration of the local church program should receive a minimum of the missionary's time. Time spent on such perfecting ministries will not eventuate in expanding church growth, unless these ministries are always bent toward evangelism.

A second feature of their work has been the missionaries' dedication to a rigid expression of the classic indigenous principle of no financial subsidies. This principle created unusually difficult circumstances for the small groups of Christians in the cities where facilities for meeting were available only at exorbitantly high rent. The year 1965, however, saw a significant breakthrough when the church in Tucumán was able to begin the purchase of a choice piece of property. This was the last of the city churches to acquire their own property. Approximately half of the fifty churches have been able to purchase property and are building their own meeting places without outside financial assistance.

A third characteristic of this work has been the emphasis on lay leadership. Baptism and the Lord's Supper are administered by these unordained laymen. The preaching is also largely their responsibility and privilege. These men are the pastors of the churches. In a recent survey it was discovered that there were 129 lay preachers, or more than 10 per cent of the total membership. The ability of many of these is minimal; however, the Mobile Institute is designed to meet this need at least partially. An elaborate extension program of the central Institute is being developed which will permit these men to study the same curriculum as the students in the mother school.

Another feature of the work in these three provinces is the emphasis on training broadly. Every church is conceived of as a Bible school, with emphasis on public Bible study and individual correspondence-type courses administered both personally and through the mail. These studies prepare the body of Bible students from which the candidates for the Mobile Institute come. Through this emphasis on study in the local church, several have felt the need for further studies in the Bible Institute. The annual men's and women's retreats, with separate attendance of around 250, have also provided a three-day opportunity for training and inspiration.

This summary of the principal characteristics of the Conservative Baptist work in northern Argentina would be incomplete without mention of the strong emphasis on tent evangelism. Two tents are constantly in use for evangelistic meetings. Not all campaigns are equally effective, but the aggregate impact of these campaigns plus the broad training program for the laymen continue to produce new churches. Broad-contact evangelism is also conducted by weekly radio broadcasts over five radio stations in the area. However, a significant breakthrough such as could be expected under today's conditions has not occurred. Under the favorable circumstances which the Evangelical Churches are facing in Argentina and all of Latin America as a whole, greater church growth should be normal. These have been fairly good beginnings but as yet they are far too small to provide us with any secure ground for rejoicing. The potential of the area produced by migration and increased urbanization has not been fully exploited. Rigorous attention must be paid to church growth principles. This is especially true of the urban areas where up to the present growth has been minimal in the face of conditions of high potential.

There seems to be an increasing disorientation and bewilderment among the missionaries working with these very young churches. The simplistic interpretation of classic indigenous principles has not produced the apostolic results that were expected. The missionary finds himself more and more involved in activities designed to hold gains already attained. Furthermore, the racial and cultural diversity and complexity of the area has contributed to this disorientation. The significance of the heterogeneous nature of this area must be correctly understood in order to develop the policies and methods which will eventuate in rapid church growth. The homogeneous units must be identified and approached in ways congenial to each. The identification of these segments and the development of adequate programs of evangelism for each will bring the desired results. The experience of the Mennonite Church among the Tobas is an eloquent example of how this principle can operate.

In 1957 the Baptist General Conference began work in northern Argentina in the provinces of Santiago del Estero, La Rioja and Catamarca. This area, contiguous to the Conservative Baptist field, is similar in racial and cultural background, with the exception of the Bolivian and Chiriguano immigrations. The two missions envision working together in the formation of one fellowship of Baptist Churches in this remote corner of the Argentine. In 1966, after ten years of active missionary evangelism, there were four churches with an increasing number of communicants, numbering about 75. Just as their Conservative Baptist neighbors, they should expect greater church growth after ten years of evangelistic effort.

CHAPTER 8

The Disciples of Christ

A. ERA OF COOPERATION INAUGURATED

The Christian Women's Board of Missions in 1904 made a decision to enter the country of Argentina to propagate the message of Christ. This decision was largely the result of correspondence with a Miss Embree, a Disciple who served in Argentina with the then interdenominational Christian and Missionary Alliance. The missionaries began their first permanent witness in the Belgrano district of Buenos Aires in 1906. These early years were filled with thrilling reports of evangelistic advances resulting in a growing church. Upon dedication of their first church building in 1911, evangelistic services were conducted by the outstanding Evangelical leader and pioneer Bible colporteur, Francisco Penzotti. Twenty-six new members were received into the church by baptism during the first month that services were conducted in the new building. Another feature which later became prominent in the Disciple's multiplying ministries in Argentina, the primary school, was inaugurated in the facilities of this church in the same year (Montgomery 1956:46-59).

The emphasis sounded at the Panama Congress on Christian Work in Latin America in 1916 was to characterize the subsequent years of Disciple activity and vision in Argentina. At the Congress a new strategy was formulated which called for increasing cooperation between the missions and churches. Montgomery tells of the reaction of delegates of most of the Christian missions working in Latin America:

The conviction of those attending the Congress was that it "has breathed new courage and hope into the hearts of lonely and scattered workers. It has led to a clearer discernment of the need of cooperation in tasks which are too great to be compassed in aloofness. It has sounded a call to a fuller fellowship of faith and race and to a recognition of the fact that not geography, nor science, nor trade, nor political sympathy, nor commercial interests, but only Christ can ever unite the nationals of North and South or of East and West" (1956:61).

Growing out of this vision and emphasis, the Committee on Cooperation in Latin America was formed which was faithfully served by Disciple personnel for many years.

During the next ten years (1917-1926) three cooperative ventures were entered into with the Methodists. The Disciples joined the Methodists in the Colegio Americano in 1917 and in the Union Seminary in 1918. Both of these institutions were already in operation, but expanded their efforts at this time. The third effort of cooperation, the Instituto Modelo, a training school for women, began in 1922. This common Christian effort in the Seminary and the Colegio continues to this day. In 1942 the Seminary and the Instituto Modelo were united to form a coeducational institution for the training of ministers for their Church. The seminary is known as the Facultad Evangélica de Teología and continues as a cooperative venture of several Churches and missions. Other cooperative ventures which have enjoyed special encouragement and assistance from the Disciples are La Aurora Bookstore, the Liga Argentina de Mujeres Evangélicas and the Federación Argentina de Iglesias Evangélicas. The Disciples' investment in these ventures has been extensive and sacrificial.

This decade (1917-1926) saw the extension of other aspects of the Disciples' work. During these years, 17 of the total of 45 missionaries who had served in Argentina up to 1955 began their terms of service. Expansion was the keynote, but only two new churches were started. One of these was known as the "Italian Band" since it was composed largely of Italian immigrants. It was soon a thriving church with 50 to 60 members and completely self-supporting. The emphasis on evangelism continued, but the large majority of the missionary force was dedicated to the growing and demanding institutional efforts of the Disciples. These years saw the development of thinking which was to produce a progressive decrease of positive evangelism in deference to other ministries.

C. Manley Morton, a Disciple missionary, wrote in 1917:

> Of course, the work of evangelization must not be forgotten, but a program that is broader than has ever been laid out for any Latin American field must be launched if we would take advantage of the greatest opportunities in this field (Montgomery 1956:70,71).

B. ANALYSIS REVEALS FAILURE TO GROW

1. Institutionalism Detracts from Main Task

In subsequent years a "broader" program was launched which included, according to Montgomery (1956:71), "strategic educational work, the preparation of a better-trained national ministry, the betterment of social standards through the education of women, the production of more adequate literature and an aggressive program of evangelism." Although balanced in its projection, the implementation of the program seems to have relegated evangelism to a place of secondary importance. This "aggressive program of evangelism" achieved few if any results, as the level of membership remained almost stationary. During these same years the Plymouth Brethren through their lay-oriented program saw substantial growth through their vigorous evangelistic program. The potential for growth represented by the responsiveness of the newly arrived immigrants, as amply demonstrated in the Italian Band, was present in Buenos Aires, but it wasn't being taken advantage of by the Disciples, who turned their attention to specialized institutional ministries. From 1920, a few years after the inauguration of this program, to the year 1965 (Figure No. 5), the membership of Disciples churches grew from 110 to 426, a total of 316, or at an average decadal rate of 35.2 per cent, or slightly over 3 per cent per year. The decade immediately following the war in Europe (1918-1927) set the tone and temper of all future Disciples work in Argentina.

In an editorial comment in *World Call* (1925:30), in anticipation of the Congress on Christian Work in South America which met in Montevideo in 1925, it was observed that a middle class was emerging in Argentina. The writer of the editorial continued to delineate the mood of renaissance in the social, economic and

Figure No.5

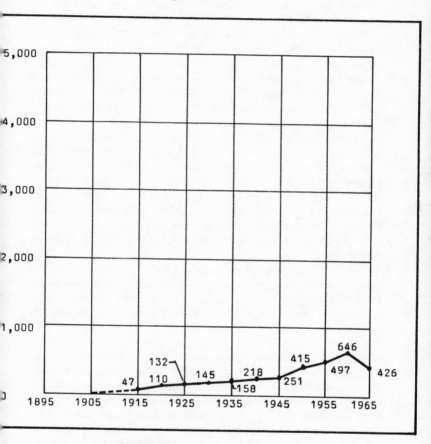

DISCIPLES OF CHRIST

COMMUNICANT MEMBERS
DATE OF ENTRANCE - 1906

ᴊURCE
ᴣ16-1965 DC YEARBOOK

educational fields brought on largely through universal public education. Since the editorialist felt that the Roman Catholic Church was antagonistic to broad education, he asserted that it was the highest mission of the Evangelical Churches to bring these tremendous changes under the domination of spiritual influences. There was an optimistic hope that the best and the most effective "evangelism" would be to bend these humanistic trends to the service of Christ through the pressure exerted by educational influences.

But the hope of creating a new community of redeemed men through a radical change of religious loyalties and motivations, who in turn would affect their environment, began to suffer serious reverses. The trend which has led to today's perverted view of evangelism was initiated. Only time was needed to arrive at interpreting evangelism as social involvement and change of social structures. The evident failure to affect radically the social structures would be a good lesson for other Evangelicals to learn. In contrast, the Pentecostal Churches of Chile who have dedicated themselves to pure and simple evangelism exert strong influence through sheer numbers. A similar situation is that of the primitive Church in the Roman Empire during the first centuries of the Christian era.

The chief instrument of this emphasis on broad education was the Colegio Americano, later known as Colegio Ward, a school established by the Methodist Church in 1913 for students from kindergarten through high school. In 1928 there were 250 students studying in the school, and today that figure stands at more than a thousand. The youth of some of Argentina's finest families are educated in this school. Missionaries were keenly aware of the prestige advantages of the school. One wrote, "It is also the one school in the whole River Plate region which forms a connecting link between Evangelical Christianity and the more well-to-do and educated classes" (DC 1928:461,462). The school was heavily supported by North American businessmen working in Buenos Aires. The influence of the school has been broad but too ambiguous to assess properly whether or not it has contributed substantially to the growth of the churches.

2. Retrenchment and Curtailment

The static growth pattern of these years can in some measure be attributed also to the excessive turnover in personnel and the uncertainty surrounding the decision as to whether or not the Disciples should continue working in Argentina at all. The rapidly evolving and expanding program became burdensome to administrate. Arising out of these changes of direction and personnel, some degree of tension and struggle developed which also affected the growth of the churches. Doctrinal divergences evident in the Congress at Montevideo in 1925 were the cause of separation of two of the Argentine pastors and disquieting influences among the churches. These factors and those mentioned above placed strong limitations on the expanding program of evangelization.

The years encompassed by the Great Depression and World War II were years of curtailment and retrenchment. Funds from the churches in the United States were reduced sharply. The reaction of the Argentine pastors, however, was encouraging in the face of reduced subsidies. They voluntarily took cuts in their salaries and sought part-time work rather than close down some of the churches and dismiss part of the staff of pastors.

3. Encouraging Trends

In 1944 there were marked changes in the work of the Disciples. First, the church in Resistencia, approximately 800 miles to the north of Buenos Aires, was begun. This evangelistic outreach by the Argentine Disciples, which began in 1945, contributed to the upsurge in the curve of growth on the graph (p. 109). This was a welcome break in the pattern of stagnation which had lasted almost thirty years. It also demonstrated to the Disciples that growth was possible. Another contributing factor was the ministry of Dr. Paul Andress in the Colegiales church which grew to become an active congregation of between 150 and 200 members (Liggett 1967, Tatlock 1967). Colegio Ward and the Union Seminary continued to enjoy marked growth and influence. The number of young people preparing for Christian service also increased. These were years of encouraging trends. Had the vision of evangelistic potential among the newly arrived urban masses been captured, these good beginnings might have been extended into a movement toward Christ. But the structures developed during thirty years were too dominant to allow for the full release of this latent dynamic which sought expression.

Recent years have been characterized by a de-emphasis of evangelistic outreach and an encouragement of theological dialogue and communication as the principal mission of the Church. In the handbook published by the United Christian Missionary Society (1965:109) it is stated that "the task in Latin America with its 200,000,000 people is so great that there is need for all believers to join forces," including Roman Catholics and Jews. When the task is interpreted as social justice over against winning men to allegiance to Christ, the emphasis on evangelism will unquestionably diminish. However, the principal reason for decline since 1960 is also attributable to a cleanup of church registers. All the churches were encouraged to drop all inactive members from their rolls (Tatlock 1967).

4. Characteristics of Disciple Presence

What have been the outstanding features of the Disciples' ministry in Argentina? First, we must mention the strong emphasis on evangelism which characterized certain periods, especially in the early years of development and the decade immediately following World War II. This emphasis, however, was not always strong. Had it been, there might have been an entirely different pattern of development.

Another feature has been the emphasis on general education and the advanced training of men and women for service in the Church. Among the results of this program are a body of sympathetic people in the community-at-large who have been affected by this general educational program, and consequently are cordially disposed to the Evangelical movement, but almost entirely separated from active participation in Evangelical Church life. Just how this growing body of sympathetic people has contributed to the growth of the Disciples' churches is difficult to ascertain. The dedication of missionary years to this task has rather detracted from the evangelistic extension of the Christian Churches in Argentina. Their program, however, has been effective in producing a few outstanding religious leaders in Argentina.

The growing emphasis on interdenominational cooperation at the expense of aggressive evangelism has hindered the growth of the Christian Churches in Argentina. This observation will undoubtedly meet with strong reactions, but it seems to this observer that the drive to evangelize is sapped by these emphases. These need not and indeed must not be mutually exclusive if broad church growth is to be achieved. We do not make a judgment as to the correctness or falseness of this position, but it is valid to point out this detrimental effect on evangelism. Liggett (1967) asserts that these cooperative efforts have "produced other fruits of significance in the fulfillment of the mission God has given to His Church." This cannot be disputed. Yet, is not the price of denominational stagnation too high? Can we not design our program of cooperation so that it accomplishes both goals? It seems that when theological dilution takes place, only interdenominational contacts satisfy the Christian desire for growth, and consequently evangelism suffers.

Another factor adversely affecting this Church in Argentina has been the excessive turnover of missionary personnel. Only one missionary couple has retired from active service after completing their full term. The Disciples would be well advised to evaluate seriously their own work in Argentina in the light of what is happening in the other Churches. Growth is being achieved, and not at the expense of cooperation. There exists a cooperation among Evangelicals in Argentina which produces growth, but in which the Disciples do not feel they can be involved. The issue in the end is not cooperation *per se,* but an affirmative decision to seek the expansion of the Church of Christ in Argentina. This can be accomplished when evangelism is returned to its proper meaning and prominent place in the life of the Church. The clergy must be trained to meet the genuine spiritual needs and aspirations of the people through forms which are cordial to Latin American life and thought. Contemporary European theological trends do not often coincide with these aspirations and needs, especially in the case of people who are just now becoming Evangelical Christians.

CHAPTER 9

The Lutheran Church—Missouri Synod

A. IMMIGRANT CHURCH DEVELOPS

The Church of particular interest in this profile will be the Lutherans, affiliated with the Missouri Synod Lutheran Church. Brief mention will be made of the other Lutheran Churches, as together they represent the second largest family of Protestant Churches in Argentina, smaller only than the combined Pentecostal Churches. One characteristic generally common to the various Lutheran Churches is the fact that they largely minister to ethnic groups. In many cases, the services in the churches are conducted in languages other than Spanish. The majority of their constituents are the descendants of European immigrants who arrived during the fifty-year period beginning roughly with the last quarter of the past century.

Lutheran beginnings in Argentina, however, go back to the year 1843, when a group of German immigrants met to worship, guided by a Pastor Siegel sent to Argentina by the Bremen Society for German Protestants in South America. The King of Prussia gave an amount equal to approximately 10 per cent of the cost of a Gothic church building, and the congregation became affiliated with the State Church of Prussia. In 1848 the Church numbered 400, and by 1896 it had increased to 6,500 members. This fact is not reported in the *World Atlas of Christian Missions* (Dennis 1911) from which our figures for 1911 in the chart of the communicant membership of the

114

Evangelical Church in Argentina were taken (see p. 178). This German Church sent 400 marks annually to the Leipzig Society for missions during the latter years of the nineteenth century (Lenker 1896:757-759).

1. Missouri Synod Mission Enters

The Missouri Synod Lutheran Church made its first contact with the Lutherans in Argentina in 1905 from Brazil, where Missouri's mission outreach began in 1901. A Pastor von Matthesius approached the German Lutherans, who by this time had organized the La Plata Synod, about serving one of their churches as pastor. Shortly before joining, he made contact with the Missouri Synod Lutherans in Brazil and requested help from them. This help arrived in 1905 in the person of Pastor Wittrock and eventually led to the formal identification of Pastor von Matthesius' church with the Missouri Lutheran Synod. The continuous stream of Lutheran immigrants and the help of North American missionaries produced a steady rate of growth.

Through the years the area of concentration of the Missouri Synod missionaries and the Argentine District of the Missouri Synod (established in 1926) has generally been the German immigrant population. Most of these people have been of the lower middle class and have farmed on ground they were able to acquire on short-term leases from Argentine landlords. This meant that the work during the early years was almost exclusively in rural areas. Few of these leases lasted for more than four years, and many for a shorter period of time. As the leases expired and the tenant farmers moved on to new ground, the churches spread the length and breadth of the pampas. In more recent years, with the increased tendency toward urbanization, the Missouri Synod has found itself working more and more in the urban centers such as Buenos Aires, Bahía Blanca and Córdoba. This increased mobility and social contact with Spanish-speaking Argentines has led inevitably to the progressive adoption of the national language in their worship. It is the opinion of the missionaries that within but a few years all worship will be in Spanish.

Urbanization and the inevitable acculturative pressures exerted on these German Lutherans have had beneficial effects. There is a growing interest in the evangelization of the non-German population. The Belgrano church in a suburb of Buenos Aires has made serious adjustments in her life and worship patterns which should eventually produce positive results in winning the non-German community. The traditional Lutheran ethnic orientation of this congregation made evangelistic outreach difficult. The members of this church are now spending one Saturday a month at door-to-door tract distribution. They invite the leisurely Argentine suburbanite to a post-siesta meeting at 4 o'clock Sunday afternoon. A service at 11 o'clock in the morning would cut into the late sleep and large Sunday dinner. The 4 o'clock service catches the *porteño* ready for his Sunday afternoon stroll. Attendance at this neighborhood mission meeting has been encouraging.

2. Education Program Develops

The education program of the Lutheran Church has involved both parochial and ministerial training. During the earlier years, until 1935, there was a strong emphasis on the parochial school in each parish. This program of private education of the German community suffered under growing nationalism in Argentina. There were 20 parochial schools in 1935 with 854 pupils, which by 1950 were reduced to 7 schools and 296 students. In 1965 the number of schools had increased again to 14 with 484 pupils (LCMS 1935, 1950, 1965). The increased identification of the German immigrants with Argentine life and culture is reflected in this reduction of emphasis on parochial education.

The Church also operates secondary schools and a seminary. The first such school was the Colegio Concordia, which began in Crespo in 1926 with the purpose of training workers for the churches. After completing their course, they continued their seminary training in Porto Alegre, Brazil, in the German language. In 1942 it was seen that a seminary would have to be started to train the Argentine pastors in Argentina, and in the Spanish language as well as in German. Thus the Concordia Seminary in Villa Ballester came into existence. According to Scopes (1962:100), in 1961 the Seminary had eleven students who received their instruction primarily in the Spanish language. The earlier language medium, German, had been almost totally abandoned, another sign of the absorption of the Lutheran community into Argentine life. Today the secondary school formerly located in Crespo is operated in conjunction with the seminary. Another preparatory school was opened in Oberá, Misiones, in 1956.

Figure No.6

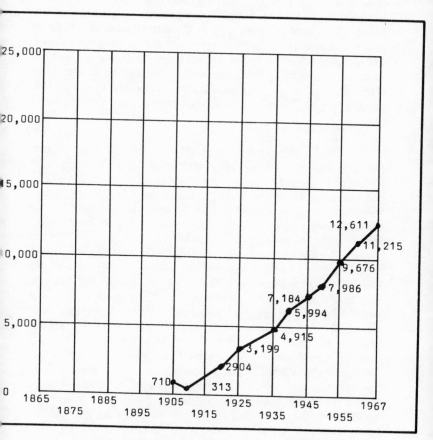

LUTHERAN CHURCH MISSOURI SYNOD

COMMUNICANT MEMBERS
DATE OF ENTRANCE — 1905

OURCE
905-1965 LCMS YEARBOOK

Although the educational program certainly has aided in maintaining many of the children of Lutheran families in the Church, it has served also to reinforce the ethnic quality of the denomination, thus frustrating positive outreach into the community, which certainly would have resulted in greater church growth. In fact, the entire educational program of this Church has contributed to its ingrown characteristic. There seems to be some break in this pattern, but if this is not accompanied by aggressive evangelism and pastoral care, the Lutheran families which have left the rural, ethnically oriented religious communities, instead of becoming bridges for people into the Church, might rather be lost to the Church entirely.

3. Internal Growth

The illustrative graph (Figure No. 6) of Lutheran Church (Missouri Synod) growth in Argentina presents few surprising variations. The early drop in membership of more than 50 per cent remains unexplained, as Lutheran histories fail to make mention of it. It is my feeling that the tensions between the older Prussian State Church in Argentina and the newly arrived Missouri Synod might have produced a return of some members to the Church they formerly attended. Let me clarify that this is purely a guess. The fact that this curve rises at a constant rate means that this Church, which represents a potential for broad evangelistic expansion, barely confirms all the children of Lutheran families. Statistical tables seem to confirm that its outreach into the Spanish-speaking community of non-Lutherans is insignificant. The rate of growth between the years 1945 and 1955 was 34.5 per cent, or 3.01 per cent per year. However, internal growth through the confirmation of the children of Lutheran families should produce a rate near 3.01 per cent per year, which has been the rate of population growth from 1911 to the present. This means that their growth from the world is less than one third of their increase. During the next ten years it dropped to 30.3 per cent. With tendencies of the Lutheran community toward growing urbanization and cultural identification, especially the use of Spanish in worship, we should see a sharp departure from this rather static pattern of growth. The greatest problem facing this Church, namely, how to capitalize on growing cultural identification for church growth, is going to become accentuated in the coming years and merits the serious consideration of all concerned.

B. OTHER LUTHERAN CHURCHES

1. Ethnic Groups

Other Lutheran Churches which direct their ministries to ethnic communities are the Danish, Norwegian and Swedish Churches. The United Lutheran Church in Argentina ministers to several ethnic minorities of more recent immigration, but actively seeks to carry on a ministry among the general Argentine community. The Danish Lutheran community dates back to 1882 when the first congregation was started in Tandil (Goslin 1956:41). Although the World Christian Handbook (Coxill 1962:126) lists 20,000 communicants in this Church, both Davis (1943:79-91) and present-day observers indicate that the number of active members is far below this. On the basis of reports of these observers it seems fair to estimate their strength at 1,000.

Other ethnic groups include the German Evangelical Church (La Plata Synod), which has a communicant membership of 11,239 (WCH 1967), and the smaller Swedish Lutheran Church, with approximately 600 communicants (SK 1967). The German Church is the successor of the first Lutheran body in Argentina, the Prussian State Church, and has maintained a strong emphasis on the German language until very recently. The Swedish Church concentrates its activities largely within the Swedish community located in Buenos Aires and the town of Oberá in Misiones. The parochial school in Oberá, however, educates the children of the Argentine community in the North, where it is located (SK 1967). There is also the smaller Norwegian Lutheran Church with about 300 members (WCH 1967).

2. United Lutheran Church

The United Lutheran Church in America began its ministry in Argentina in about 1919, with the arrival of Dr. Edward Miller. Work of this organization has met the needs of many ethnic groups including Slovaks, Hungarians, Latvians and Estonians, especially since World War II, which produced increased Lutheran immigration to Argentina (LCA n.d.:63-65). The majority of the churches, which achieved synodical stature in 1948 with the organization of the United Evangelical Lutheran Church in Argentina, worship in the Spanish language. In many instances they use the facilities of the ethnically oriented bodies to reach the Spanish community. Today there are 3,995 active communicant members (WCH 1967). With other Lutheran bodies in Latin America they operate a seminary known as the Facultad Luterana de Teología in José C. Paz, a suburb of Buenos Aires. Dr. Henry S. Gehman's reflections on a sabbatical year spent teaching in this seminary give an interesting and authentic account of Lutheran life in Argentina (Gehman 1958:35-43). The seminary serves students of several language traditions including Germans, Danes, Swedes, Hungarians, as well as Argentines. In 1961 there were nineteen students enrolled (Scopes 1962:99,102).

The total number of communicant members of the different Lutheran Churches is difficult to calculate accurately. This is due largely to the fact that some of the ethnic communities have almost totally lost their national identity. This has greatly affected their active participation in religious life, and many have almost completely lost contact with the Church. This is especially true of the Danes. The Swedish and German Churches, on the other hand, have maintained their national identity to a greater extent. This is even more true of the recently arrived Eastern European Lutheran immigrants who remain almost entirely unassimilated into Argentine life and continue to maintain their strong church ties. If we were to take the World Christian Handbook—1968 (Coxill, Grubb 1967) figures for 1967, there would be a total of 52,731 communicant members and a community of 195,314 in the six Churches listed. Religion, for a large portion of the Lutheran community, is identified with nationality, and as this sense of ethnic identity is lost, their active participation in church life diminishes. This is a broad generalization and certainly there would be exceptions. Our corrected estimate on the basis of this study would be 17,684 active communicant members and a Christian community of 68,536 in 1967. This does not include the Lutheran Church—Missouri Synod, which is listed separately. The table on page 121 is a summary of Lutheran Churches in Argentina.

Briefly let us look at the outstanding features of the Lutheran Churches, and more particularly, of the Missouri Synod Church. First, these are Churches of ethnic specialization, oriented to meet the needs of their own national communities. Their early interest in Argentina was not in evangelizing the general community, but in ministering to the needs of their own people. Recent years, especially since World War II, have seen a general opening to the Argen-

LUTHERAN CHURCHES

Communicant Members–1967

Church	Communicants	Source[1]
Danish Church	1,000	1
German Evangelical Church–La Plata Synod	11,239	4
Lutheran Church in Argentina	3,995	4
Norwegian Church (Norske Kirk)	300	4
Swedish Church (Svenska Kyrkan)	600	3
Synod of Evangelical Lutheran Church	550	5
SUB-TOTAL	17,684	
Lutheran Church–Missouri Synod	12,611	2
TOTAL	30,295	

tine people reflected in the adoption, more and more, of Spanish as the language of worship and instruction. We would add that this tendency to identify provides this great body of Churches with a growing opportunity for evangelism.

The potential community to be served has been so great that the acute shortage of pastors has become the prime concern of the churches. This lack of adequate ministerial care for vast numbers of immigrants has produced a dilution of Lutheran understanding and identification in many of the immigrants. The two Lutheran seminaries are a step in the right direction. However, if the proper approach to the education of these pastors is not discovered, the Lutherans can expect even greater problems in the future. The seminaries must discover ways to meet the pastoral needs of the scattered Lutheran families in the growing urban centers. Development of a responsible lay ministry under pastoral supervision in these cities could contribute to the end of maintaining their Lutheran identification. This, however, would have only limited effect among a Christian population which in some instances tends toward mere confessionalism. One who reflects on past revival movements within the Lutheran Churches in Europe, especially in Scandinavia, would long for an Argentine Hans Nielson Hauge to bring new life into this potential field of great spiritual and numerical growth. New spiritual dynamic and life such as that

[1] Sources: 1. Estimate; 2. Graph (p. 117); 3. SK 1967; 4. WCH 1967:130, 131; 5. CGRILA.

released in the Lutheran reformation is desperately needed for substantial church growth.

It is encouraging to see the growing interest in evangelism. This third feature of present-day Lutheranism in Argentina is the most positive, although very limited in extent. Lutheranism's adherents have traditionally formed tight colonies where they live in ethnic isolation. Fillol (1961:32) observes that these non-Latin communities, as a result, have had only a very negligible influence as agents of cultural change. The long period of ethnic isolation is breaking down, however, and an opening into the general Argentine community is being made. Lutheranism's great hope is a growing emphasis on evangelism based on and born of a revived Church.

CHAPTER 10

The Mennonite Church

A. MENNONITES LOOK SOUTHWARD

Mennonite interest in missionary work in Latin America began near the turn of the century. It did not become a reality until two missionary families, Shank and Hershey, sailed from New York on an August afternoon in 1917 for Buenos Aires. Previous to their departure, Shank had made an extensive survey trip of several Latin American countries including Perú, Bolivia, Chile and Argentina. His commission from the Mennonite Board of Missions and Charities directed him to make an investigation of the possibilities of initiating missionary work in those lands. These were years of increasing Protestant interest in all of Latin America. The Panama Congress on Christian Work in Latin America in 1916 marked the beginning of a new era of Evangelical missionary activity. The Mennonite pioneers were arriving at a pivotal point in Protestant mission work in Latin America.

After a preliminary period of language study in the burgeoning capital of Argentina, these two sons of Menno Simons began their exploratory travels in search of the area which would become Mennonite territory in Argentina. Investigations and the sympathetic counsel of other Evangelical missionaries led them to concentrate on the area served by the Western Railroad, which ran between Buenos Aires and the *pampa* city of Santa Rosa, four hundred miles to the west. This zone is located in some of Argentina's richest cattle- and grain-producing country. Rural life in this area was organized around and oriented to the large land holdings of a few rich families. Life on these *estancias* revolved around two foci: the family of the large landowner and their social contacts with other landed families on the one hand, and the weary but gay *gaucho peon* and his family on the other. The *peon* worked the lands and herded the cattle while the cultured landowner's son studied in France.

A genuine middle class as we know it in the United States was practically nonexistent, although some smaller farmers were able to secure sufficient land to survive with a modest agricultural operation. In the towns occupied by the Mennonites, the small businessmen also represented the emerging middle sector of economic and social life. Weber, quoting Merle Davis, writes concerning this rural area:

> The most baffling problem to the Evangelical Church in Argentina is the scattered rural population. Some of its seemingly insoluble aspects are . . . the hundreds of thousands of *peons* and small tenant farmers who labor or live upon the lands of the *estancia* owners; the landed aristocracy who control every condition and activity upon the estates and who are bitterly opposed to the coming of Protestantism upon their property; the widely scattered hamlets and villages made up of desperately poor *peon* families eking out a bare existence by *peon* labor or by small shopkeeping for their neighbors, and the small independent farmer whose acres are often a day's walk from his neighbor. Among such conditions the Gospel finds difficult soil for lodgment and growth and an organized Evangelical Church, self-supporting and indigenous, is a remote prospect (1945:143).

This was the area and these the difficult conditions prevailing when the Mennonites began their missionary work. Towns as large as 20,000 inhabitants had developed along the railroad lines and became the centers of Mennonite work. The first such town occupied was Pehuajó, near the western border of the province of Buenos Aires. Early ideas of beginning an agricultural mission to provide for the partial support of the pastors of the young churches were later abandoned, but certainly influenced these sons of immigrant farmers in their choice of this particular area of Argentina (Hershey 1961:35).

1. Bright Beginnings

The first break came in Pehuajó through the ministry of an Argentine evangelist "loaned" to the Mennonites by another mission. These converts were baptized in late 1919. From Pehuajó the missionaries extended their missionary outreach to Trenque Lauquen, Santa Rosa (the end of the railroad line) and Carlos Casares. Early methods largely involved gospel tent meetings, distribution of literature, Sunday School services in homes and Bible readers. Halls rented by the mission served as church meeting places until funds from the sending churches made it possible to purchase land and build permanent buildings for places of worship.

These were years of good church growth. The early pioneers were men with vision and tireless drive. During the first ten years the original group of four missionaries was quadrupled (MBMC 1964:247). They were able to expand their outreach during these years to four additional towns. By 1935 there were 21 churches with a total membership of 584 communicants. This represents almost three-quarters of today's total membership in the central provinces. This same year a church was begun in the province of Córdoba. Expansion continued. In 1941 the city of Buenos Aires and in 1943 the Toba tribe in the Chaco became the objects of Mennonite concern and mission. Occupation of the large urban center was motivated chiefly by the observation that many of the members of the provincial churches were migrating to the city. This internal migration of church members to the urban centers has been one of the problems that has continuously frustrated growth in the rural churches.

2. Years of Struggle

Incipient Mennonite Church organization appeared in the year 1923 when the first Argentine Mennonite Church Conference was held in Trenque Lauquen. This young Church of only 44 members manifested a vibrant passion and concern for evangelism. Consequently, subsequent years saw their vision become a reality (Shank 1943:88-91). The churches continued to grow from conference to conference, which continued as annual events. Growing out of the desire to advance toward full financial independence, The Argentine Board of Evangelization and Finances of the Mennonite Church was organized in 1931. Difficult financial conditions in the churches of

the United States forced the Argentine Church, along with the
missionaries, to seek a broader financial base among the emerging
churches. The 20 Year Plan instituted in 1933 was a part of the
solution of this pressing financial need of the depression years and
the evident desire of the missionaries and the Argentine Church to
become financially more independent (Shank 1943:156-159).
During the mid-thirties economic strain led several pastors to begin
small mission-financed businesses to help with their support. These
ventures failed and the churches suffered. Dissension and disorientation resulted in stagnation among the provincial churches. It has
been impossible to make any appreciable break in this stationary
situation to the present time. Mennonite growth since 1940 has
taken place almost exclusively in the urban areas around Buenos
Aires. Mennonite methodology provided a steady rate of growth as
long as additional finances and missionary personnel were forthcoming. When these diminished, stagnation resulted.

An attempted fresh start for the Argentine Church came in 1954.
A new constitution was adopted in the interests of developing a
truly national church. Principal changes provided the Argentine
Church with the necessary legal authority to transact business and
hold property. Previously these functions were performed by, and in
the name of, the mission organization. Unfortunately, the mental
attitudes of a subordinate Church had already been formed, and it
will take years to shatter these chains that frustrate the kind of
church growth that is commensurate with the evident potential of
the Argentine scene. The new constitution was a step in the right
direction and called for a division of the churches into six zones,
each with its respective director (Wenger 1961:47). This event
marked the end of the Mission Council meeting as a separate entity.
The Church continues to function under basically this same
structure.

3. Shortage of Leadership

During the years of organizational struggle and innovation, and
even into the present, the Mennonite Church in Argentina has had
difficulty maintaining a resident fulltime pastor in each of its
churches. Early Bible school training began in a simple way in
Pehuajó and continued there, in Trenque Lauquen and finally in
Bragado. By 1942 the Bragado Bible School was functioning with a
full three-year course with five students in attendance. Because of

the shortage of teaching personnel and the reduced number of students, the school was closed temporarily in 1952 and 1953. Although the school continued to function in the provincial center of Bragado, it became increasingly evident that in order to be where the Church was growing, the school should be located in the city of Buenos Aires. At this same time growing contacts with other Mennonite Churches in Uruguay, Brazil and Paraguay gave birth to the idea of a single Mennonite training center. In 1959 the Bragado school merged with the Biblical Seminary of Montevideo to become the Montevideo Evangelical Biblical Seminary (Wenger 1961:53), serving the Mennonite community in Argentina and the three countries mentioned above. This emphasis on Bible training was designed to meet the continuing shortage of fulltime pastors. In 1958 there was no national leader between the ages of 25 and 40. Hopes were placed in twenty youths preparing for Christian service (MBMC 1958:105).

Even with these recent hopeful signs, leadership continues to be one of this Church's principal problems, particularly in the provincial churches. Reduced missionary personnel, coupled with expansion into the Chaco and Buenos Aires, has left the rural churches shorthanded. Lay pastors in churches accustomed to professional leadership find it difficult to stimulate their fellow Christians to new and expanding Christian experiences and missionary exploits. Yet an effective training of lay pastors is what is needed to meet this shortage.

B. ADVANCE AMONG THE TOBA INDIANS

1. Drought in the Midst of Plenty

To be complete, the Mennonite work among the Toba Indians of the northern Chaco merits a separate chapter (or book), but our purposes are served adequately by several paragraphs. The original purpose in sending Mennonite missionaries to the Tobas in 1943 was to establish an agricultural colony. The Indians were to be settled on a farm, with a view to teaching them better agricultural methods. Strict moral standards would be required of those Indians wishing to settle on the Mennonite farm. It was the Church's expressed hope that they could be brought "into the Christian way of life" (Weber 1945:114). Progress was slow, and at times the enterprise became very discouraging.

At about the time the Mennonites began this work, using a

traditional institutional approach, a people movement of the Tobas into the Christian faith took place which literally surrounded the colony. The Tobas had made contact with Christianity through Pentecostal missionaries in the cities along the Paraná River and in the city of Roque S. Peña. The principal inspirations of this movement to Christ were Juan Ricardo Lagar, an independent Pentecostal missionary from the United States, and the Toba chief, Pedro Martínez. The power of Martínez, a charismatic leader of the Indians, was a mixture of positive and negative influences. Yet his people moved toward God and took the first steps toward Christian "influence" under his guidance. He died in the late 1950's (Kratz 1967). The Church of God, Cleveland, Tenn., reports (Conn 1959:161,162) receiving 3,800 into membership in 1946 when Lagar turned the work over to them. Hargrave (1967) reports receiving another 6,000 into this Church at a later date. Conn estimates a total of 15,000 Toba Christians in 1958. Kratz (1967) feels this to be an exaggeration, since there are hardly 15,000 Tobas in the entire tribe. By 1954, most of the adults of approximately 13,000 Tobas were Christians. My point is that the Mennonites found their methodology totally inadequate and unworkable in the light of the movement of almost this entire tribe to Christ.

2. Mennonites Modify Approach

This led the Mennonites to invite an anthropologist, William Reyburn, and his wife, both sympathetic to the goals of Christian missions and themselves active Christians, to study the situation and make recommendations. After only four months of field investigations Reyburn (1959) published a report which in practical outworkings and application is proving to be a classic example of how a sympathetic anthropologist can aid in the extremely difficult and complicated task of cross-cultural gospel communication. Essentially, Reyburn interpreted the Indian culture to the North American missionaries. His report included a plea for patience with the Toba's poor and very inadequate understanding of the Christian faith. He recommended that the Bible be translated into the Indian language for clearer understanding (Buckwalter 1955:274). A program of Christian education was introduced (Kratz n.d.) with a view to helping the Tobas understand their new faith.

As a result of this new approach and the already strained relationships between the Indian believers and the Church of God missionaries (Kratz 1967), the Tobas' hearts were won over to the Mennonites. Today, according to Hargrave (1967), not more than 1,000 Tobas are formally identified with the Church of God. The large majority of the remainder, which Buckwalter (1967) estimates at near 3,500, are identified with the Mennonite-sponsored (although independent) United Evangelical Church and various other independent Churches. The United Evangelical Church, which has approximately 4,000 members, was organized in 1962 with 24 congregations and had grown to 40 congregations by 1965 (Loewen 1965:251, Kratz 1967). The Toba Christians are not reported in the Mennonite statistical reports, neither are they included in the World Christian Handbook except for those in the report of the Church of God.

Through the Toba experience the Mennonite Church has learned to seek a clear understanding of the times and the Church's place in them. They continue to confront the problem of a chronic shortage of pastoral leadership as well as a general stagnation (Kratz 1966:288). But the Church, during the period of preparation for the celebration of their 50th anniversary in Argentina, is planning for the future (Darino 1966:880,881). Their experience with the Toba Indians should be lesson enough that correct approaches to the task of missions will result in solid results. With the proper application of church growth principles, similar movements toward Christ and His Church can be seen in the cities of Argentina.

C. ANALYSIS OF MENNONITE MISSION

1. Stalemate and Stagnation

Our statistical survey of the Mennonite Church reveals the inner dimensions of the stalemate and stagnation which have characterized the past twenty-five years of their work. By the year 1935, eighteen years after the beginning of Mennonite mission work, there were 584 communicant members (Figure No. 7). This represents 71 per cent of total church growth during the fifty years of Mennonite missionary occupation. During the subsequent fifteen years, with a substantial increase of the missionary force (more than 50 per cent over the 1935 figure), there was only a meager (13.7 per cent) increase in communicant membership. Undoubtedly the war years affected the growth rate adversely; however, much of the growth of the early period was achieved during the difficult depression years. I

Figure No.7

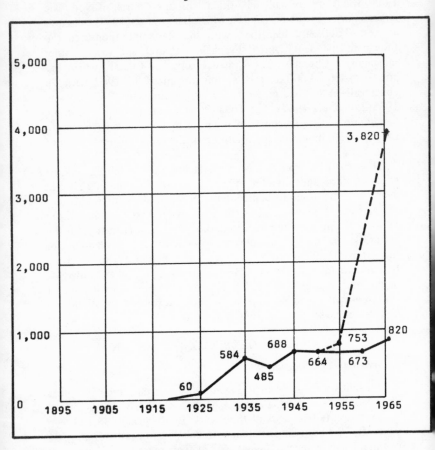

THE MENNONITE CHURCH

COMMUNICANT MEMBERS
DATE OF ENTRANCE — 1917

SOURCES

1925 BEACH 1925:119
1935—1966 CGRILA

Broken line: United Evangelical Church (Toba)

would suspect that there were other reasons. Perhaps there was a slackening of the pace and faith of the early pioneers. Or internal problems such as emerging nationalism in the Church could have influenced the growth pattern negatively. It is also true that the rural churches lost their members as they migrated to the larger urban centers which were not then occupied by the Mennonites. Mission policy had not anticipated this problem, nor was their sufficient flexibility to provide for a massive response to this new area of potential church growth. The cities still represent the highest potential for growth for all the Churches in Argentina. The fact that these were the years of the "20 Year Plan," whose purpose was to reduce mission subsidies 5 per cent, also adversely affected the mood of these churches.

2. Urban Breakthrough

In 1940, before the Mennonite Church began their urban work around this large city, there were 485 communicants in the provincial churches. By 1966, the total membership (excluding the Toba churches) reached 820 communicants. Of these, 234 were located in the large urban concentrations in and around Buenos Aires.

During these twenty-six years (1940 to 1966), the provincial churches grew by only 91 members and sustained a net loss of eight members over their 1935 membership. In view of the critical shortage of fulltime pastors for these provincial churches this loss is explained, but it is not church growth. It appears that the Mennonite churches in the provinces, although in many respects mature and stable churches, had reached a period of stagnation. The missionaries were aware of this and took the right step. They began a new outreach in the burgeoning urban conglomerate around Buenos Aires where others felt there was already too great a concentration of missionaries, and a break in this pattern of non-growth occurred in 1960. However, the Mennonite Church even now is not taking full advantage of the potential for church growth in the cities. Pentecostal growth in the urban centers is evidence of the responsiveness that prevails during these times of rapid social change and acculturation.

3. Principal Features of Mennonite Work

What have been the chief characteristics of Mennonite missionary penetration among the people of the Argentine *pampas?* Recent years have been characterized by stalemate and disorientation. By contrast the pioneer years were marked by a strong and wise emphasis on evangelism. These were the years of greatest church growth and expansion. Even though an anti-Catholic emphasis colored their evangelism, genuine conversions produced Christians who have remained faithful and provided valuable leadership to the present day. Evangelistic methods varied broadly, but the outstanding fact is that there were solid and lasting results, and the churches grew both numerically and spiritually. Institutionalism, especially during the early years, was never allowed to crowd out evangelism. Later several Christian service institutions (kindergarten, clinic and orphanage) were initiated. These slowly cut into the evangelistic thrust, especially insofar as personnel was concerned. A healthy sign in Argentine Mennonite church life at the present is the self-examination into the reasons why there is not more church growth (Kratz 1966:288). This is a strong indication that we might well see a return to this early emphasis on evangelism.

Throughout the early years Mennonite mission work in Argentina was afflicted by what I will call *ruralism*. The original few missionaries who made their way to the Argentine nation were undoubtedly strongly influenced by their own Mennonite agricultural heritage. They found the hitherto unevangelized rural communities cordial to their previous general orientation and preparation. Being people not far removed from a rural setting, they found they were naturally and congenially adapted to the rural mentality. These early years were the period of greatest growth among their newly planted churches. Their original intentions to establish an agricultural mission as partial solution to the financial problems of their emerging churches and the colony begun among the Tobas confirm this propensity to ruralism.

Economic, social and political factors converged to produce profound structural changes in the rural areas of central Argentina during the late 1930's and 1940's. The Mennonites found their churches and mission inadequately prepared. Although token moves were made into the highly responsive area around the growing centers of urbanization, redeployment commensurate with the growing responsiveness was lacking. Granted, adequate care for the already existent churches could not be neglected. From 1944 to 1966, twelve rural churches have been discontinued. Membership in the rural churches remained nearly constant while the newly occupied urban areas provided the Mennonite movement with four new churches and a total of 193 new communicants. This ruralistic mentality moved too slowly into the high potential urban areas from which almost 100 per cent of Mennonite church growth since 1944 has come. During the early years ruralism coincided with responsiveness, but it became an obstacle to realization of the growing potential among the new arrivals in the cities.

A further characteristic of Mennonite missionary penetration was their Germanic bent toward closely structured and meticulous order in church life. This proclivity expressed in administrative organization produced a highly efficient church within the first few years. It was highly commendable that Argentine leadership was incorporated into this organization almost from its very inception. Although there was rather strong and close mission influence and supervision, the positive aspect was that they were working closely with the emerging leadership of the churches. Yet the Mennonite missionaries felt that there was an acute shortage of leadership capable of assuming the responsibilities of the key leadership positions. Property was held in the name of the mission until the early 1950's.

As this progressively elaborate structure passed from stage to stage, it became increasingly evident that there were not sufficient adequately trained Argentine leaders to assume the positions of leadership left vacant by the decreasing missionary force. Here we observe that where structure precedes and suppresses dynamic, the growth of the church is frustrated. This problem has been common to many of the missions ministering in Argentina. Church organizational structure at any given stage of development should never be so complicated or elaborate as to preclude every task being done by members within the emerging Church. The proper function of structure is to preserve and channel the power and new life released by the dynamic of the new spiritual order which is coming into being. Knowing how much and when to organize the emerging church is the great and heavy burden every missionary organization must bear, especially during the years the Church is coming into existence.

Coupled with this hesitancy to turn over the control of their church organization, an inherent tendency to idealize Anglo-Saxon values and customs produced several barriers to continuing church growth. This idealization of foreignness made it possible for the missionaries to use direct translations of Church documents from the

sending churches when establishing the new church organization
(Shank 1943:82). Weber (1945:28) asserts that early missionaries
sought out people of Teutonic racial strain because they felt that
their qualities of thriftiness and faithfulness made the best Christians. This and the preceding factors were certainly in some way
involved in the church split of 1940.

4. Future Opportunities

Mennonites would do well to give serious attention to the following areas during the next few years. They should concentrate on the
areas of greater responsiveness. This is clearly borne out by their
own experience among the Tobas and in the area around Buenos
Aires. Future expansion would consequently not be determined by
secondary factors such as remoteness, with its appeal to the exotic
or the "need" of unoccupied areas. The rapid acculturation process taking place among the Tobas and the recently arrived city
dweller provides ready opportunities for church growth. These
opportunities are ripe now and the iron must be struck while still
hot.

Mennonites could well learn to apply the lessons learned among
the Toba Indians to their missionary efforts in general. Their own
Bishop Nelson Littweiler sums up the most important lessons:

> Several truths stand out in bold letters. The Toba church and
> leaders desire and must be unfettered from foreign control.
> The essence of Christianity, in faith and practice, should not
> be forced into a certain mold by the missionary, but rather
> liberty must be given to the Toba brethren to live their
> Christianity within the norms of Toba culture. The missionary
> must be only and continually the fraternal brother who
> teaches, cooperates, and advises with all kindness, under-
> standing and sympathy (MBMC 1958:102,103).

Extreme caution would well be exercised in the matter of the
education of leadership. Whether or not it will finally prove wise to
have trained a leadership for an Argentine Church composed almost
exclusively of non-Mennonites (with regard to ethnic origin) along
with the leaders of the ethnically oriented Mennonite immigrant
Churches of Brazil and Paraguay, will be answered by the practical
results. It would appear, however, that such leadership could further
contribute to the stagnation of the Argentine churches. While it was

undoubtedly a wise decision from the standpoint of improving the caliber of the Bible training received by the students, its advantages might be far outweighed by this other potentially negative consequence. The Mennonites of Argentina cannot fail to consider this possibility.

CHAPTER 11

The Methodist Church

A. BUILDING ON A FIFTY-YEAR HEAD START

The Methodist Church was one of the first Churches to preach the Evangelical message in Argentina. When other missions entered Argentina in the last fifth of the past century, Methodism had already enjoyed fifty years of ministry to the English-speaking community and had witnessed the beginning of services in Spanish under their guidance. The development of Methodism prior to the twentieth century has been handled briefly in Chapter IV. Here our interests are directed primarily to the developments in the history of this established Church during this century.

Methodism in Argentina has pertained to four different administrative districts since 1893. From 1893 to 1909 Argentine Methodism was a part of the South American Annual Conference. Work in the Southern Hemisphere progressed, and the area was divided in 1910, assigning Argentina to the Eastern South American Annual Conference until after World War II. In 1946, another administrative adjustment was made and Argentine Methodism was grouped with the neighboring country, Uruguay, in the Rio de la Plata Annual Conference. This arrangement continued until 1955 when these two countries were separated and the Argentine Annual Conference was organized. This Argentine division of Methodism is not autonomous as are the Churches in Mexico and Brazil, but is administratively dependent on the General Conference of the Methodist Church of the United States. The Commission on the Structure of Methodism Overseas has under study a project which will finally lead to the formation of an autonomous Argentine Methodist Church (*Pampa Breezes* 1967a). The Argentine Conference also forms part of the Latin American Central Conference (Derby 1960:147). I have chosen to follow these divisions chronologically in this profile of the Methodist Church in Argentina.

The membership of the Methodist Church after 64 years in Argentina and 33 years of ministry to the Spanish-speaking community had reached almost 3,000 by 1900. The first statistical survey available to us of world missions is dated 1911, when the Church had a communicant membership of 3,817 and a community of 11,829 (Dennis 1911:96). A seminary founded in 1884 (Glover 1960:376) functioned exclusively as a Methodist institution at this time. In 1903 the Church procured the legal recognition of the Argentine authorities and secured her incorporation papers (IMA 1960:754), and continues to operate under similar legal arrangements today.

1. Cooperation and Institutionalism

With the administrative change of 1910, an era of considerable change and innovation was inaugurated. The key word of the succeeding period was "cooperation." The Methodist Church in Argentina and the rest of Eastern South America took its keynote for the period from the Panama Congress on Christian Work in 1916. There followed a period of cooperative efforts, especially with the Disciples of Christ, but which also included the Presbyterian Church (Church of Scotland) and the Waldensians. With the Disciples they entered into an arrangement of joint responsibility in the Colegio Ward, as indicated in the profile of the Disciples' work (Chapter VIII). The other joint effort was the Union Theological Seminary. The Seminary was small when B. Foster Stockwell assumed the presidency in 1926 and began to build it into the most influential theological institution of the "established" denominations. According to Browning (1928:78), the Methodist Church, although the strongest Church in the region, reported a net gain of only four ordained ministers in the 10 years preceding 1928, and twelve in 34 years, including both national and foreign. The years following 1928 began to see new life in the Seminary under the new and imaginative leadership, although there was no corresponding increase in church

Figure No.8

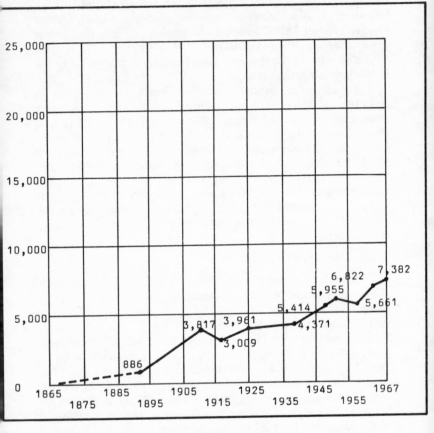

METHODIST CHURCH

COMMUNICANT MEMBERS
DATE OF ENTRANCE - 1836

SOURCES

1893	BARCLAY	1957 Vol.III:320
1911	DENNIS	1911:96
1916	BEACH	1916:72
1925	BEACH	1925:119
1938	PARKER	1938:82
1949	GRUBB	1949:304
1952	GRUBB	1952:216
1957	BINGLE	1957:115
1962	COXILL	1962:126
1965	MC	n.d.:355

membership for 10 to 15 years. Training was improved, but immediate results in Methodist church growth were not seen.

The Methodists, following contemporary mission trends, were fully committed to the policy of education. Besides the school in Buenos Aires, they operated another such school in Rosario, known as the Colegio Americano, with 150 students. There was also a school for poor children in this same city known as Gleason Institute (Browning 1928:69). In addition, they were involved in an extensive parochial school program. The system included 12 schools with a total of 800 students and staffed with five foreign and 35 Argentine teachers. Browning gives the reason for the existence of these schools: "No doubt the real apologetic lies in the fact that the evangelical schools educate, while the Government institutions merely instruct." The contemporary emphasis in education made its impact on Methodist missionary thinking. This institutional emphasis became the dominating influence for subsequent years. Personnel were diverted from necessary evangelism and the potential of these years was largely missed.

The communicant membership of the churches grew during this period from 3,817 in 1911 to 4,371 in 1938 (Parker 1938:82), or a net growth of only 20.5 members per year (Figure No. 8). The rate of growth per decade was a low 5 per cent. The rate of Methodist church growth stood far below the rate of population growth. On the other hand, during this same period other denominations, particularly the Baptists and the Plymouth Brethren, were achieving their highest rate of growth. It is surprising that Methodist leadership did not take notice of this and make necessary modifications of policy. This is an outstanding illustration of how desperately research is needed to guide in determining policy. It should be noted, however, that the sharp drop in membership between 1911 and 1916 was most likely due to a purging of inactive members (Derby 1967). It could not have been due to an administrative adjustment, as no change of organizational districts was made during those years. The policy of cooperation and education was not producing the results which should be the aim of all Christian mission, namely, the reconciliation of men to Christ. Undoubtedly the incipient trend toward dilution of the biblical content in theology was also having its effect.

2. Organizational Growth

In 1932 the first Argentine bishop came into office. Bishop Juan

E. Gattinoni, whose two sons actively and positively serve this Church today (one as pastor of the Central Methodist Church, and the other as manager of the publishing house), led the Church until 1944. The participation of Argentine leadership in Methodist church government on a par with the missionary begun in 1925 continued toward its logical goal in this step (Monti 1967:9). An arm of the growing literature ministry, La Aurora bookstore, also a cooperative venture, began in 1927. Browning (1928:53), summarizing the position of the Methodist Church in 1928, said: "Today, as regards numbers and influence, it ranks first among the distinctly evangelical groups of the region." This position of privilege and prestige was already in serious jeopardy, especially with regard to numerical strength. Browning seems to have been unaware of the swelling tide of Plymouth Brethren growth. Membership in this lay-oriented group then stood very near 6,000, or half again as much as the Methodists. This seems to have been a period of great growth potential, but the Methodists, as well as other Churches, were not alert to the opportunity.

The period when the Church in Uruguay and Argentina functioned as the Rio de la Plata Annual Conference (1946-1954) was largely a time of transition. A very energetic and capable young bishop, Sante Uberto Barbieri, was appointed in 1949. Much of the new orientation of the Methodist Church both in Argentina and Uruguay can be attributed to his vision, imagination and drive. It was largely through his encouragement that the Uruguay Provisional Annual Conference was organized in 1954. He was also the motivating spirit behind the later formation of the Patagonia Provisional Annual Conference (1963), which was organized to stimulate the "extension of the Church in the southern part of Argentina" (MC n.d.:355). Many of the Welsh Protestant immigrants of a century ago form part of this Conference today.

3. Multiplying Ministries

With the year 1955, the Argentine Annual Conference was organized and the present period of Methodism in the *pampas* was inaugurated. Recent years have seen the rapid unfolding and increase of the multiplied ministries of this active Church. Today they have no rivals in terms of sheer variety of projects which receive of her vision, finances and organizational ability. The earlier institutions, such as the Colegio Ward and Colegio Americano, continue to function. The school in Rosario celebrated its 92nd year of operation in 1967 with well over 500 students in the primary and secondary programs. The Buenos Aires school, with over 1,100 students in the two-level program, is the only other secondary school operated by the Methodists.

Social services receive increasing attention in the face of persistent need in certain regions of Argentina. The Boca Mission begun by William Morris in 1898 continues to operate under the auspices of the Methodist Church. There are three community centers operating to meet the need of less fortunate elements in the Argentine community. Of special interest is the center for the Toba Indians in the Chaco opened in recent years at J.J. Castelli in the province of Chaco. This center, operated by an international team of doctors, nurses and teachers from Switzerland, the United States and Argentina, provides a wide variety of social services, adult education, medical care and an evangelistic outreach (MC n.d.:359). This ministry is carried on largely among Toba Christians who came into the Christian faith through the influence of Pentecostal evangelistic efforts. Today they are organized in the Mennonite-sponsored United Evangelical Church. The Methodists consider this thrust a service and do not seek to organize their own congregations along the lines of Wesleyan order. In the rest of the country the Methodists operate student hostels for university students near four of the national universities.

Other ministries include the Methopress Publishing House, which benefits the entire evangelical community, as does La Aurora Bookstore, which in 1966 became the distribution branch of the publishing house. The Church also operates a home for children and for the aged in Mercedes, as well as an agricultural center.

B. ANALYSIS OF METHODIST CHURCH GROWTH

In 1965 the Methodist Church in Argentina had a communicant membership of 7,382 which, with the 3,208 preparatory members, made a total of 10,590 including the Patagonia Conference (MC n.d.:355). This represents an increase of 1,721 since 1957, or a rate of 38 per cent per decade, just slightly higher than the annual rate of population increase. The drop in membership of 294 in 1957 is not an administrative adjustment caused by the organization of the Uruguay Conference, as in both figures the Uruguay Church was listed separately. Derby (1967) feels that this numerical decline is due to an effort on the part of the churches to "clean out" their membership rolls of inactive members. It is interesting to note that this occurred during the years of greatest Pentecostal growth. The net increase in Methodist membership since 1911 is 3,565 members, or 17 per cent per decade. This rate of increase is below the growth rate of the national population for the same period, which is about 2.1 per cent annually. When this rate of growth is compared with the rate for the most recent period (above) it is seen that present-day Methodism shows signs of new life. With other denominations growing even more rapidly, it would be worthwhile for Methodists to ask themselves if they are taking advantage of the existent potential to the fullest extent. Per capita giving in this Church was $16.90 (U.S. dollars) in 1960 (Derby 1961:90). The present staff, which includes some outstanding leaders (among them, José Míguez Bonino, president of the Union Seminary since 1960), is made up of 55 fulltime pastors and other officials, 22 supply pastors, one doctor and one nurse. In addition, the foreign staff numbers 32 mission-aries, including wives.

What are the characteristic features of Methodism in Argentina? First, they seem to have the big-church complex. Being there first, and seeing all the newer missions enter has given them a sense of being the elder brother, which in many respects is justified. It was already a Church of approximately 2,000 members when the other missions entered, and still feels that if it is not the largest from the standpoint of numbers, it is surely the most influential and most important Church. The Methodist Church has consequently ne-glected evangelism for perfecting ministries as she stretches herself to maintain this image and this position of leadership. Attention is given to evangelism in the Easter and Spring campaigns and through a program of *avanzadas* (mission outposts), but the Wesleyan passion is missing in this established Church of third and fourth generation Christians. There are insufficient pastors for the churches already operating, and expansion, which largely depends upon a highly trained clergy, is painfully slow and generally tragically late to respond to opportunities. It is significant that some of the most spectacular evangelistic breakthroughs have been the result of the vision and sacrificial dedication of laymen (*Pampa Breezes* 1967b). This type of expansion must be encouraged and a training program designed for laymen in all the churches to prepare them for these opportunities. Evangelistic outreach in part is sacrificed to a desire to maintain the prestige of leadership among other Evangelical Churches. One of the beneficial results of this emphasis on a highly trained clergy has been the emergence of the "River Plate Theologians," all products of the Union Seminary in Buenos Aires. Their contributions to Latin American theological thought are generally significant, as well as controversial, but usually reflect modern European theological trends far more than distinct Latin American approaches and thought. This type of thinking, however, does not seem to fit the needs of a Church that is growing slowly in an area that is proving to be more responsive for other missions. There is great emphasis placed on quality over against mere quantitative growth. This "quality," when directed primarily toward maintaining and strengthening the elaborate structures that have already developed, frustrates genuine church growth.

Another aspect of Methodist work in Argentina is the early emphasis on secular education. The school in Rosario has been functioning for almost a century. Parochial schools have functioned in conjunction with some local parishes. Although curtailed in recent years, during the first forty years of this century the schools received special attention. Much of this educational effort, especially that directed toward the influential middle-class families, has made almost no direct contribution to the numerical or spiritual growth of the Methodist Church. Its significant contribution in the lives of the students cannot be debated.

Still another feature of Methodism in Argentina has been the diversified program with its multitudinous ministries. These began during the early years and continue their progressive development. These Christians of sensitive heart and conscience saw the needs of certain sectors of Argentine society and reached out in genuine charity to help. As outlined above, these services are highly diversified and yet inadequate to meet the social demand. They are interpreted as expressions of Christian concern instead of the full answer to Argentina's problems, which, at present, would be too large a task for the entire Evangelical community to pretend to solve apart from genuine spiritual revolution and regeneration resulting in broad church growth. This is a concern which depends on the entire world community of Methodists, especially North American financial help, and is expressed by this younger Church in Argentina.

The Methodist Church in Argentina has allowed itself to indulge in the expensive luxuries which even among the older sending Churches have produced a state of near stagnation and even decadence. Involvement in such a diversified program of specialized services has obligated them to devise training programs and leadership patterns to meet these needs. There has consequently been a shift of personnel away from those activities which produce church growth. The average pastor finds himself busy fulfilling the image of one involved in every activity of a growing establishment. Little time remains for evangelism which springs from genuine Christian concern for man's ultimate welfare. Training should be bent to produce the Pentecostal passion which has been a distinctive Methodist heritage. The theological shifts which take place in a young seminarian's mind often annul his passion to evangelize.

The Church must discover the masses in the new urban *barrios,* not merely as examples of social dislocation and discrimination but as men who are the object of Christ's passion. A situation which largely includes churches among a relatively comfortable middle class and a social concern for the unfortunate masses is not full-orbed concern. The Methodists should seek to extend their program of *avanzadas* through the training and direction of laymen out into these urban *barrios* in evangelistic outreach. The potential for church growth and expression of integral Christian concern is phenomenal.

This is the profile of a Church that is alert, well versed on current tensions and issues, identified sympathetically with the world about her and yet seeking to reform it; but it is also the story of a Church that does not grow in proportion to her potential or the responsiveness of today's Latin America. The Methodist Church has all the institutions and ecclesiastical accouterments of a sophisticated church, but seems to have lost its passion to disciple the people of Argentina and bring them into a meaningful spiritual relationship with Christ.

CHAPTER 12

The Plymouth Brethren

A. SPECTACULAR GROWTH OF LAY MOVEMENT

The Plymouth Brethren movement had its beginnings in 1882 when Mr. J.H.L. Ewen began his evangelistic travels in the first horse-powered "Bible coach." This method of spreading the Gospel became characteristic of Brethren expansion across the *pampas* of Argentina. Ewen, before coming to Argentina, had studied in the Missionary School which operated under the vision and direction of Grattan Guinness (Clifford 1954:79-81) in London. He was "commended" for missionary service in Argentina by a Plymouth Brethren assembly in England, as were the large majority of his growing number of colleagues. Others in subsequent years came from other Commonwealth countries and the United States. Although not a mission organization in the commonly accepted sense, these missionaries were related to the administrative organization known as Christian Missions in Many Lands.

Upon his return to England Ewen visited the assemblies of the Open Brethren, the spiritual descendents of George Müller, describing the need and opportunities for evangelism in Argentina. The quality of the young men inspired by his preaching to join him in his labors in Argentina was outstanding. Among these first volunteers the Brethren number some of their most distinguished missionaries: Payne, Torre, Clifford and Langran.

With the arrival of these men and the blessings of God, this group

of assemblies, which was to become the greatest single force for the
Gospel in Argentina, began quietly but solidly. The first formal
meeting in the characteristic Brethren style began in Buenos Aires
in 1889. This assembly moved from place to place until 1903, when
a lot was purchased on Brazil Street and a tent was installed for
gospel meetings, with Mr. Payne preaching. This was the beginning
of what became the first permanent assembly in Argentina. Mr.
Payne commented at the time on the caliber of men needed for this
type of evangelistic ministry:

> For those who are thinking of taking up evangelistic work in
> Argentina I would like to impress upon them the fact that the
> people of Buenos Aires are well educated and intelligent ...
> the upper class man is a great admirer of the teaching of
> Comte, the Positivist. In order to reach these we must be able
> to deal with them from their own standpoint, and, unless able
> to hold an audience with some ability, he will very soon find
> difficulty in getting people to listen. The idea that anything
> will do for the mission field has, I trust, quite passed away
> (1904:8,9).

The growth of the assemblies, as they are called by the Brethren, is
eloquent evidence that Mr. Payne's message reached the hearts of
high caliber young men who thereafter spent their lives in effective
service for Christ.

1. Brethren Assemblies Spread

The next Brethren assembly started in 1896 in the river-port city
of Rosario, north and west of Buenos Aires on the Paraná River. It
began largely under the inspiration and vision of the recent widow of
George Spooner, an employee of the railroad, who died six years
after his arrival in Rosario in 1888. Under the inspired leadership of
missionaries the work has grown and prospered. The assembly in
Quilmes, a suburb of Buenos Aires, began in 1894 with an
orphanage, the vision and burden of Charles Torre. Later, in a
borrowed church building used by the English-speaking Protestant
community, Torre began services in Spanish in 1902. Torre was one
of the first of a long line of self-employed Brethren missionaries in
Argentina who contributed greatly to the expansion of their
assemblies. Many Brethren employees of the British-built and
-operated railroads which reached throughout Argentina considered it

their Christian responsibility and privilege to witness for Christ. Through dedicated and sacrificial efforts they established assemblies on their own without missionary assistance.

The first decade of this century saw a phenomenal increase in Plymouth Brethren missionary activity. Young men and women in the assemblies of England and Scotland, undoubtedly influenced by the writings of Payne, began to flood into an Argentina that was ripe for the Gospel. By 1911, according to the World Atlas of Christian Missions (Dennis 1911:96), the organization Christian Missions in Many Lands had 38 missionaries in Argentina, and all were reporting good results. In 1900 there were congregations in Córdoba, Buenos Aires, Tucumán, Rosario and Quilmes. At the close of this decade of advance, there were at least 24 congregations, mostly in the provinces of Buenos Aires and Santa Fe, but also extending west to Mendoza and north as far as Jujuy and Salta. This was just the beginning. The seed had been planted and it was finding unusually fertile soil in Argentina, where the Brethren were employing effective methods. Gospel meetings in tents were the chief evangelistic tool of outreach. Payne, speaking of the effectiveness of gospel meetings in the "wooden-sided, canvas-roofed" tents pitched in the populous districts of Buenos Aires wrote:

> This has proved to be one of the best means of getting the people to hear the Gospel that has yet been tried in Buenos Aires. At the end of five months' meetings the interest has in no way abated, and our difficulty at most of the meetings is to provide seats for those who wish to sit and listen to the Gospel. At least 400 persons hear the message of salvation at each meeting. We have had some trouble with a number of young men who came to oppose, but the police have given us every assistance in keeping order. This element has rendered the holding of after meetings almost impossible, and so most of the following up of the work has to be done by visiting (1904:7).

Although the Methodists had been in Mendoza since about 1885, the Brethren were the first to penetrate the interior of the country of Argentina in force. Many of their converts were from among the recent immigrants from Europe, and Italian family names are common among them. In 1900, the 25 converts in Tucumán represented eight different nationalities (*Echoes of Service* 1900:272). In Buenos Aires that same year Torre reported that the

39 participants in the "Breaking of Bread" represented 11 different nationalities (*Echoes of Service* 1900:320).

2. *Conference Is Immediate Success*

The year 1910 marked the beginning of the Brethren conferences. This annual gathering in most of the central churches has become one of the key institutions in the growing strength of Brethrenism in Argentina. Generally held at the time of one of the national or religious holidays, these two- to four-day concentrations draw believers from all the surrounding churches, including other central churches that have their conferences at another date. It is a time for Bible messages and fellowship between the believers; a genuine highlight in the lives of the Christians. It has afforded the opportunity for young people to become acquainted and consequently has produced a number of marriages between the sons and daughters of Brethren families. The first of these conferences was held February 6th to 8th, 1910, in Rosario and proved to be an immediate success. Observers at the conference felt it was a harbinger of even greater blessings for the Brethren work in Argentina.

By 1915 there were at least 40 local assemblies and their number was increasing rapidly. A publication ministry was begun in Quilmes in about 1905. During these early years some of the single women missionaries such as Miss Miles conducted schools for under-privileged children, but these were later discontinued. In the past ten years primary and secondary schools started largely under Brethren initiative and dedication are functioning both in Córdoba and in Buenos Aires. During this period an orphanage was begun in Quilmes and continues to render valuable service today. Orphanages have been operated in Jujuy and Córdoba also.

3. *Immigrant Character of Assemblies*

Open air campaigns and street meetings continued. In 1915, when the Socialist Party was active and growing, a law against political agitation was used against the Brethren (*Echoes of Service* 1915:78). Yet their tent campaigns continued with increasing success. The international character of the Brethren meetings was reflected in the ten different nationalities participating in the Lord's Supper in Tucumán in 1915 (*Echoes of Service* 1915:336). In the northern part of the country, first contacts were made with the hill people of

Jujuy in a place called Guayacán. Until 1920 there was very little Argentine leadership in the meetings, with almost all active work being carried on by the missionaries. During these years attendance at the open-air meetings was unusually good. At times there were as many as 700 present, in contrast to today's mere handful as the Brethren persist in this traditional approach.

In 1920 the first contact with the Syrian merchants who were to become influential in the northern churches, in particular, was reported. Findlay, the missionary, writing from Santiago del Estero says:

> A number of Syrians still come to nearly all the meetings in the hall, and assent to all they hear, and yet somehow do not come out clearly for Christ. Please pray for them (*Echoes of Service* 1920:258).

Jujuy also reported interest among the Syrians at this time. Today the leadership of this church and a large percentage of the membership consist of these Syrians. Again we have a reference to the immigrant nature of this growing Church. At the funeral of Doddrington, one of the missionaries in Salta, the coffin was carried by six brethren representing the Dutch, French-Swiss, Scotch, English, Anglo-Argentine and Argentine racial strains.

4. Numerical Increase Continues

Such sustained growth was indeed unusual in Argentina up to this time, but in the next years it continued at an even more accelerated pace. Tent meetings in Buenos Aires were extended for longer periods. William Payne, who was to die within nine months while on a missionary tour into Bolivia (Lear 1951:142), reported his last campaign in that metropolis. The response and general effect of the effort were nothing less than phenomenal. The campaign of 1923 was the greatest movement Buenos Aires had ever seen. It was reported that thousands heard the Gospel. The after-meetings lasted for two to three hours and 300 inquirers were present at a specially called meeting. The newspapers gave the campaign a full half-page coverage and it was believed that some 200,000 of the two million inhabitants of Buenos Aires heard the Gospel. The general response was excellent and attendance increased in meetings in the assemblies after the campaign (*Echoes of Service* 1924:19,20,44,69).

Attendance at the conferences continued to increase. Córdoba reported that 500 partook of the Lord's Supper at their conference in 1925, and 640 in Lanús, a suburb of Buenos Aires (*Echoes of Service* 1925:157). By 1930 each assembly had her special date for the conference. In Jujuy it was at Easter, in Santiago del Estero on the 25th of May, a national holiday, and in Córdoba at Carnival, the three days immediately preceding Ash Wednesday. People were invited from increasingly longer distances and the British railroads delivered them on time.

The young people began their annual conferences in Córdoba in 1930. These provided the emerging young leadership with their opportunity to organize, direct and preach at the conference. This single effort aided greatly in preparing young Argentines, and the sons of the missionaries, for service in the assemblies. There were 400 to 500 youth present at the first conference. By 1950 they had grown to over 2,000 in attendance.

During the 1930's evangelism with the tent continued, sometimes for 34 nights straight, with over 350 present nightly. Group baptisms became normal and membership in the churches increased. Reports of nearly 200 in communion in a single assembly became common. These were years marked with growing opposition also. Letters from the field report difficulties with the priests. The priests in Tucumán, in an attempt to arrest Brethren growth, imitated the Brethren evangelistic methods. Much of this reaction was inspired by the fanatical religious fervor generated by the Eucharistic Congress held in Buenos Aires by the Roman Catholics in 1934. These years also witnessed the beginning of monthly city-wide prayer meetings. Missionaries were generally very optimistic about the prospects of the work. Five new churches were started in the Belgrano district of Buenos Aires alone. These encouraging signs continued right up to the beginning of World War II, when the British missionaries felt the pressures of hostilities and a tighter economic situation.

5. Signs of Slowdown

Since the War growth has continued, but there is a different spirit evident. After 1945, the older missionaries in Argentina found themselves in semi-retirement and almost no young men coming out from England, Canada and the United States to replace them. The work passed more and more into the hands of a very capable body of Argentine Christians that had been trained in the churches. As of the early months of 1967 there were 49 missionaries from sending countries, including wives and widows. The average age of these would probably be over the 60 mark since many of the retired personnel, who continue to live in Argentina, are counted in the figure. The number of Argentine personnel who serve in the capacity of "missionary," since in Brethren church government there is no place for "pastors," now stands at about 75. Their average age would be much lower as younger men are "commended" for missionary service.

In spite of what appears to be a general slowdown in Brethren growth in Argentina, there have been significant breakthroughs in recent years, one of them rather spectacular. The Chaco town of Palo a Pique in the province of Salta is located some sixty miles from the nearest Plymouth Brethren assembly in Orán. Palo a Pique is quite isolated as there is no regular means of public transportation out of the Chaco into Orán. A rancher, Cristóbal Matórraz, was traveling to Orán in search of medical help at the regional hospital. He passed the Brethren assembly while their annual conference was going on and entered to buy a Bible. On returning he shared his discovery with the tavern keeper only to discover that he had a copy of the same book. Their study together led to their conversion and that of many of their friends who, with them, formed a congregation which met in the bar. The missionaries and church leaders from the assemblies in the surrounding area continued to visit these new Christians to teach them. People throughout the entire area were becoming Evangelicals and soon there were congregations 75 miles farther into the Chaco and in many intervening towns (*Bible Society Record* 1967:13, Harlow 1964:39). Recent reports indicate that there are at least 10 congregations and approximately 1,000 Christians in this area. Only ten years have passed since Mr. Matórraz walked into the Brethren hall in Orán.

B. UNDERSTANDING PLYMOUTH BRETHREN GROWTH

The attempt to construct a statistical graph of the growth pattern of Plymouth Brethren expansion meets with certain insurmountable obstacles. The first obstacle is one of principle. The Brethren feel it less than fully spiritual to "count the sheep." Consequently it is difficult to find statistical information. Data on the missionary activities of the Plymouth Brethren in Argentina are almost entirely absent from the available surveys of missions. However, the basis of our study is a Plymouth Brethren estimate of the number of

Figure No.9

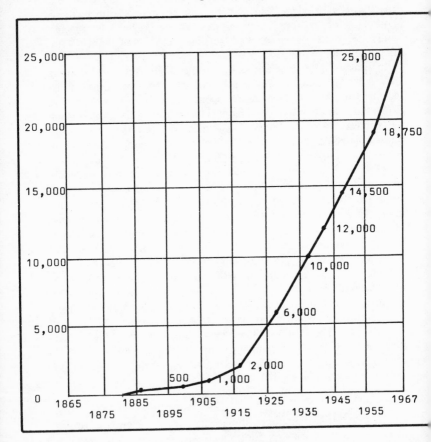

PLYMOUTH BRETHREN

COMMUNICANT MEMBERS
DATE OF ENTRANCE — 1882

SOURCE
ESTIMATES of PLYMOUTH BRETHREN LEADERS IN ARGENTINA

missionaries and assemblies or churches (Harlow 1964:34). Although it is quite incomplete, it is the only statistical chart on Argentina that we have seen in Brethren writings. This data, with other information from various sources, formed the basis of a questionnaire sent to twelve of their leaders in Argentina. Of the six who returned the questionnaire only two attempted a statistical reconstruction which could serve as a basis for the graph we have prepared (Figure No. 9). Four of the six who returned the questionnaires are in agreement on the final figure of 25,000. The graph indicates that the growth in the Brethren assemblies from 1947 to 1957 was 29.9 per cent. This is contrasted with a growth of 33.3 per cent for the following ten years. These figures would seem to indicate a steadily mounting surge of Brethren strength in Argentina. However, an analysis of their growth dynamics through the years indicates to this writer that further investigation by those most intimately acquainted with this movement is needed in order to arrive at a more accurate delineation of the growth pattern. The observations contained here could provide several guidelines for the beginning of such an investigation.

There were at least two general growth periods among the Brethren which are not reflected in the graph curve as it appears in this study. There was the very strong beginning movement of the first decade of this century, which might have been sharp enough to be reflected in the curve. The movement's proportionately small size could have hidden the upsurge in relation to the rest of the graph curve. The other burst of growth, which was certainly more marked than the present rate of growth, was the period beginning with the campaigns of the 1920's. It is my opinion that this upsurge as reconstructed on the graph is not marked enough in relation to the period following 1947. The curve reflects rather artificially only a very steady rate of growth, beginning in 1917.

1. Disorientation Threatens

Today there seems to be a spirit of disorientation which is overwhelming the Plymouth Brethren in Argentina. It is manifested in the growing spirit of dissension evident among them which polarizes chiefly around two issues. First, what should the Brethren attitude be toward the denominational organizations? Traditionally, they have felt they were not a denomination and should not associate with the other Churches too intimately. The cooperative evangelistic campaigns in Buenos Aires with Oswald Smith, Cecilio Arrastia and Billy Graham have forced them to "judge the issue." This, together with other dimensions of the same problem, is producing a degree of dissension among them and a resurgence of traditional Brethren independence and exclusiveness from the denominations.

The other issue which has concerned the Plymouth Brethren is the training of young Argentines for national missionary service. A group of leaders, largely Argentines, had the growing conviction that some formal training should be given the young men and women even though it represented a departure from traditional Brethren procedure. A Bible school was opened in Villa María, Córdoba, in June, 1960, with a vision of supplying the need for missionaries, since the overseas supply was diminishing. This curtailment was largely due to the fact that the Brethren leadership in the sending countries did not feel that missionary personnel were needed any longer in Argentina, although economic reasons surely had their effect also. It was specifically stated that the school would not be training "clerics." Six girls and four young men enrolled. The school has met with good success although some of the traditional leadership in the churches possibly see these "highly" trained young men as a threat to their authority, as well as a threat to the traditional Brethren concept of leadership, and view the school coolly. Brethren observers feel that the matter of this school is no longer an important issue although it has left its marks and helped to define camps within the Brethren assemblies. The fact that the school has continued at all with some measure of general support is a significant step away from traditional Brethren practice and augurs well for the future.

The Plymouth Brethren are partially victims of their own success. According to their own observers the phenomenal growth of the assemblies in Argentina has backfired and the Brethren in England feel it is no longer necessary to send missionaries. Men of the spiritual and leadership quality of the early pioneers such as Payne, Torre, Clifford and Lear could still make significant contributions. This would be particularly true of specialists in the field of teaching which are available in England and North America.

2. Outstanding Features of Brethrenism

What have been the outstanding features of the Plymouth

Brethren work in Argentina? First, the influence of the British in Argentine life and commerce during the years of Brethren expansion cannot be passed over lightly. The years of growth were also the years when it was in a certain measure advantageous to be identified with their enterprises and institutions. This was particularly true of the railroads with which many of the self-employed Brethren missionaries worked. Ewen mentions transporting his Bible coach free of charge on a British-operated train from place to place. This influence should not be overstressed, however, because other British-based missions such as the Evangelical Union of South America did not experience great growth during these same years.

Another feature which has already been alluded to was the high degree of fellowship and intercommunication between the different assemblies. The Bible conferences which began in 1910 became the distinctive mark of Brethrenism. They seemed to fit the mood of the new movement as it spread from area to area. Recent converts from one area would visit their relatives in another center where the conference was being held. It was natural to invite them to the meetings and many were reached for the Gospel in this way. The youth conferences were the normal extension of this, as were the citywide prayer meetings in the larger urban centers. The conferences were an effective functional substitute for the religious festivals common in Catholic countries, and many times through deliberate planning their dates coincided. Merle Davis (1943:98,99) considers this feature of the Brethren "the most striking practice of this group." One feature of the success of these conferences has contributed to the development of a degree of ingrownness. The visiting youth in attendance allowed their hopeful eyes to drift from the preachers toward the other young visitors. The resulting pattern of intermarriages, although it has produced strong Brethren homes, has also contributed to the development of certain aspects of a ghetto complex. The subsequent younger generations, desiring greater contact with the Argentine world about them, have defected in increasing numbers. There are other reasons which have contributed to these defections, such as leadership tensions and the generally low level of preparation of the preachers of the second and third generations, but the fact of the isolation of the Brethren cannot be overlooked as the key factor.

During the first fifty years of expansion the Brethren evangelistic tent was ubiquitous. This was the symbol of advance. In recent years, the evangelistic efforts have been almost entirely confined to the buildings of the regular meetings, although some have been conducted in public halls such as theaters and sports arenas. The crusading zeal characteristic of the early missionaries has diminished somewhat in this regard. Other methods used were extensive itineration, both with the tent and the Bible coach. There is some reason to believe that this decrease of public evangelistic efforts at the local level is a further consequence of the "blessed" isolation which seems to be developing.

Probably the most outstanding feature of this movement is their effective use of laymen in all aspects of the ministry. Plymouth Brethrenism is a lay movement and nothing could be better suited to the needs of the mission situation where the national church is just emerging. The missionaries themselves were unordained although receiving offerings to meet living expenses. The large number of self-employed British missionaries reinforced the missionaries' teaching that the layman could serve God actively and effectively. The hundreds of Brethren lay preachers have contributed greatly to the growth pattern. The formal training of these men was nil, but they learned on their own and in the meetings, which were divided into four basic categories: evangelism, ministry (teachings on the Christian life), Bible study and worship. The central service of worship was the weekly celebration of the Breaking of Bread. This weekly worship of the crucified Christ was also an unintentional but highly effective functional substitute for the mass. Laymen became unusually adept at leading and at preaching or teaching at each of these types of meetings. The personal libraries of some of their outstanding leaders would rival those of the seminary professor, including the volumes in Greek and Hebrew.

Finally, the fact that there was no mission organization greatly aided the indigenous development of this movement. The missionaries did not form or participate in some power structure that stood over against the churches and their emerging leaders. They became members of these churches and participated as equals with their Argentine brethren. When some particular missionary could get financial help from overseas for the building of meeting halls, this was given freely and with no strings attached. No organizational control or pressure was applied by a mission. Loyalty to the Brethren movement and Brethren principles was based strictly on spiritual motivations. The common mission-versus-church tensions have been almost totally absent.

3. Projecting Into the Future

The Brethren leaders might consider the following suggestions to meet the mounting need in these areas with a view to breaking the threat of stagnation. There is no human reason why this movement could not double its strength within the next 20 to 30 years if the correct steps are taken. To rise to the occasion of the opportunity which lies before the entire Evangelical Church in Argentina the Brethren should dedicate themselves to the discovery of ways in which the present-day leadership can be trained "on the job." This would greatly aid in stopping the leakage to the world of many of the youth. It would also provide the present leadership with a greater sense of strength from which to express positive instead of negative leadership. Concerted effort must be dedicated to the preparation of the youth for more effective leadership. International Brethrenism can and should play an important role in this together with their Argentine counterparts. At this second and third generation stage of the work, the Brethren leadership could well invest energy and finances in such a project. Some departure from traditional Brethren patterns will be necessary but this group of practical Christians has already demonstrated that this is possible. This is particularly true in the area of increased giving and support of the ministry.

In the light of the phenomenal growth pattern evident in the development of the Plymouth Brethren movement in Argentina, other Churches would do well to make a close comparison of their methods with these which have proved so fruitful in Argentina. It is equally important for the Brethren to ask whether they have achieved the full potential for church growth under today's conditions. Or will the Pentecostal movement prove to have the key to expansion? The experience and observation of each demonstrates that great growth is possible now. What is needed are the proper techniques, methods and spiritual attitudes to exploit this opportunity fully.

CHAPTER 13

The Seventh-Day Adventists

A. MAKING SABBATH KEEPERS ON THE PAMPAS

Argentina was the first South American country entered by the Seventh-Day Adventists. The first Adventists to enter the River Plate country were North American farmers of German origin from Tampa, Kansas. There were four families, making a total of ten persons, who decided to make this move to spread the Advent message and to "make other Sabbath keepers." One of the men in the party, Jorge Riffel, had been in Argentina before and through correspondence with friends had found one person who had promised to keep the Sabbath with him. When the ten immigrants arrived in Diamante, Entre Ríos, they were met by Riffel's friend, Hetze, and the very next day they held the first Sabbath school service. This was early in 1890 (SDA 1966:Vol. 1,54). One of the descendents of the Riffel family came to occupy important positions in the international division of the Adventist Church (Aitken 1967).

This unofficial beginning was soon followed up by the Seventh-Day Adventist Board of Foreign Missions, who designated funds for beginning work in South America and appointed a study commission to determine the most feasible means to begin work on that continent, Mexico, the East Indies, and Africa. It was this same commission that appointed three colporteurs, Snyder, Nowlin and Stauffer, to pioneer the work of selling literature in Argentina. They arrived in Argentina in December of 1891. Their door-to-door labors also carried them to Brazil and the Falkland Islands. Colportage work has become the hallmark of Adventist expansion in Argentina as elsewhere. Again and again people in even the most remote areas have brought this writer a timeworn book which they believe to be the Bible, which turns out to be a copy of Mrs. E.G. White's writings. The successful ministry of these booksellers indicated to the leaders in the United States that they were in a potentially responsive field. This led them to the appointment of the first ordained Adventist minister, F.H. Westphal, who in 1894 began his ministry among the German immigrant communities (Olsen 1926:561).

The community into which Westphal entered was made up of German and Russian colonists living around the town of Crespo in Entre Ríos. The original inhabitants were Roman Catholics, but the immigrants were Lutheran and Baptist. Some within these denominations, according to Adventist sources, had earlier (1885) practiced Sabbath observance. This was especially true of a group of French-Swiss Baptists in the province of Santa Fe whose pastor was the outstanding Baptist pioneer leader, Pablo Besson (SDA 1966:Vol. 1,53). Through the ministry of Westphal a church was quickly organized with 36 members. This was the first Seventh-Day Adventist Church in South America. The incipient faith of these early Sabbath keepers burned white hot under the discriminatory practices of the community, especially on account of the seventh-day issue. Their foreign extraction contributed to their feeling of being discriminated against. The positive values derived from this and parallel martyr-like experiences have provided the Adventist movement with strong compensatory religious drives which are reflected in their rapid growth rate (SDA 1966:Vol. I,53-54).

From this beginning in Entre Ríos, which currently is probably the strongest center of Adventism in Argentina, the movement has spread throughout the entire republic. The greatest concentration of members in proportion to population is still in this same area and the neighboring province of Corrientes. From Crespo the movement spread to the province of Santa Fe, the issue of decision always being the keeping of the Sabbath. The technique used in seeking conversions was tent meetings. Most of the early converts came from the immigrant groups then flooding Argentina, and many of them were from Protestant or Evangelical Churches. One of the first missionaries conducted services in French, German, Spanish and English (Olsen 1926:561-563).

As the churches multiplied, the administrative structure was modified several times and progressed from a mission to a conference both on the national and the continental level. Today Seventh-Day Adventist churches in Argentina are in the Austral Union Conference, which is a part of the South American Division. The Austral Conference is composed of the Buenos Aires and Central Argentine Conferences and the Cuyo, North Argentine, Paraguay, Uruguay and Patagonian Missions. The Seventh-Day Adventist organization is efficient and highly departmentalized, meeting the diverse needs of the churches (SDA 1966:Vol. I, 55-56).

Today an extensive support program for their evangelistic outreach comprises the diversified ministries of the Adventist churches. Medical work was begun in 1901 upon the arrival of the first missionary doctor. His first work was among the scattered inhabitants of Entre Ríos. Finding it difficult to have his medical license validated in Argentina, he at first helped only those who demanded his services. A sanatorium was built in Puiggari, Entre Ríos, in 1908. In 1959, another sanatorium was inaugurated in the city of Buenos Aires. Adventist medical facilities today are staffed with Argentine trained doctors and have been for over thirty years (Olsen 1926:567,568). The emphasis on health among the followers of Mrs. White has produced an industry which processes health foods. The Granix Health Foods company in Argentina has proved to have side benefits also, providing a source of revenue for church expansion.

Education has been an integral part of Adventist work in Argentina, as it has in other parts of the world. There are three large institutions providing primary and secondary education for the children of Sabbath keepers and others in three widely separated areas. The first of these schools was begun in 1899 and is presently functioning in Puiggari, Entre Ríos. The second of these was founded in the Buenos Aires suburb of Florida in 1914, and the third in the North in 1923 (SDA 1966:Vol. I,56). Other smaller schools are also in operation, such as the primary school in Tucumán. Total enrollment in elementary and secondary schools in Argentina in 1965 stood at 2,861 (SDA 1965:25).

The Adventists of the River Plate are also involved in extensive publication and colportage work. From the original three colporteurs who began their ministry in 1891, the number of active colporteurs increased to 108 in 1960. These 108 sold almost 300,000 pieces of literature, including 7,000 Bibles, that year (SDA 1966:Vol. I,56). The approach as salesmen of religious literature has given the Adventists initial contacts with many Protestant families. The Sabbath issue is then presented and becomes the key question people must decide (SDA 1956:319).

The radio ministry and the Sabbath schools have been effective tools for disseminating Mrs. White's interpretations of the Scriptures. In 1960 the *Lecciones para la Escuela Sabática* were taught each Saturday to nearly 12,000 Sabbath school students. The Voice of Prophecy, known as the Voice of Hope (*Voz de la Esperanza*) in Argentina is closely tied in with the correspondence school. Between 1958 and 1962 the broadcast was being aired on 32 different stations (some in Paraguay and Uruguay), with 9,113 active correspondence school students. In addition to these avenues of outreach, they also maintain an active program of social work through the Seventh-Day Adventist Welfare and Philanthropic Work Society (SDA 1966:Vol. I, 54). Among the welfare programs is a Five Day Plan to Stop Smoking. It has been so successful that it has "captivated the attention of the leaders and statesmen" (Aitken 1966). The Plan is being taught in universities and civic centers. Among those who claim to have been cured is a woman 140 years old who was a victim of "smoking slavery" for more than 100 years (Aitken 1966:8).

These ministries have provided the Adventist movement with a great part of its drive and growth. The direct evangelistic approach, however, has been used with extraordinary success generally, and in some cases with outstanding results. One such case is the movement in late 1956 in the northern city of Tucumán. A team of seven young men and one girl organized and led an evangelistic campaign in this church of 35 members which in two years brought the membership to 250. The sensational breakthrough particularly reached the youth including the university community, and especially a group of Peruvian medical students. Today the Adventist church of Tucumán is housed in a large modern building and is growing (Emmerson 1957:16,17; Damboriena 1962:131).

B. INSIGHTS INTO ADVENTIST GROWTH

The growth of the Adventist churches, as reflected in the graph

Figure No.10

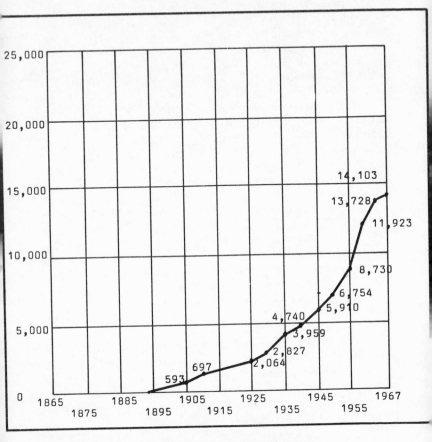

SEVENTH-DAY ADVENTISTS

COMMUNICANT MEMBERS
DATE OF ENTRANCE — 1894

SOURCES

1905–1965 SDA Statistical report
1966   SDA 1967:194,195,196

(Figure No. 10), has been steady and at a regular rate. The slight increase in the growth rate after 1950 could be attributed in part to the conversion of the disillusioned followers of Perón when almost all the other Protestant Churches experienced similar growth. The growth rate for the decade 1945 to 1955 was a strong 50.2 per cent. The rising rate for the subsequent period, 57.2 per cent per decade, would indicate increasing vitality in this movement. It is the highest rate of growth of those churches with over 10,000 members, with the exception of some of the Pentecostal Churches.

1. Salient Aspects of Adventist Mission Thrust

Among the chief characteristics of the Seventh-Day Adventist churches are several that distinguish them from the other Protestant Churches. Probably the most outstanding is their organization, which consists of divisions, conferences and missions. The organization of personnel, beginning with the recent graduate of their training school and moving progressively up through the different categories of leaders, is unparalleled by the other Protestant Churches. Damboriena (1962:123,124) attributes the phenomenal growth of the Adventists to this organization and the program of tithing. The amazing outcome in this era of mission versus church problems, is that this Washington, D.C.-based organization does not have acute problems between the national and foreign leadership. Not only is the organization well structured, but the Argentines have been incorporated into the organization along with the missionary even at the international level.

The next feature of Adventism in Argentina which demands our attention is the fact that the vast majority of the members are strict tithers. Annual giving in Argentina during 1965 was $383,654 (U.S. dollars) or a total of $27.20 per capita (SDA 1965:12). With such giving their program progresses rapidly. The excellent organization, combined with the generous giving, has probably contributed more than any other factor to the harmonious relationship between the mission and the churches. The lesser disparity between the salaries received by the Argentina pastors and those received by the few missionaries, in addition to the fact that the salaries are of Argentine origin, has undoubtedly contributed largely to this harmony. Davis (1943:93) records an interview with an Adventist leader in which this important aspect of their life is emphasized as a key to their strength.

Another feature of the Seventh-Day Adventist organization in Argentina is the institutional program, which supports the general work of the Church. Perhaps outstanding in this division of their ministries is that each phase is bent and oriented to the prime mission, that of making more Sabbath keepers. Interpreted in this way, each person involved sees himself as a communicator of Adventist doctrines. This organization, possibly more than that of any other Church, has achieved a total integration of these specialized ministries into the principal goal of their Church. Some would criticize them for this, accusing them of impure or double motives. But no one can deny that while serving people in their needs, they are accomplishing their chief purpose of evangelization.

Permeating their entire program of outreach is the strong emphasis on proselytism. This was evident in the very beginning of their work in the tent campaigns, where people of other Churches were convinced of the imperative necessity of keeping the Sabbath. Today they use public halls to give lectures on subjects of broad public interest, but the seventh-day message is always dominant in the end. The general Evangelical public is always invited through the personal contacts of the members of the Adventist churches and not infrequently become the converts of these efforts. The radio and correspondence school ministries are also oriented to this same approach and purpose.

The Adventists have, from the very beginning, provided a place for active lay participation. This involves the day-to-day witness of every church member, but has also led to more extensive activity such as colportage and preaching. There seems to be a degree of commitment and active dedication on the part of the average Adventist not paralleled in other Protestant Churches, with the possible exception of the Pentecostals. One of the favorite techniques of the Adventist laymen is to visit the other churches and strike up friendships with the members with the view to convincing them later on the issue of Sabbath keeping.

2. What Can Adventists Teach Us?

But probably the chief reason for their success is the religious temperament of this group. A burning religious zeal largely born of a persecution complex, plus the simplified single issue (Sabbath keeping), forms the basis of every conversation and is manifested in an intensified religious experience. But although these factors have determined the favorable growth pattern to a great extent, because they result from negative motivations they do not approach what God can do through a movement when positive spiritual power is released.

Although definitely outside the mainstream of Evangelical Churches in Argentina, this Church provides illustrations of several keys to church growth. The purpose of this chapter has not been to make necessary critical judgments of erroneous Adventist doctrine, but rather to analyze their growth dynamics in the hope that all Evangelical Churches might learn from their example. The reasons for the steady and increasing rate of growth they are achieving should interest all who desire to serve Christ in the most effective way possible in Argentina.

CHAPTER 14

The Southern Baptists

A. BAPTIST IMMIGRANTS INITIATE MOVEMENT

The Southern Baptist Foreign Mission Board entered Argentina largely through the vision that was born in the hearts of two young theological students at the Louisville Seminary. Even though the Board had attempted to discourage them from beginning new fields of service, their strong convictions prevailed, and they were confirmed by their fellow students who gave a generous offering toward sending them. The Board finally granted their wishes, and in 1903 Sidney M. Sowell was appointed and sailed for Argentina alone. The following year, Joseph L. Hart and his wife joined him in Buenos Aires (Means 1960:46).

1. Precursors to Mission Effort

Upon their arrival they soon learned of other Baptists already at work in Argentina under the French-Swiss pastor, Pablo Besson. They formed part of a long line of Baptists who had been active in Argentina, but hadn't extended their churches appreciably. The first of these was James Thomson, the agent of the British and Foreign Bible Society and the British and Foreign School Society, who set up the Lancastrian schools in Buenos Aires at the request of the new independence government. There was also a congregation of Baptists among the Welsh immigrants of 1864 in the South. In about 1880, a small group of French-Swiss farmers in Esperanza, Santa Fe, desired a pastor to lead them in worship in the Baptist way. They wrote to the pastor in France under whom one of the families had been converted, asking him to send someone. The young man himself, Pablo Besson, came. This was the beginning of the first permanent Baptist church in Argentina, which later became affiliated with the churches sponsored by the Board of Foreign Missions of the Southern Baptist Convention. After a year in Esperanza, Besson went to Buenos Aires, where he began a church for French-speaking people. This church, which soon began worshiping in the Spanish language, became what is known today as the Central Baptist Church. It still worships in the building built by the congregation under Besson's leadership in 1899 on Estados Unidos Street (Goslin 1956:40).

Besson, outstanding missionary, preacher and man of letters, will be remembered most gratefully by the Evangelical community in general for his accomplishments in the field of religious liberty. Dissidents from the Roman Catholic faith were almost totally without legal rights. Besson, with the support of liberal political factions, fought and won the battle for civil marriage, the right to register births and the right to bury the dead in public cemeteries. Before this, the only legal marriages were Catholic, the children of dissidents could not be legally registered and they had to bury their dead in their own gardens (Means 1960:42,43). A prolific writer (Canclini 1948), Besson left an indelible impression on Evangelical and national life through his articles, published both by the secular press and the church-related periodicals.

German Baptists of Russian origin settled in Argentina in 1878 and by 1894 had organized a church in General Ramírez. Entre Ríos, under their pastor, Juan Pedro Bruner (Canclini n.d.:19). This work prospered through the years among the German-speaking immigrants. Today they form part of the Argentine Baptist Convention.

2. Southern Baptist Mission Organizes Churches

When Sowell arrived in 1903, he began a door-to-door evangelistic visitation ministry which resulted in the first Baptist church established through the efforts of a missionary related to the Southern Baptist Mission. It is worth noting that this church at Plaza Constitución and the Plaza Once church were established near separate railroad stations in Buenos Aires. This enabled these growing churches to engage in an extensive missionary program along the rail lines out into the suburban areas. The Once church by 1948 had begun six daughter churches (SBC 1948:67). To the south of the Constitución church, also along the lines of rail transportation, the churches of Lanús, Banfield and Adrogué were established (Canclini n.d.:20).

The missionary staff grew as did the number of new churches. In 1908, five churches met and formed the Argentine Baptist Convention (Canclini 1958:59). This was the first national Baptist organization and has been the basis of subsequent work in Argentina. The churches which joined to form the convention were two newly established churches in Rosario, two churches from Buenos Aires and Besson's former church in Santa Fe. During the sessions of the first convention it was decided to publish a denominational paper and to collect funds for mission work in Chile. These were the preliminary steps to the formal organization in 1911 of the missions board and in 1912 of the publications board, both of which are active and significant aspects of the total program of Baptist work in Argentina today (Means 1960:47). Missionary work was initiated in Paraguay in 1910 by Maximinio Fernández and funds were sent to Chile in 1913 to support a Baptist missionary from Scotland (Canclini n.d.:21,26). During the decade following the formation of the convention, work was begun in Entre Ríos and Mendoza.

By 1920 the first stage of Baptist work had been accomplished. An embryonic organization was functioning, and churches were established in a large part of the country, including the provinces of Buenos Aires, Santa Fe, Entre Ríos, Córdoba, Mendoza, Corrientes and San Juan, with a foreign ministry in Paraguay, Uruguay and Chile. By this same year, there were 1,452 baptized members. Baptist work was established in Argentina and growing. Much of the growth could be attributed to the faithful colporteurs who sold the Scriptures in the remote parts of the country.

B. SOUTHERN BAPTIST EFFORT GROWS

1. Strong Leadership Expands Base

The decade which followed were years of solid growth. Membership grew from 1,452 to 4,207, at a rate of 190 per cent per decade (Figure No. 11). The principal factors contributing to the growth probably were that the missionary force held steady and that they

Figure No.11

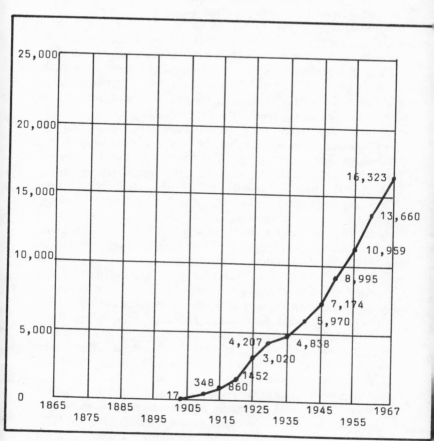

SOUTHERN BAPTISTS

COMMUNICANT MEMBERS
DATE OF ENTRANCE - 1903

SOURCES

1903-1955 CARROLL 1959
1960-1965 SBC   1967

were gaining in experience and maturity in the work. Furthermore, the staff of Argentine pastors was growing and maturing, and the economic conditions in the country were stable. There were not so many new geographic extensions of the churches, but rather a multiplication of churches in areas already occupied. Another development during this decade was the immigration of hundreds of Slavic Baptists from Russia, the Ukraine and Poland. They established their homes around Buenos Aires and in the provinces of Misiones, Santa Fe and Mendoza. In 1948 they affiliated with the Argentine Baptist Convention (Canclini n.d.:22).

During these years one of the outstanding men was J.C. Varetto. An unusually effective preacher, he was used extensively in tent campaigns which contributed to the growth of the churches. His writings have been numerous and are still widely used by all the Evangelical Churches. His influence on the Baptist work has been especially significant in calling a body of able men into the ministry. With the growth of this body of Argentine leaders the churches spread out into other areas of the republic. The board of missions entered the Chaco (1930) in the North and Patagonia (1934) in the South. From 1940 to the present, new areas such as Tucumán, San Carlos de Bariloche and Santa Cruz have been entered, but the principal factor contributing to growth has been the multiplication of churches and membership increase in areas where the Baptists had already concentrated their work. The latter years of the Perón government saw concerted attempts to place severe limitations on Baptist and all other Evangelical work, but determined efforts under the leadership of an outstanding Baptist pastor largely frustrated these attempts (Canclini n.d.:24).

Although the years of the Perón government were times when the churches experienced difficulties and saw their religious liberties threatened, they were also years of growth. Between 1940 and 1955, the year the *peronistas* were expelled from power, the communicant membership rose from 5,970 to 10,959, or at a rate of 50 per cent per decade. Communicant membership growth during the next 10 years has been from 10,959 to 16,323, or 48 per cent per decade. The increase in the number of Argentine pastors between 1940 and 1955 was particularly significant, rising from 45 to 154, or over 200 per cent. Although the North American missionary staff increased between 1955 and 1965 by 68 per cent, there was a surprising drop of Argentine pastors from 164 to 146 between 1960 and 1965.

Severe economic conditions were probably the chief cause of this decrease, the newer churches unable to carry the financial burden. What effect this might have in the future on the growth pattern of these churches strongly oriented to a professional ministry cannot be fully interpreted for the present. A crash program of pastoral training for laymen aimed at full participation in the ministry of the churches would certainly aid in maintaining the momentum of growth begun during previous decades. Southern Baptists generally have not seen the advantages of exploiting the potential for extensive church growth in a voluntary lay clergy. Lay leadership has produced solid results for other denominations and merits careful study by this organization. It could very well prove the key to continued expansion at an even more accelerated rate.

2. Development of Full-Orbed Program

Today the Southern Baptist related Argentine Baptist Convention through its mission program has extended its witness throughout the entire republic. It is probably the national Church which covers more areas of the country than any other, with the possible exceptions of the Methodists and the Plymouth Brethren. The breadth of her ministries is also extensive. The most influential institution operated by the Argentine Baptists with the Southern Baptist Mission is the International Baptist Seminary, which in one form or another has been in continuous operation since 1912. Today this seminary serves the Baptist churches of Argentina, Chile, Paraguay and Uruguay from its unusually fine facilities in Buenos Aires. In recent years there have been more than 100 students in the three principal programs of study. The Women's Training School (Davis 1943:104) which began in Rosario in 1936 now functions as a part of the Seminary.

The publications operation and the primary and secondary education program of the Convention deserve special mention. The publications ministry began with Pablo Besson before the Southern Baptists arrived. Publications have included magazines, lesson materials, books and tracts. Today they operate three bookstores located in Buenos Aires, Rosario and Córdoba. The elementary schools began functioning very early in Argentine Baptist history, but had to close. Since 1957, when the effort was renewed, six elementary schools and one high school have been established. In 1966 there were 60 students in the secondary school. There is also a program of social work involving a retirement home and a home for children (Canclini n.d.:42,43).

The structure of the Southern Baptist work in Argentina involves a mission organization which represents the Southern Baptist missionaries. Independent of this organization are two interdependent parallel organizations representing the Argentine Baptist churches. First, the Convención Evangélica Bautista to which we have already referred and second, the Confederación Evangelica Bautista, which is the legal representative of both the convention and the churches. A Council of Coordination, representing both the mission and the *Convención,* exists for the purpose of studying plans which are of interest to both organizations. The Council of Coordination administers the funds supplied by the Southern Baptist mission through a program of *Ayuda Fraternal* (Fraternal Aid). Financial assistance for the budgets of the local churches includes subsidization of pastoral salaries and occasional grants in support of specialized programs, especially evangelistic thrusts. Funds for the construction or purchase of buildings for worship are supplied by the mission directly to the local churches. A modification of this arrangement whereby such funds would be distributed by a committee of the *Convención* is under study at present (Anderson 1968). Locally, the churches organize associations with other churches for the purpose of achieving common goals, for mutual help in larger tasks, and to elect one representative to the board of directors of the *Convención.* Nationally there are auxiliary conventions for the women and the youth.

3. Principal Characteristics of Movement

The outstanding feature of Southern Baptist work in Argentina is the diversified program which is the expression of both the North American enterprising spirit and the growing desire of the Argentine Christians to "nationalize" their churches. Each Southern Baptist related church is characterized by certain common practices and methodologies. The promotion and execution of these specific programs become the driving burden of both foreign and Argentine leadership. Many features of these programs have become a genuinely indigenous part of Argentine Baptist church life. Others have not, and have become the issues of tension between the mission and the churches. The seminary curriculum is successful in preparing the young church leaders to become effective promoters of this highly specialized program. Where successful, this growing and ever more diversified program is in large measure responsible for the splendid growth rate of these churches. The question arises, however, whether or not this program has achieved the optimum results possible. It hardly seems feasible that a program which by and large is "imported" could meet Argentine church needs in the best way. Undoubtedly, as the *Convención* becomes stronger, the program will incorporate forms that are more cordial to Argentines.

Another aspect of Southern Baptist work in Argentina has been the program of evangelism. From the early years, when J.C. Varetto was the chief evangelist for these advancing churches, to the present, the revival meeting has been common in all the churches. Pastors often "trade" pulpits to help each other with these campaigns. The Board of Evangelism of the *Convención,* which was founded in 1957, now carries on a diversified ministry involving campaigns, tract publication, institutes of evangelism, and radio and television evangelism.

The strong and effective training program has produced another characteristic feature of this movement, namely, a solid Argentine leadership. These men, well trained and indoctrinated in the dynamics of the developing program, become efficient administrators and effective promoters. The biblical and theological teaching provided by the Seminary, largely by foreign missionary staff, also prepares them well for an effective preaching ministry. Among these pastors are several who have distinguished themselves among the entire Evangelical community as outstanding leaders.

Still another feature of this group of churches is the strong emphasis on giving. The training program of the local church and the promotional thrust of the *Convención* are geared to encourage the practice of Christian financial stewardship. Their per capita giving in 1965 was $17.18 (U.S. dollars), approximately $10 less than the Adventists.

The continuing misunderstandings bordering on open tension between the missionary leadership and the Argentine pastors must be resolved to ensure a steady rate of church growth. There are signs that these are diminishing, but the pressures which accompany the introduction of foreign funds continue to contribute to misunderstandings. Yet no one desires to see this supply of funds cut off. The convention's position has been strong and independent in Argentina due in part to the non-Southern-Baptist-mission oriented Baptist leadership of the early days in the forceful personality of Besson. The influence of Juan C. Varetto and his family has contributed greatly to the strength of the convention, also, as have the non-Southern-Baptist oriented churches which have joined the national organization through the years. This has contributed toward establishing a healthy balance between the churches and the mission. The burden of resolving these remaining tensions, however, rests chiefly with the missionary since it is the Argentine organization which must become predominant in every respect to ensure greater growth. Such growth will be both numerical and qualitative, as this dynamic fellowship of churches discovers forms of church life more congenial to the Argentine situation. In this changing situation the role of the missionary will have to be interpreted in terms of these new forms in order for him to make a positive and growing fraternal contribution.

CHAPTER 15

Church Growth Trends in Argentina

A. NUMERICAL STRENGTH OF ARGENTINE EVANGELICAL CHURCH

The discussion in Part II thus far has provided us with brief analytical profiles of ten mission-related Churches in Argentina. Each has been presented with a view to discovering the reasons for its dynamic and spelling out the chief characteristics of its church life and program. The purpose of this concluding chapter is to present a comprehensive statistical comparison of the present situation of the Evangelical Church in Argentina, especially with regard to its numerical strength. The Churches treated in the profiles are then classified according to other criteria in an attempt to discover additional dimensions of the church growth patterns that have been operative in Argentina. Among these criteria are length of occupation, interdenominational affiliation, religious temperament, theological and ecclesiastical identification and, finally, whether a given Church is of Latin American origin (indigenous) or if it began through the efforts of overseas missionaries. With the presentation of each of the analytical graphs the criteria employed will be defined and explained more fully.

1. Communicant Membership Passes Quarter Million

Figure No. 12 presents the communicant membership of the ten different Churches for which a profile has been presented. However, in addition to the ten Churches which have been the principal objects of this investigation, other Lutheran Churches treated only cursorily in the profiles have been included in this analysis. This has also been done in the case of other Pentecostal Churches. These Churches plus the ten Churches specifically studied in the profiles represent the first line of totals in the chart (Figure No. 12).

In addition, all Churches and missions which maintain missionary activity in Argentina are included. These groups are listed as "Other Churches." The totals represent the entire communicant membership of the Evangelical Church in Argentina. These figures are presented for four distinct dates in its development: 1911, 1925, 1949 and 1967. The statistical data for "Other Churches," for which profiles are not included, are from the survey sources listed at the foot of the table. In the interest of clarity and comprehensive treatment of the year 1967, a complete listing of the Churches and their communicant membership is given here. This listing, with the list of Lutheran Churches (p. 121) and Pentecostal Churches (p. 83), plus the ten Churches covered in the profiles, identifies all the Evangelical Churches active in Argentina in 1967. Altogether there are approximately seventy-four distinct Evangelical religious bodies working in Argentina to present the Gospel of Christ.

OTHER CHURCHES

Name	Communicants	Source[1]
Armenian Brethren	96	5
Armenian Congregational Church	40	1
Armenian Evangelical Church	55	5
Asambleas Bíblicas	1,800	7
Baptist General Conference	75	3
Brethren (Ashland, Ohio)	283	1
Brethren (Winona Lake, Ind.)	498	1
Church of England	2,500	5
Church of God (Anderson, Ind.)	–	8
Church of the Nazarene	983	2
Church of Scotland	1,600	5
Concilio Evangélico de Iglesias	760	1
Congregational Christian Board	8,844	1
Convención Evangélica Bautista	1,677	5,6

[1] Sources: 1. CGRILA; 2. CN 1965; 3. Estimate; 4. Flagg 1968; 5. WCH 1967:130,131; 6. SBC 1967; 7. Schisler 1967; 8. López 1967:14.

Evangelical Union of South America	600	1
Iglesia Reformada	1,850	1
Irish Baptist	306	5
New Testament Missionary Union	2,000	1
Reformed (Dutch)	540	5
Reformed (French)	100	1
Salvation Army (inc. Brazil, Uruguay and Paraguay)	4,211	5
Slavic Gospel Mission	250	5
South American Missionary Society	2,500	4
Waldensians	6,460	5
TOTAL	38,029	

The Churches treated in the profiles represent a total of from 83.4 to 97.8 per cent of the total Evangelical communicant membership, depending upon the year being considered. This proportion of the total membership of Evangelical Churches in Argentina forms an adequate basis for drawing firm conclusions about church growth in that country. The procedure has been to take a broad sampling only, namely the ten profiles and supplementary information about the Lutheran and Pentecostal Churches. This sampling represents the vast majority of the membership of the Churches in Argentina. All of the larger organizations are included, and several of the smaller ones, to provide a spread in the sampling.

By way of further clarification, it must be stated that the statistics in some cases represent figures of one to three years before or after the year under which they are listed. This means that the figures for some denominations in the year 1949 might actually be their membership for the year 1950 or 1951. This is also true of the year 1967, where the data for one denomination is from the year 1964. This variation can be checked by comparing the table with the growth graph of the respective denomination under the particular year that is being considered. In every case the data given in the growth graph of a particular Church and for the respective year formed the basis of that used in the table. To this degree, which is minor, the data is not comparable. This small variation will not significantly affect the general conclusions.

It is appropriate here to caution that the growth graphs included with the profiles in general are not comparable. Two separate scales have been employed. The Churches with a membership of between 400 and 5,000 are plotted on the same scale. This is also true of the

Figure No.12

THE EVANGELICAL CHURCH IN ARGENTINA
STATISTICAL SUMMARY

MISSION or CHURCH	COMMUNICANTS								COMMUNI
	1911	%	1925	%	1949	%	1967	%	1967
Assemblies of God	—	0	——	0	348	0.4	4,582	2.0	18,328
C & M Alliance	125	1.7	214	1.1	513	0.5	1,022	0.4	4,088
Conservative Baptist	—	0	——	0	365	0.4	1,183	0.5	4,732
Disciples of Christ	9	0.1	132	0.8	415	0.4	426	0.2	1,704
Lutheran Mo. Synod	313	4.6	3,199	17.2	7,986	8.3	12,611	5.4	50,444
Lutheran¢	—	0	53	0.4	10,326	10.8	17,684	7.6	70,736
Mennonite	—	0	60	0.4	698	0.8	820	0.4	3,280
Methodist	3,817	54.9	3,961	21.2	5,414	5.7	7,382	3.2	29,528
Pentecostal+	—	0	——	0	24,500*	25.5	93,890	40.3	375,560
Plymouth Brethren	1,400	20.1	5,500	29.5	15,000	15.6	25,000	10.7	100,000
Seventh-Day Adventist	697	10.0	2,064	10.8	6,754	7.0	14,103	6.0	56,412
Southern Baptist	348	4.9	3,020	16.2	8,995	9.4	16,323	7.0	65,292
Subtotal	6,709		18,203		81,314		195,026		780,104
Other Churches	260	3.7	432	2.3	14,628	15.2	38,029	16.3	152,116
Total	6,969	100	18,635	100	95,942	100	233,055	100	932,220

Sources for Other Churches: 1911   Dennis 1911:96
                            1925   Beach   1925:119
                            1949   Grubb   1949:304,305

Explanation: ¢ Less Missouri Synod
             + Less Assemblies of God
             * Estimate

Churches with from 5,000 to 25,000 members. Within each grouping of Churches comparisons of graph curves may be made. To facilitate the comparison of growth curves, they have all been projected on the same scale in Figure No. 13.

2. Growth Patterns Worthy of Imitation

One of the most significant discoveries revealed by this study is the emergence of what is known widely as the "third force" of Protestantism. In 1925 the Pentecostal family of Churches was almost impossible to count because of its small size. Our table records no figures, since no reliable data for this early period were available. As mentioned in the profile of the Assemblies of God, Merle Davis estimates Pentecostal strength in 1943 at 15,000. By 1949 there were nearly 24,500 members in their churches according to my calculation. This represented 25.5 per cent of the total communicant membership of the Evangelical Churches. However, in 1949 the largest single Church was the group of Plymouth Brethren assemblies, which alone comprised 15.6 per cent of the total Evangelical Church membership. Even in 1967, with 25,000 communicant members, the Brethren still represented the largest single group of churches, although percentagewise they dropped to 10.7 per cent of the total. Both the Pentecostal and Plymouth Brethren Churches reflect growth dynamics which will receive fuller treatment later. The fact that these two rapidly growing Churches reflect radically divergent approaches to the Christian faith means that their results should be studied by all Churches desiring to achieve greater growth. Growth in Argentina is not exclusively a Pentecostal phenomenon. Every Church seeking to win men to Christ in Argentina and to bring ever increasing numbers into His body would do well to give serious consideration to the reasons for such healthy growth.

By contrast, the Church which has been "present" in Argentina the longest period has not experienced a growth rate commensurate with the potential of Argentine responsiveness. This is evident when contrasting Methodist growth with the Plymouth Brethren or the Southern Baptists. The Methodists, who represented 54.9 per cent of the total Evangelical communicant membership in 1911, by 1967 were only a low 3.2 per cent of the total. The Southern Baptists began their work in Argentina in the year 1903. By 1911 their membership had grown to 348, or less than one-tenth of the

Figure No.13

COMPARISON OF GROWTH GRAPHS

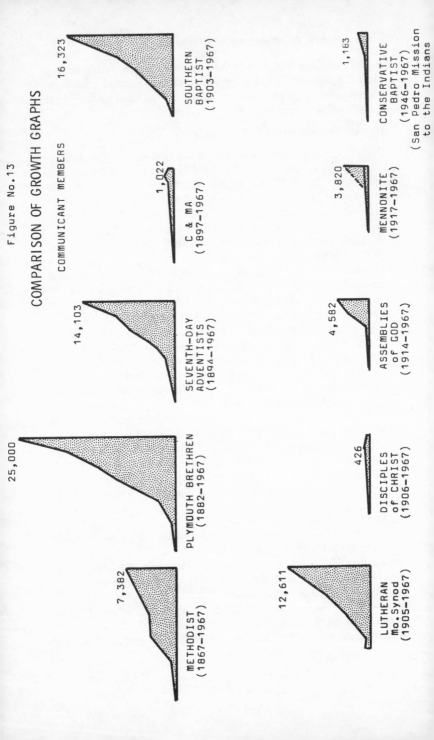

COMMUNICANT MEMBERS

25,000

PLYMOUTH BRETHREN
(1882-1967)

7,382

METHODIST
(1867-1967)

14,103

SEVENTH-DAY
ADVENTISTS
(1894-1967)

1,022

C & MA
(1897-1967)

16,323

SOUTHERN
BAPTIST
(1903-1967)

12,611

LUTHERAN
Mo.Synod
(1905-1967)

426

DISCIPLES
of CHRIST
(1906-1967)

4,582

ASSEMBLIES
of GOD
(1914-1967)

3,820

MENNONITE
(1917-1967)

1,163

CONSERVATIVE
BAPTIST
(1946-1967)
(San Pedro Mission
to the Indians)

Methodist membership at that time. Today, after 64 years of aggressive evangelism, their communicant membership stands at more than twice that of the Methodists. The advance of the Plymouth Brethren assemblies is even more spectacular. In 1911, after 29 years of occupation, the Brethren had 1,400 communicant members as compared with the Methodists' 3,817. By 1925 the Methodist Church reported a net increase of 144 for a total of 3,961. The Brethren, who experienced an evangelical breakthrough during these years, now had 5,500, for a net increase of 4,100. Today the Plymouth Brethren membership is more than triple the Methodist communicant total. Furthermore, the Plymouth Brethren assemblies are far less dependent on foreign funds and leadership, although strong fraternal ties exist between them and their brethren in Latin America, Spain, North America and England. It might be argued that the Methodists were more concerned with quality than quantity. This is probably true. It was not a "quality," however, that was capable of reproducing itself as vigorously as Brethren "quality." Theological dilution was taking its toll on the momentum of Methodist growth. When such sharp divergences in the growth rate occur, answers to questions about policies and practices lying behind each are urgently needed. Such answers are relevant to each Church and mission working in Argentina. In fact, we ought to be clamoring for the secret of such growth. When the astonishing surge of the Pentecostal Churches of recent years is added to this picture, it is evident that a firm understanding of Argentine church growth principles is desperately needed. All Churches have seen their proportion of the total communicant membership diminish as the "third force" surged, but none quite so noticeably as the Methodists since 1911 (Figure No. 14). Today the predominant mood is dialogue and social involvement. Will a survey of the growth of the Churches in Argentina taken 25 years from now expose the failure of these methods also?

3. Growth Rate Exceeds Population Increase

When the growth rate of Evangelical Church membership during the three different periods is compared, it becomes evident that the period between 1925 and 1949 reflects the greatest percentage increase. Figure No. 15 provides us with a comparison of these three periods. The two columns on the right indicate the rate of increase, first for each of the three periods and then for the entire 56 years.

Figure No.14

PROPORTIONATE SIZE OF CHURCHES

COMMUNICANT MEMBERS

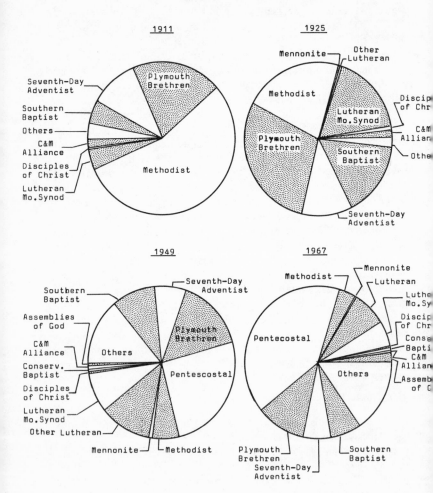

Both are figured at the annual compounded percentage rate and are comparable even though the three periods differ in length. The principal reason for the surge between 1925 and 1949 is the sudden appearance of Pentecostal statistics in the table. The established mission organizations and Churches as a whole were not experiencing radically improved growth patterns as might appear superficially. The second half of this table provides us with the national population increases for roughly the same periods. When these two are compared it is seen that the Evangelical population is growing 3.1 times as fast as the national population.

The proportion of Evangelical communicant members to the national population is increasing slowly. It still remains at just barely over 1 per cent. Communicant membership represented .097 of 1 per cent of the total population in 1911. This percentage grew by 1925 to .18 of 1 per cent and in 1949 to .59 of 1 per cent. At present Evangelical Church membership stands at 1.03 per cent.

The Christian community, which is listed in the column on the far right of Figure No. 12 (p. 178), reflects the broad influence of the Evangelical Churches. The Christian community is interpreted as meaning those persons who, through family or friendship ties of a broad variety and of varying intensity, are related to the Evangelical Churches through their members. This body of interested people forms the human reservoir from which converts are won and added through Christian baptism to the communicant membership. In the case of the Lutheran and other Churches which practice infant baptism, the community includes all infants baptized although not confirmed.

4. Argentina Lags Behind Other Latin American Countries

There has been considerable discussion as to how large the community is in proportion to the communicant membership. In church growth studies taken on a worldwide basis this figure has varied from a ratio of 2 to 1 all the way to 5 to 1. When the particularly responsive situation of Latin America is considered apart from the rest of the world, there has been a tendency toward calculations at the upper parts of this scale. Rycroft (Kessler 1967:336) estimates this body of adherents at three and one-half times the number of communicants. This seems to be a conservative estimate. In Perú, the government census in the department of Puno in the year 1949 indicated there were 29,000 persons who stated

Figure No.15

COMPARISON OF GROWTH RATES

Evangelical Communicants and National Population

Period	Number of years	Beg. of Period	End of Period	Increase	Annual Compounded %	
EVANGELICAL POPULATION—COMMUNICANTS						
1911–1925	14	6,969	18,635	11,666	7.3%	⎫
1925–1949	24	18,635	95,942	77,307	7.1%	⎬ 6.5
1949–1967	18	95,942	233,055	137,113	5.1%	⎭
NATIONAL POPULATION						
1911–1927	16	7,171,910[1]	10,348,189[2]	3,176,279	2.3%	⎫
1927–1947	20	10,348,189	16,107,936[3]	5,759,747	2.3%	⎬ 2.1
1947–1967	20	16,107,936	22,691,000[4]	6,583,064	1.7%	⎭

POPULATION SOURCES

1 STUNTZ   1916:206
2 BROWNING   1928:124
3 IRVINE   1948:506
4 LONG   196 6:594

that they were Seventh-Day Adventists; yet the Church's records showed a total slightly under 6,000 (Kessler 1967:240). This is a ratio of almost 5 to 1. The Church Growth Research in Latin America team feels that the dynamic manifested by growing Pentecostalism would indicate that the ratio should be at least 5 to 1. Therefore, in these calculations a conservative estimate of 4 to 1 has been chosen. This reflects the fact that some of the Churches in Argentina fall far short of the dynamic evident among their sister Churches in Brazil and Chile, where 5 to 1 might be a correct calculation. Using this calculation as a basis, a fair estimate of the Evangelical community in Argentina would be 932,220, or 4.1 per cent of the national population.

This places the Argentine Evangelical community well behind such countries as Brazil where the percentage is 7.1 (6,000,000), Guatemala with 9.5 (426,307), and Chile with 7.0 per cent (620,000) of the national population. Argentina is just slightly ahead of Colombia and Costa Rica with 3.2 and 2.9 per cent, respectively. The annual compounded percentage rate of growth of the Christian community in Argentina during the years 1949 to 1967 stands at 5.0 per cent. This is in contrast to the present rate of 11 per cent in Guatemala, 6.5 per cent in Chile, 8 per cent in Brazil and 11.5 per cent in Colombia.

If it is later conclusively demonstrated that there is a direct relationship between the size of the community and the dynamic present in any Church, then it follows that future growth potential or trends should be reasonably predictable by an accurate measurement of the community. This observation also serves to help the present administration of any Church or mission determine whether or not its policies are effective. Programs and methods which tend to turn the vision of the Church in on itself result in a reduction of the size of the community and consequently represent a tragic decrease in dynamic. Those activities which contribute to the continual increase in the size of the Christian community eventually affect church growth.

B. INTERNAL DIMENSIONS OF CHURCH GROWTH TRENDS

Church growth trends in Argentina have not reflected a direct relationship between the length of occupation and growth achieved. In several instances tragically little growth has been achieved by Churches which have been present in Argentina for more than half a century, and some even longer. Figure No. 16 graphically reveals these trends. The object here is not to emphasize failures, but to demonstrate clearly that conditions for solid growth have been present in Argentina since shortly after World War I which have only partially been taken advantage of. This reveals the urgent need for research and a clear understanding of those methods and practices which will contribute to the growth of the Church.

Generally the Churches are too inclined to accept their own rate of growth as normal for Argentina and for their own Church. A *status quo* mentality makes them its prisoner and nothing seems strong enough to break the chains that bind them to this static condition. That radical and encouraging breaks can and do happen is

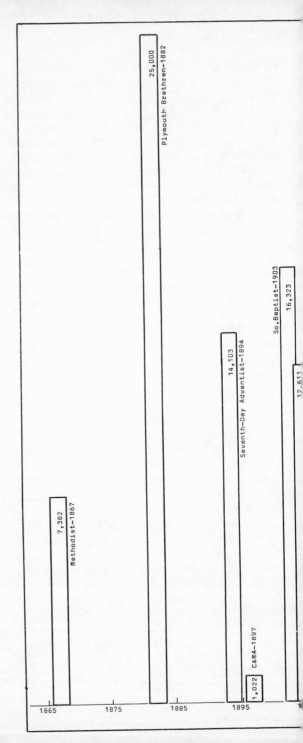

7,382
Methodist–1867

25,000
Plymouth Brethren–1882

14,103
Seventh-Day Adventist–1894

1,022
C&MA–1897

16,323
So.Baptist–1903

12,611

1865   1875   1885   1895

Figure No.16

COMPARISON OF DATE OF ENTRANCE

AND

GROWTH ACHIEVED

TOTAL COMMUNICANTS 1967

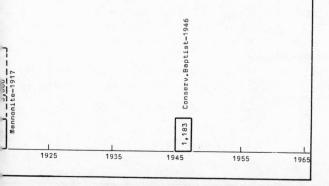

evident in the case of both the Mennonites and the Assemblies of God. Both missions entered the Argentine at the time of World War I. Neither seemed to achieve spectacular growth during the early years. These were years when the Plymouth Brethren and the Southern Baptists were experiencing phenomenal growth. Conditions conducive to growth were operative, but these two newly arrived groups did not seem able to take advantage of them. Thirty years later, both the Mennonites and the Assemblies of God were experiencing healthy growth. The Mennonites through a cordial anthropological understanding of the Toba people movement to Christ have been able to give these Christians organizational identity and educational help. There are now 3,000 Toba Christians identified with the Mennonite-sponsored United Evangelical Church. The Assemblies of God have also broken their pattern of forty years of stagnation. Through the evangelistic efforts of the Tommy Hicks campaign a new attitude of faith and expectancy has characterized this Church. Churches which have experienced little growth to date need not be satisfied. They can break the chains that bind if careful attention is paid to church growth patterns in Argentina. Bold administrative decisions are essential to implement the insights gained from the study of the experience of others. Our loyalty to Christ demands that old wineskins be discarded where they have been demonstrated to be ineffective to contain or carry the new dynamic of the Gospel.

1. External Pressures Forcing Polarization

One of the burning issues in the Evangelical Church of Argentina and of all of Latin America today revolves around the matter of interdenominational affiliation. Essentially this is not a Latin American problem in its origin, but it eventually will concern all Christians in that part of the world. Ecumenical pressures are building and the essentially Evangelically oriented Church in Latin America cannot be aloof from it. Alignments foreign to the Latin American Churches are being forced upon them and they are urged to decide. This continental problem has become acute since the 1961 Latin American Evangelical Congress in Lima, when the issue began to polarize. Argentina is not free from these pressures which are forcing a polarization.

For more than twenty years the only interdenominational organization in Argentina has been the Federación Argentina de

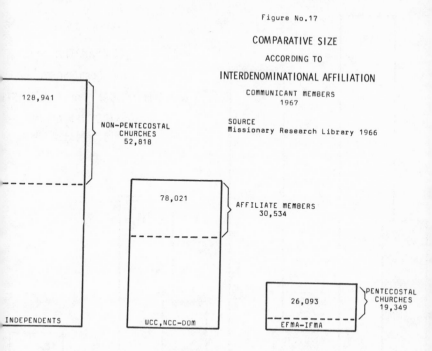

Figure No.17

COMPARATIVE SIZE

ACCORDING TO

INTERDENOMINATIONAL AFFILIATION

COMMUNICANT MEMBERS
1967

SOURCE
Missionary Research Library 1966

128,941

NON-PENTECOSTAL
CHURCHES
52,818

78,021

AFFILIATE MEMBERS
30,534

26,093

PENTECOSTAL
CHURCHES
19,349

INDEPENDENTS   WCC,NCC-DOM   EFMA-IFMA

Iglesias Evangélicas. This organization generally reflects an orientation toward the World Council of Churches and related entities, but includes Churches of both Evangelical Foreign Missions Association and Pentecostal identification. This body has in the past predominantly represented a third position of nonalignment on an international level, but this picture is changing rapidly. There is a growing disenchantment among several of the component Evangelical Churches with the leadership (which is largely from the "historic" denominations) as they lean toward the WCC pole more and more under the pressures of the ecumenical movement. Today not more than one-third of the total membership of the Evangelical Churches is affiliated with the Federation.

Figure No. 17 presents the 1967 membership of the Evangelical Churches in Argentina according to the interdenominational identification of the parent body or mission (MRL 1966). The three

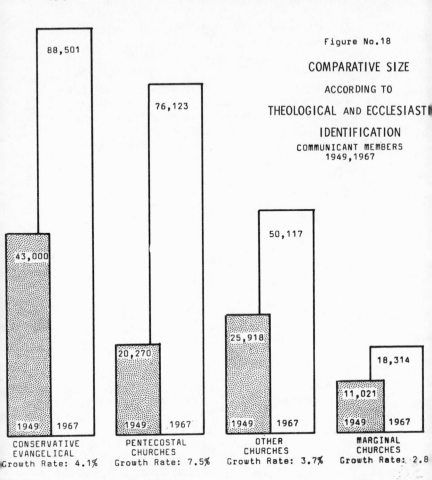

Figure No.18

COMPARATIVE SIZE

ACCORDING TO

THEOLOGICAL AND ECCLESIASTI

IDENTIFICATION

COMMUNICANT MEMBERS
1949,1967

88,501

76,123

50,117

43,000

25,918

20,270

18,314

11,021

1949   1967   1949   1967   1949   1967   1949   1967

CONSERVATIVE   PENTECOSTAL   OTHER   MARGINAL
EVANGELICAL   CHURCHES   CHURCHES   CHURCHES
Growth Rate: 4.1%   Growth Rate: 7.5%   Growth Rate: 3.7%   Growth Rate: 2.8

groupings represent the two principal international positions of polarization, the WCC entities and the Evangelical and Interdenominational Foreign Missions Association, plus the independents. The Pentecostal Churches within the EFMA-IFMA grouping account for three-quarters of the total. The Plymouth Brethren and Southern Baptists plus several other smaller independent Churches account for 52,818 in this largest group. The affiliate members of the WCC group are the Seventh-Day Adventists, Missouri Synod Lutherans and the Mennonite Church including the Toba United Evangelical Church of Pentecostal orientation. These four Churches alone have a membership of 30,534.

For a clearer and more meaningful understanding of the identification of the various Evangelical religious bodies working in Argentina, the information supplied in Figure No. 18 must be added to the foregoing paragraphs. Here the Churches have been divided according to their theological and ecclesiastical identification. In the light of today's fluctuating situation with regard to alignments, criteria other than ostensive identification must be applied. Due to the essentially biblical orientation which the Evangelical movement has taken in Catholic Latin America, there is a greater sympathy for the classic Evangelical position. Consequently, an attempt is made to demonstrate this basically conservative Evangelical position of Latin American Protestantism in Argentina. "Conservative Evangelical" is understood to mean those groups which maintain a conservative theological position with regard to the inspiration of the Scriptures, remain aloof by and large from the international ecumenical movement and are slow to become involved in social problems, especially in advocating revolutionary solutions. These Churches, with 88,501 members, represent by far the largest single group of Evangelical Churches.

The "Pentecostal Churches" are the second largest group with 76,123. From these Churches several have been added to the Conservative Evangelicals and the "Other Churches" since they formally maintain ties with these groups. The Other Churches in the graph are generally the historic denominations which maintain active relations with the WCC entities. These might be identified as Progressive Protestants. The fourth group are the Salvation Army and the Seventh-Day Adventists and are identified as "Marginal Churches" because of their unique ministry and theological position respectively.

When the growth rates between 1949 and 1967 of these four categories are compared, it is seen that the Pentecostal Churches are growing the fastest at 7.5 per cent per year. This is partially accounted for by the fact that many of the Pentecostal Churches in existence in 1949 did not figure in the statistical table for that year. This tends to inflate their growth rate. Nevertheless, this group of Churches accounts for almost the entire surge in Argentine church growth. The other three groups of Churches grew at a rate below the average of 5.0 per cent for the Evangelical Churches as a whole (see Figure No. 15). There is a similarity between the growth rates of the Conservative Evangelicals and the Other Churches (4.1 and 3.7 per cent respectively per year). This seems to indicate that neither ecumenical involvement nor a desire to maintain theological purity alone are the keys to church growth. The low rate (2.8 per cent per year) of the Marginal Churches is due to the drop in Salvation Army membership.

2. Mission-Related Churches Can Expect Growth

Since the late fifties it has become increasingly common to refer to the indigenous Churches of Latin America. The characteristics and strengths of this movement have received the sympathetic attention of a growing number of students of the Evangelical Churches in this part of the world. A result of this interest has been a flood of literature which seems to convey the idea that the only church growth taking place in Latin America is among this body of Churches. This propensity can produce an "anti-mission" attitude on the part of the missionaries and students of missions themselves. A possible consequence of such thinking can be the erroneous conclusion that the missions no longer have a ministry in Latin America. Furthermore, it can lead to the false assumption that growth is not possible for the established non-Pentecostal missions and Churches. It consequently produces an atmosphere in which policy decisions are geared to consolidation and perfection instead of to church growth.

Figure No. 19 presents evidence which seems to refute the observation that the principal dynamic for growth in Latin America is among the Churches which sustain no ties with an overseas missionary organization. This is at least the case in Argentina. The fact that these indigenous Churches are not growing as rapidly as their sister Churches in other parts of Latin America may in some measure account for the slower overall growth rate in Argentina, compared with Brazil and Chile. When this same classification is applied only to the Pentecostal Churches, there are 45,972 communicants in the mission-related Churches and 52,500 in those Churches which have no mission ties. In this case the Latin American Churches are larger. When the annual growth rate is calculated, the mission-related Churches show a slightly higher percentage. The

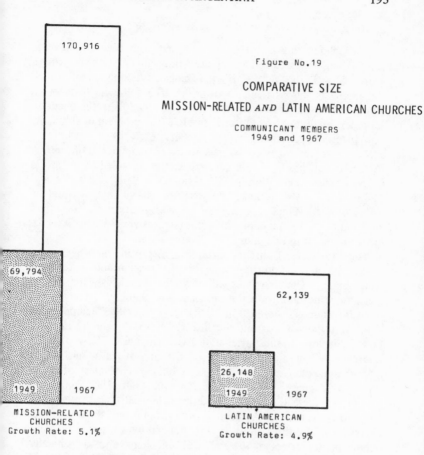

Figure No. 19

COMPARATIVE SIZE

MISSION-RELATED *AND* LATIN AMERICAN CHURCHES

COMMUNICANT MEMBERS
1949 and 1967

170,916

69,794

1949   1967

MISSION-RELATED
CHURCHES
Growth Rate: 5.1%

62,139

26,148

1949   1967

LATIN AMERICAN
CHURCHES
Growth Rate: 4.9%

Churches which sustain mission ties have grown at an annual rate of 5.1 per cent since 1949, while the Latin American Churches are growing at 4.9 per cent per year.

Mission-related Churches need not necessarily expect to experience a slower growth rate. Among this group of Churches which maintain fraternal ties with mission organizations are some which are growing at a rate considerably higher than the general average. Mission ties *per se* do not affect growth adversely when this relationship is not one of paternalistic dependence or subjugation.

3. Religious Temperament Affects Growth Rate

Throughout this investigation one fact continued to manifest itself. There appeared to be a direct relationship between the growth achieved and the nature of the religious temperament which characterized the particular movement. The following categories, which have been developed in an attempt to explain this phenomenon, are presented in a tentative fashion. The problem of subjectivism involved in attempting to classify each of the Churches according to these categories needs further and finer definition. A further investigation of this question would be aided by a careful study of the application of Kluckhohn's (1954) *Dominant and Variant Value Orientations.* The concepts she develops would be valuable in developing categories of classification which would contribute greatly in eliminating the subjectivism which is recognized as present in this preliminary presentation.

The Evangelical Churches working in Argentina have been categorized on a three-position scale of values according to religious temperament. The first is called *dogmatic* and encloses the idea of convictions bordering on the fanatical. The theological convictions of this group are radical in that they generally include some significant departure from the historic creeds of the Evangelical Church, if not in substance, at least in emphasis. Many of these Churches reflect an expectancy of the almost daily miraculous intervention of God. The second group is characterized by a *moderate* degree of religious fervor and zeal. The theological position of these Churches is traditional biblical conservatism and tends to emphasize an intellectual comprehension of these doctrinal expressions. The third group is characterized by a *tolerant* religious temperament reflected in a liberal theology and a generally progressive attitude toward the Church and its place in the world (Figure No. 20).

The first group consists of the Pentecostal family of Churches and the Seventh-Day Adventists. The traditionally conservative Evangelical Churches are classified in the second category. This second group also includes the Missouri Synod Lutheran Church because of their conservative theological position. The final group of Churches comprises largely the historic mainline denominations, most of which have been active in Argentina for many years.

During the years that these Churches have been in Argentina they

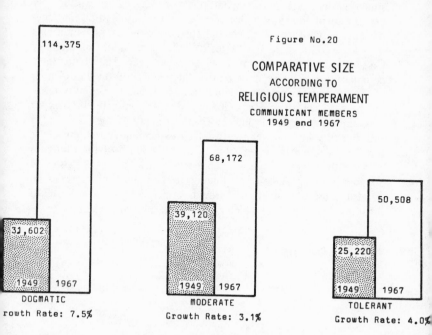

Figure No.20

COMPARATIVE SIZE
ACCORDING TO
RELIGIOUS TEMPERAMENT
COMMUNICANT MEMBERS
1949 and 1967

have achieved a degree of growth which reflects a direct relationship to the nature of their religious fervor. Those characterized by a more intense religious temperament account for the larger part of the communicant membership in Argentina today. As might be expected, the Churches categorized as "dogmatic" represent the largest group and the "tolerant" Churches the smallest group. When the growth rates of the three categories of Churches are compared a very different picture comes into view. True to form, the first division of Churches, largely comprising those of Pentecostal emphasis, reflects the most rapid rate of growth. Since 1949, this group of Churches has increased at an annual rate of 7.5 per cent. In part this high rate is accounted for by the fact that many of the Pentecostal Churches have been "discovered" statistically since 1949. It seems fair, however, to conclude apart from this fact that this is the fastest growing body of Churches in Argentina. Surprisingly enough, the annual growth rate of the second body of Churches is considerably below that of the third group. Since 1949 the "moderate" Churches of conservative theological convictions have grown at an annual rate of 3.1 per cent while the "tolerant" Churches of liberal theology have increased at a rate of 4 per cent per year. The comfortable complacency of these conservative "defenders of the faith" is in need of penetrating analysis and radical revision. A mental outlook on the work which might be designated as the minority complex, or remnant thinking, is turning the vision of many of the Churches in this category in upon themselves. That expanding church growth is possible in Argentina is reflected in the experience of the Churches in the other two categories, but conservative "status quo-ism" is apparently not capable of responding to the opportunities available. Careful attention to church growth principles will contribute to breaking this mental set which goes with stagnation.

Part III

AN EVALUATION OF ARGENTINE
CHURCH GROWTH DYNAMICS

CHAPTER 16

Previous Surveys of Evangelical
Churches in Argentina

The Evangelical Churches in Argentina have been studied extensively on two previous occasions. In 1928 Webster E. Browning, in his book *The River Plate Republics,* surveyed the Evangelical Churches in Argentina, Paraguay and Uruguay. This was the first survey of the whole area ever attempted. The next survey, covering the same three countries, was conducted by J. Merle Davis and reported in his volume *The Evangelical Church in the River Plate Republics,* published in 1943. The purpose here is to consider their appraisals and recommendations with a view to evaluating their judgment and insight in terms of the subsequent development and growth of the Evangelical Churches. First let us consider Browning's treatment.

A. BROWNING'S EVALUATION

1. Highly Trained Clergy Misses Responsive Segment

His procedure is to present the general characteristics of the region including the religious life. He then traces the development of the Evangelical Churches in the area from their beginning in the River Plate countries to 1928. The main concern here, however, is his evaluation of the Evangelical movement in Argentina at this stage of its development. This he accomplishes by an enumeration of the Church's main problems and a discussion of the reasons for slow growth (Browning 1928:78-98). This latter aspect, in which he utilizes the studied opinions of four different persons, is of particular interest as it touches on their estimate of the dynamics of church growth at that interval (1928) in the development of the Evangelical Churches in Argentina.

Browning lists several problems facing the Churches in Argentina. The first is the need for the development of a stronger national leadership for the Churches through stepped-up educational efforts. At the time of the writing of these lines the Union Seminary in Buenos Aires was being progressively improved under the guidance of a new president. The level of the ministry has certainly improved since that time. There is, however, justification for the belief that to a great degree the young pastors trained in this seminary have suffered from what might be called cultural dislocation. The improving educational program obeyed the current trends in education and theology then popular in the home country of the missionary personnel and of Europe. The improvements were largely the result of influences from the outside. They did not result from a detailed analysis of the cultural context in which the seminary graduates were to minister. This fact contributed to a growing breach between the Churches sponsoring the seminary and the increasingly responsive lower segments of the social spectrum. The pedagogical effectiveness of this improved educational program cannot be disputed. The graduates are eloquent proof. Their contribution to the Evangelical Church in Argentina has been significant. One wonders how many more might have been brought to Christ had their eyes been directed toward this responsive segment which represented opportunities for growth, especially in the light of political events of the following decades.

Furthermore, it is doubtful that the higher classes they had hoped to reach through a more highly trained ministry have come to Christ in sufficiently increased numbers to justify the apparent neglect of the poorer masses. It is these masses that form the congregations of the lesser educated Pentecostal clergy which are experiencing the phenomenal growth. Education is unquestionably essential to the development and growth of the Church. Those responsible for the training of candidates for the ministry can, however, adversely affect the growth pattern of the Church. This has happened to many Churches which were not the chief object of Browning's suggestions and thought that their essentially biblical training would bring many men to Christ. This happens when the educational program is overbalanced in its emphasis on the internal development and perfection of the Church (be it program or doctrine), to the exclusion of aggressive evangelization of the non-Christian masses.

2. Nationalism Orients Missions

Another problem developed by Browning is the growing nationalism which was present during the years immediately preceding the writing of this book. This was a development concomitant with the emergence of the Radical Party, the political party which represented the new middle sector in Argentine life. Browning's insight here is perceptive even if limited. The increasing participation of the Argentine leadership in the Churches of Browning's principal concern has been good. A significant step in this direction was the appointment of the first Argentine Methodist bishop in 1932. Where misunderstandings developed in several of the Churches, tensions rose to the boiling point. We have seen how this affected the Christian and Missionary Alliance mission particularly, in a negative way. This same spirit of nationalism was being harnessed by some of the nascent Pentecostal Churches who permitted broad expression of indigenous leadership and ideas. The newly found faith was permitted to manifest itself in forms congenial to Latin culture. When nationalism is expressed through strong church leadership and worship forms which fit the host culture, growth of the Church is the happy result.

3. Two Perennial Concerns

Browning also mentions the relationship with the dominant Roman Catholic Church and the obstacles to greater development of the social implications of the Gospel as problems to be overcome. The latter met with some technical difficulties in a country whose legal requirements were frequently difficult for the missions to meet. It is interesting to note that with the emergence of Evangelical Argentine doctors trained in Argentine universities, several of the Churches have found it feasible to establish clinics. The obstacles created by the Argentine authorities proved to be the means to an indigenous expression of this concern, freeing the missions for their principal task of discipling the nation. Even now, forty years later, these social issues remain unsolved and are becoming increasingly acute. The energy-consuming preoccupation of many of the Churches to discover their Christian responsibility in these issues is directing them away from the primary Christian duty of spiritual reconciliation.

Relations with the dominant Church, although never extremely violent in Argentina, were somewhat less than cordial on the part of much of the leadership of the Evangelical Church as well as the Catholic leadership, both lay and clerical. Much of the anti-Catholic polemic literature existent today was the product of these years when relations were less Christian. In contrast, Browning advocates an increase of friendliness and an effort to cooperate in solving the problems of the day. This desire for cooperation and greater friendliness had to wait for its fulfillment until it found its echo in Pope John XXIII and the decrees of Vatican Council II. The improvement of relations with Roman Catholicism has indeed been welcomed by all segments of the Evangelical Church, although some find it mixed with new fears. This proper and characteristic Christian attitude has provided an atmosphere in which large segments of the population with only minimal exposure to Christian thinking can now be meaningfully evangelized.

Browning next quotes the views of an Argentine lawyer, an Argentine educator, a foreign missionary and a national pastor. They each express what appears to them to account for the slow progress of the Evangelical Churches. Their desire is to find that which will stimulate a more accelerated rate of church growth. It does not serve our purposes to develop fully each of their different views. It will be adequate here to point out several which appear to be among the more significant.

4. Aiming for the Intellectuals

The principal cause which in one way or another is developed in each of these appraisals is the lack of an adequate preparation of the pastors of the Evangelical Churches. This confirms Browning's own position and judgment and seems to have been the chief burden of all concerned during this period. The chief criticism is that the Argentine pastors had little effect on the intellectual classes of Argentina. Even the young people from the Evangelical Churches were unable to go to them to find satisfying answers to their intellectual doubts. The other reasons presented by these observers as causes of the slow growth during this period are all related in some way to this basic reason.

The principal audience of Browning's comments, the established denominations, apparently learned their lesson well. The Methodists,

Disciples, Waldensians and others tooled up their educational facilities and began to attract higher caliber students. The most obvious results are the body of Evangelical scholars known as the "River Plate Theologians," presently active in this region, and the pastors of the churches which reflect this same intellectual formation. It has not, however, either produced the expected advances in church growth or begun a significant breakthrough into the intellectual classes. Argentina's intellectuals by and large continue to resist God while large numbers of the masses turn to Christ. The vast majority find new life in the Pentecostal Churches through the preaching of poorly trained pastors. A deliberate look at this puzzling discrepancy would prove rewarding to the historic Churches.

B. DAVIS' EVALUATION

1. Ghetto Complex Church

This brings us to our second survey, the study completed by J. Merle Davis (1943:106-116). His general emphasis is on the economic needs of the growing Churches, especially as reflected in the need for self-support. Davis also mentions three other areas of need among the Argentine Evangelical Churches. First he cautions the Churches not to become ingrown and separated from the people. Here Davis' judgment is precise and his criticisms of the tendencies toward a ghetto-complex church incisive. This tendency, present then, continues today, especially in some of the Churches of ethnic orientation and those Plymouth Brethren and other conservative Evangelicals who lean heavily in the direction of exclusivism and separation. It has become difficult in some churches and assemblies for the sinner to come to Christ. The "gospel of perfection" has taken the place of the gospel of grace and forgiveness. This tendency in one degree or another haunts all of the Churches. Man's basic need is to be forgiven by God, and to forgive, and this truth tends to be obliterated or clouded where the ghetto complex develops. There is nothing like forgiveness (both experienced and offered to others in the name of Jesus, in the same way we have been forgiven by Him) to open the doors of the church to the entrance of the repentant sinner. This is genuine church growth. Davis' observation is well taken, but the full solution still escapes the grasp of the Churches.

2. Expensive Luxuries

Davis next mentions the need for a full and comprehensive parish program. Although it is highly desirable that each church have a fully developed program, it is difficult to see how this will appreciably contribute to the continued growth of the churches. Unless the program springs from indigenous roots, it is doubtful that it would be multiplied in a sufficient number of churches to affect the overall growth of the Church. As the church grows, diversified programs will develop that are cordial to the needs and expectations of the emerging Church. Programs are the result, not the cause of church growth. It can be observed in the Argentine church scene that programs have not produced significant increase of church membership. The possible exception is the elaborate program of social services of the Adventist churches. And even here, the real cause of growth is probably the religious zeal and fervor of the adherents, and not the programs of social service.

Cooperation and ecumenical solidarity are also suggested by Davis as factors essential to a mature Argentine Church. This is a reflection of a growing contemporary theological and ecclesiastical opinion rather than the result of an analysis of what makes the Church develop to maturity in Argentina. Historical and statistical analysis of the different Churches in Argentina indicates that the Churches which do not cooperate are experiencing greater and more rapid growth (Figure No. 17) than the Churches oriented to both the WCC and the EFMA-IFMA organizations.

C. PROPER EVALUATION PRODUCES BASIS
FOR CHURCH GROWTH

In conclusion it should be added that these earlier evaluations of the Evangelical Church in Argentina are too exclusively based on contemporary theological, educational and ecclesiastical trends then popular in North America and Europe. They have not taken seriously the task of analyzing the historical, religious and sociological background with a view to discovering the particular dynamics which have been operative in Argentina. Of course, the key question is: Does the history of the Argentine Evangelical Church have something to tell us? A comparison of the Argentine scene as developed in Part I, with the development of the Churches in Argentina as presented in the profiles in Part II, will demonstrate the validity of this procedure. If the line of reasoning were followed which only reflected contemporary theological and ecclesiastical opinions and emphases, the solution for today's lack of growth in the Evangelical Churches in Argentina would be an involvement in a radical change of the social structures. Although this is a pressing and growing need in all of Latin America, it is not the key to a vibrant and expanding Evangelical Church. Such a Church, however, is the key to permanent and long-range solutions for these pressing and urgent problems. Any solution, however attractive, if it neglects the spiritual dimension of a growing Church, will always be less than satisfactory to Christ, who desires that all men come to Himself.

In the following chapter several factors will be developed which are crucial to producing a growing and vital Church, a Church capable of effecting radical changes in Argentine life, both individually and collectively.

CHAPTER 17

Factors Affecting Church Growth in Argentina

A careful analysis of the contextual setting and the historical development of the Evangelical Church in Argentina has resulted in the discovery of several factors which affect church growth, both quantitatively and qualitatively. An understanding of these factors provides interested persons with the proper orientation for actively and beneficially entering into the work of building Christ's Church in Argentina. It will be the purpose of this chapter to delineate these factors, illustrating them with concrete examples from the denominational profiles and background materials of the previous chapters.

A. UNDERLYING SPIRITUAL FACTORS

1. Sovereign Working of God's Spirit

The preliminary insistence on the sovereign workings of the Holy Spirit as an underlying factor in church expansion in Argentina cannot be interpreted as naiveté or superficial analysis. After careful observation of the development of Evangelical Churches in Argentina and the rest of Latin America, it must be boldly concluded that God's Spirit is indeed working. In Argentina, spectacular breakthroughs as well as solid, steady growth are evidence of the Holy Spirit's operation. The large evangelistic movements of the Plymouth Brethren in the 1920's and the Hicks campaign in 1954, although vastly different, were both sovereign breakthroughs by God. The

Spirit blows where He wills. This is how every man comes to life in Christ whether singly or by people movements such as among the Toba in the Chaco.

The conscious presence of the Spirit in each Christian's life is a determinative factor of equal importance to the general working of God's Spirit in the Churches. The power of the Spirit in the lives of simple and often ignorant Christians has made them tall towers of spiritual strength. It has transformed the common man into an effectual instrument of God. Such changed lives have brought hundreds into the Church of Christ in Argentina. Matórraz in the Chaco, Martínez among the Toba, and their hundreds of unsung spiritual ancestors and brothers have demonstrated and are demonstrating this fact.

With such broad statements, the hasty reader might conclude that no other factor is relevant when considering the dynamics of God's movement among men. This would be the conclusion of that superficial judgment which feels that God's Spirit operates only through His Church. Granted, this is precisely where His Spirit should enjoy the greatest freedom. However, God is operative by His Spirit in the affairs of men, arranging circumstances and situations for His greater glory. It is less than completely accurate to treat the work of the Spirit in church growth as a separate category. His sovereign purpose and plans reach and affect every aspect of life. Each of the separate factors which follows is the special area of the Spirit's operation. Not only must we seek to experience the freedom of the Spirit in our lives, but also to understand His broad movements in the affairs of men and of nations.

2. Dedicated Lives Sacrificially Spent

A second underlying factor influencing the growth of the Churches in Argentina has been the personal contribution of the lives of particularly outstanding men. Spectacular increase of the Church is the result of dedicated lives spent sacrificially for Christ. Almost every denomination could point to one or more who significantly altered the course of developments in their movement in Argentina.

Among the outstanding men of the early years in Argentina were Gardiner, Thomson (John F.) and Morris. More recently men like Payne, Lear, Varetto, Stockwell and Hicks have left their beneficent imprint on the growing Evangelical Church in Argentina. The caliber of the men involved in the life of the Church affects the patterns of growth. In the same way others have made their contribution to the growth of the Church, new opportunities await the investment of vision and dedicated lives. Opportunities for effective and meaningful expenditure of life clamor for the attention and response of today's Spirit-guided youth. There is no single factor in church growth as crucial as a life of intense spiritual dedication abandoned to the purposes of the Spirit of God. A charismatic figure of this caliber finds its echo in the Hispanic personalism present in the Argentine basic personality. People are waiting for the outstanding spiritual leader who can bring them into a meaningful Christian experience in Christ.

These two spiritual factors are basic and previous to all other factors involved in church growth. Men have been astute in analyzing the times and suggesting solutions. Only those who combined their insights with charismatic power and dynamic leadership have been able to effect any great movement for church growth. Church growth is the coincidence of God's man with God's method in a moment especially prepared by His Spirit. The presentation of the following factors is specifically designed to help those missionaries who labor in Argentina to read their times as God moves among them, and a call to place themselves at His disposal.

B. TEN KEYS TO CHURCH GROWTH

1. Effectively Mediating the Forgiveness of Christ

The first specific factor affecting the growth of the Evangelical Church in Argentina centers around the Christian doctrine of forgiveness of sins and the removal of guilt. Saravia (in Part I) developed the theory that the soul of the Argentine is sick because of a poor integration of the value system. A Christian analysis of his arguments would soon lead to the conclusion that Saravia is essentially speaking about the symptoms of guilt. He develops the Argentine personality characteristic which he calls moralism, or the strict advocacy of a particular position or point of view. As a corollary to this, he demonstrates that these almost absolute principles are lightly and systematically disobeyed. The resulting ambivalence of moral compromise is manifested in tensions and complexes. This moral conflict is the tragic consequence of the defective religious experience of the vast majority of professing Catholics. The effective indoctrination of the majority of the youth by the dedicated and sacrificial labors of the catechists has been successful in inculcating such basic Christian standards as the Ten Commandments. The routine violation of these basic moral principles, however, has produced deep feelings of genuine guilt, although they are generally not recognized as such. Coupled with this, the general neglect of the confessional on the part of the average Catholic bars him from even a superficial assuagement of his guilt.

Some observers of Argentine society feel that shame is a more dominant emotion than guilt. Fillol (1961:9) makes this observation in contrasting Argentine society with Anglo-American culture. He cautions, however, that shame is not as dominant among the Argentines as it is among the Japanese or the American Indians. Shame is essentially the reaction of the self-oriented person who feels that his *honor* or *dignidad* is threatened. On the other hand, a person oriented to the Christian concept of God and the moral standards He demands senses guilt after his moral lapses. Shame drives the individual to employ rationalization, self-justification and even lying to shore up his sagging image. This reaction underlies the average Argentine's haunting fear of "*¿Qué dirán?*" (What will others say?) (Enns 1966:4). The social pressures built up by this fear keep many from following Christ. It just isn't socially the thing to do to follow Christ in the Evangelical Church. Genuine guilt, the result of the violation of biblical moral standards and the fracture of man's relationship with God, demands the justifying grace of Christ. This must be the heart of the message of the Evangelical Church. It addresses itself to a basic need in the Argentine personality and when properly communicated will issue forth in genuine qualitative church growth. This in turn will bring increasing numbers into Christ's Church.

Against this background, the popular image projected by the average Evangelical church that they are a very good people, if not even a perfect people, is devastating. We have reverted to what appears to the outsider as a salvation by works, rather than by forgiveness through grace. The dimension of forgiveness in Christ needs to find its central place in all Evangelical proclamation. This forgiveness must be made meaningful in the realm of daily life, not just in religious terms and cultic or ecstatic experiences which too frequently do not get at the heart of the matter.

One of the surprising consequences of this incorrect emphasis and failure to give central place to the doctrine of forgiveness is the growing introversion of the Evangelical Churches. The example Christ used for this type of introversion was Pharisaism: "God, I thank thee that I am not like other men." There must be a constant reminder that God's people are, originally, essentially and always a forgiven people. The person who knows himself to be forgiven by God's grace alone will unceasingly (provided that he continues to experience this forgiveness) seek for others to enjoy his continually fresh experience of God's grace. Antinomian tendencies are no acute danger where there is authentic forgiveness in place of only superficial assuagement of guilt and where cordial adherence to biblical norms is observed. This is the essential message of the Evangelical Church and it addresses itself to a desperate need of the Argentine person. Church growth will be forthcoming to the degree that this message is effectively mediated and communicated in and through the lives of Argentine Christians.

2. Meeting the Argentine Need for Community

A second factor influencing church growth is the presence or absence of a new fellowship or community spirit which is based on, and springs from, genuine forgiveness. The observations regarding the absence of a social consensus and the almost pathological inability to approach urgent common problems with a community spirit, as pointed out in Part I, are relevant here. This deficiency, springing from the extreme individualism present in the Argentine basic personality profile, impinges directly upon this factor. Taylor (1948:320-322) observes that in rural areas dominated by Catholic religious influence, local churches and school were almost never built by the people. The lack of community effort created a habit of dependence on the higher authorities for such facilities. This seems to be confirmed by the fact that in areas of the provinces of Santa Fe and Misiones recent Protestant immigrants have sprinkled the *pampas* with church buildings for worship. Fillol (1961:3,12,14,22) and Mafud (1965:372,273) confirm this lack of social togetherness and inability to find common solutions to problems of mutual interest. In varying degrees, this is a problem in most Latin American countries.

The significance of this fact is crucially important for church growth. It is both an obstacle to be overcome in the formation of genuine redeemed communities as well as the precise object of one of the Gospel's major emphases: reconciliation between men. When this fundamental need in the Argentine basic personality profile is met by the genuine forgiveness offered in Christ, church growth results. Mackay (1935:195) points out that this absence of community and fellowship in Latin American culture is the supreme need of the Evangelical Church in that part of the world. He states that the "early Christian community was a *koinonia,* a fellowship, before it was an *ecclesia,* an assembly." If this view of the Church, which is the only biblical possibility, does not replace the tendency toward division into social classes as is the case in some local congregations, evangelistic stagnation will suffocate the little life remaining. Such divisions are evident in the seating arrangement and leadership patterns in many churches. This situation sounds the death knell of healthy church growth for these churches. Roman Catholics of progressive mentality also are keenly aware of the need for the formation of a community spirit. Small Catholic Action groups and the Christian Family Movement are steps in this direction, but both leave the vast majority of professing Catholics untouched and unaffected.

Related to this factor is the church growth principle of McGavran that people come to Christ most readily when they need not cross cultural or racial barriers to do so. This fact concerning how people *become* Christians is not adequate to describe how the new redeemed community must live together in unity. We do well during the early development of the Church when we address ourselves to the homogeneous units of a complex society. However, the Christian message must always eventuate in the true *koinonia* of God's people, regardless of the cultural or racial background of the members of the individual congregation. In the remaining stable communities in the vast rural areas of the underdeveloped countries the homogeneous units within society are largely determinative as to the nature of our evangelistic approach. However, in the rapidly growing urban shanty towns of Latin America with their heterogeneous masses of dislocated peoples, the determining factor in evangelism is not the former homogeneous unit (which in the city is practically nonexistent), but rather the new community of redeemed men who have found each other in the fellowship of Christ.

With continued internal migration and growing urbanization, social dislocation has become increasingly acute. The loss of the familiar orienting influences of the small community have vanished. The individual has no traditional cultural moorings to which he can tie his new life. The personal relationships of the country have been replaced by the impersonal organizations of the city. In this situation the community and fellowship offered by the Evangelical Church are heavily freighted with evangelistic potential. Much of Pentecostal growth of these recent years has been among these new city dwellers. During earlier years, the Baptists and Plymouth Brethren, as well as other Churches, grew among the masses newly arrived in growing Buenos Aires. Today it is the testimony of Evangelical Christians migrating to the city and attending churches of these denominations that it takes great patience and perseverance to penetrate the tight society of the churches and become one of them. The long-range significance of these dislocated and disoriented masses in the burgeoning urban centers of Latin America today has been pointed up by Luzbetak:

> The face of Latin America will be changed not by the isolated, snobbish, status-quo-loving aristocrats nor the tradition-upholding villagers or peons but the rapidly growing Latin shanty town dwellers, the main "power-house" of change and the potentially strongest current of communication in that part of the world (1963:298,300).

The greatest need of these responsive masses in the cities of Argentina is the sense of community based on genuine forgiveness. The fellowship experience of the Evangelical Churches is their most powerful tool of outreach into the world. Mission organizations and churches who are alert to this opportunity will see great growth in the coming decades.

Most of the Evangelical Churches have developed strong communities of fellowship which reach out in evangelistic impact. Some have evolved features in their church life and worship patterns which minister with special meaning to this need. Among these is the Plymouth Brethren conference, which has provided broad opportunity for genuine Christian fellowship. The significance of this custom for church growth among the Plymouth Brethren cannot be overemphasized. Other denominations would do well to imitate this and similar methods which have proven to provide this fellowship based on genuine forgiveness and acceptance by God and fellow Christians. Such activities provide community support for the new convert who outside this intimate circle is bombarded with ridicule and abuse. This fellowship of the new community meets the tragic deficiency of impersonal Catholic worship patterns which tend to emphasize the vertical dimension of forgiveness to the neglect of the horizontal reconciliation between fellow men. Church life must provide for the horizontal expression of the vertical faith which is professed.

Another dimension of this factor which needs further investigation is the *compadre* (godfather) and *comadre* (godmother) relationships. Most Argentines are related in some way through a web of these traditional ties. This is especially true and more significant in the rural areas and small towns.[1] When these ties are utilized to channel the community experience of the Christians out into the world of the nonconverted, solid growth will result. People who previous to their conversion already sustain some sort of tie with the Christians are more readily integrated into the life of the church. Family web relationships should be utilized in the same way to provide an ever-increasing circle of evangelistic contacts.

3. Creating a Religious Temperament Appropriate to Church Growth

A third factor, the religious temperament of an Evangelical Church, can affect the growth of that movement more decisively than most of the other factors mentioned as contributing to church growth. This is true both negatively and positively. It can either produce attitudes of faith and expectancy which stimulate growth or attitudes which frustrate growth and result in a static Church. These attitudes range from the white hot zeal or fervor which borders on religious fanaticism to a cool, sophisticated perspective of tolerant non-involvement in the religious affairs of others. It cannot be denied that such attitudes will definitely affect the rate of evangelistic expansion. The particular religious temperament of a Church will be reflected in its rate of growth.[2]

In Argentina, as in all other countries of missionary penetration, this factor has played a significant role. The Wesleyan dynamic of the early Methodists gave place to the encroachment of an expanding organization, theological liberalism and diluted religious conviction. The institutions developed by the organization were not always those which contributed to the growth of their churches. The liberal theological emphasis also contributed to the cooling off of this movement. Recent involvement in ecumenical concerns and social engineering has contributed positively to the religious temperament of this Church, but it remains to be seen if these eventuate in church growth. By way of contrast, the Plymouth Brethren, who began their work in Argentina just fifteen years after the Methodists started their outreach in the Spanish language, have enjoyed a much more accelerated rate of growth. The factors in the general environment were identical. The difference, in part, was the contrasting religious temperaments of the two Churches. In recent years the Pentecostals have been experiencing growth greater than that of either of the two previously mentioned Churches. The dynamic Churches of Argentina today are the Pentecostal Churches. There do not appear to be any signs of cooling off among them up to the present.

The discovery that the average rate of growth among the "conservative" Churches of "moderate" religious temperament is below that of the "liberal" Churches stands in contradiction to the otherwise close relationship between the religious temperament of a movement and the degree of dynamic for growth it reflects. Other factors are obviously at work which attenuate the dynamic of this body of conservative Churches. Their preoccupation with the "grammar of religion" has drained off their energy of faith into the stagnant channels of dead orthodoxy. Religious conviction, however intense, when directed only toward activities designed to maintain the *status quo,* or consolidate the gains already achieved, will make little contribution to the growing expansion of the Church. These Churches cannot expect to break this pattern of inertia until their biblical faith is quickened by the presence and power of the Holy Spirit and directed toward the unredeemed world.

A religious phenomenon closely related to this factor is revival. Revival has been used of God to bring warmth back into the religious temperament of many inactive Churches. The spiritual intensification of a traditional religious experience is the birthright of every follower of Christ. This is the chief need and most promising hope of the Churches in Argentina. Observers are divided as to whether or not the growing charismatic movement will bring new life into the Churches or merely serve as the occasion for divisiveness.

4. Mobilizing the Entire Membership for Church Growth

The fourth factor which influences growth positively is the degree to which a particular Church has achieved the participation of the total membership in the life and extension of the Church. This factor forms the basis of Kenneth Strachan's Evangelism-in-Depth principles. No Church, especially a mission Church, grows appreciably when extension and regular ministry depend principally on the paid leadership. When the members are inactive and fail to communicate their Christian experience to people on the outside, the growth pattern becomes static. Often the cleric, through the "deculturating" processes of his ministerial preparation and education, loses natural and normal contact with the real man. His role as a member of the professional clergy limits him almost exclusively to the formal religious dimension of man's experience. Since this is but a part of the whole man, only with great difficulty can he reach the whole person. The layman does not have this problem to the same degree and with careful training can overcome it almost entirely.

Those Churches in which the laymen are responsible for, and actively participate in, the different ministries of the congregation find a "bridge of God" out into the world and back into the community of Christians. Where this has taken place among the Churches in Argentina, there has been multiplied growth far beyond what one professional leader would be able to produce and maintain on his own. Here is the ideal in church growth which several of the Churches in Argentina have been able to make real.

This factor of church growth dynamic has expressed itself in several ways among the Churches. The rather young churches related to the Conservative Baptist Mission permit unordained men to administer the Lord's Supper and baptism. This has the beneficial effect of placing the key responsibilities on the members. The church becomes truly theirs. The Plymouth Brethren followed this pattern as a matter of principle from the very beginning and continue to reap positive results from its use. Among the Pentecostals the total membership is actively and aggressively engaged in evangelism. This is also true in the churches of the Seventh-Day Adventists, even though they have developed a strong professional leadership. The two are not mutually exclusive. In fact, as Kessler (1967:204-206,327) points out, the proper balance between the two is the determining factor in solid growth. Several of the other Churches have seen the urgency of achieving the involvement of the total membership in church life and evangelism, but they have not been able to eliminate sufficiently the latent impression that the layman is being used in the program of the clergy. Total participation of the membership must include authority as well as responsibility. Kessler (1967:341) cites the example of the Chilean Pentecostals who break up their churches for smaller neighborhood cell meetings as ideal for affording responsible lay participation.

This type of involvement is mentioned by Mafud (1965:360) as necessary for the total development of the Argentine personality. They need an opportunity for the exteriorization of their personalities which through frustrated social experiences have atrophied. Opportunities for participation in communal activities are a contribution which the Evangelical Churches are especially equipped to make which meets this critical need among the Argentines. Churches which have achieved this kind of involvement on the part of their membership are experiencing solid growth.

5. Utilizing All Leadership Sets Positively

Another factor closely related to this matter of total membership participation is the nature of the leadership patterns which develop among the churches. I refer especially to the leadership tensions which express themselves in any social organization. These tensions polarize around the different leadership sets within a particular social organization. The *established* leadership of the older men, often the elders, traditionally exercises the initiative within the society. The young men, who are learning to know themselves and attempt to influence their times increasingly, seek opportunities to express their leadership. They form the new and *emerging* leadership. In today's rapidly changing world of abundant cross-cultural contacts, leadership tensions are further complicated by the introduction of influences by an *external* leadership. This is particularly true of the missionary situation, and it is critically important to understand the nature and the patterns of its influence. These three leadership sets readily form bipartite coalitions of varying alignments to protect the cherished interests of each. The battle between communism and capitalism in Latin America illustrates this principle. Communism, an external political position, seeks to impose its exotic ideology largely through an appeal to the emerging leadership, especially in the universities. Capitalistic interests attempt to maintain the *status quo* by carefully cultivating their ties with the established leadership.

When these leadership categories and the dynamics involved in their interrelationships are applied to the missionary situation we have a tool for analyzing church growth. Generally, when a missionary (external leader) enters a culture and brings to bear the influence of the Gospel, he finds that the young are the most responsive. This is welcomed by the missionary as a beneficent sign of offering the possibility for developing a strong and loyal future church leadership. He remembers that this is the pattern which continues to provide leadership for the Churches in his own country. Furthermore, it was his own experience. However, the older men (established leadership) react to this foreign element and the exotic message as an ominous threat to their authority and the stability of their way of life. This is especially true when they see their sons become bound by growing competitive loyalties.

In Part I (pp. 62-63) we saw how Saravia developed this tension in Argentine society between the older and the younger. The missionary welcomes the young men since they more readily adapt to the new cultural mores of the emerging Evangelical community. A Bible training program functions so much more effectively when only the young men are involved. With the withdrawal of the young men for training, tensions develop which identify this exotic new religion as culturally disrupting and revolutionary. Reaction on the part of the older men sets in and the penetration of the society with the Gospel of Christ is made virtually impossible.

The tensions which accompany this leadership struggle at the moment of original Gospel penetration are often present subsequently between the established leaders and the younger men who exhibit a desire to participate actively and meaningfully in the life of the Church. Unless such tensions are resolved at both stages of development (initial penetration and subsequent development period), church growth is frustrated and the emerging young missionary-dominated Church settles down to slow growth patterns. In fact, such slow growth patterns are thought of as normal, since they occur so generally.

A situation conducive to rapid evangelistic expansion and solid church growth develops to the degree that this tension is resolved in positive contributions of each leadership set. The missionary must seek to win and train the established leaders for the spiritual responsibilities and ministerial duties of the emerging Church, always careful so to train that the men are not culturally dislocated and thus lose all meaningful contact with the world from which they have come. This can be accomplished by various techniques of on-the-job training. When this approach is used, there is greater assurance that the Church which develops will assume a greater percentage of indigenous forms which are cordial and appropriate to the stage of development in which the Church finds itself. Furthermore, the Church will develop institutions which are culturally relevant and congenial to the host culture. When the older men are developed and trained as leaders, their rapport with the outside community is stronger because of the greater respect which they command. A far more healthy and faster growing Church is the result.

What of the young men? They too are to be trained. But the orientation of their training is not toward occupying the leadership of the established churches immediately, where they might pose a threat to the older men. They are most effectively utilized if trained for missionary outreach. Missionary activity on the part of the young men fits the situation described for two reasons. First, the younger generation by very nature is rebellious and revolutionary. When this spirit is turned against the older men, tension ensues. However, if it is wisely directed against the pagan culture in crusading evangelistic zeal, the young anti-status-quo spirit is satisfied. The spectacular breakthrough by the Seventh-Day Adventist Church in Tucumán was largely the work of an evangelistic team of young people. The second reason is found in the reaction of the established leadership. When they observe that the revolutionary enthusiasm of the youth is turned against pagan society, they are satisfied. They know that if this is not accomplished, the youth might rebel against the established leadership and identify with pagan society. Perhaps some of the tragic leakage of young Plymouth Brethren Christians back into the world can be traced to this cause. The established leadership jealously guards its position and the young leadership finds itself frustrated. This is equally true of many of the other Evangelical Churches. The degree to which leadership tensions can be resolved in this way will be reflected in the amount of church growth dynamic which will operate in the developing Church.

A review of the development of the Evangelical Churches in Argentina confirms this principle. The Pentecostal Churches through design, accident, or experimentation have utilized this pattern of leadership accommodation to great advantage. This explains much of the growth thrust presently operative among their churches. Pentecostal observers in other Latin American countries confirm that this principle is operative there also. Combined with this is the concept of the mother church with her many satellite congregations. Some of these complexes have as many as 5,000 members. The mother church is pastored by the principal leader together with a group of older men, while the dependent congregations and the missionary churches are started and led by the younger men. The Plymouth Brethren have ably developed leadership among the older men. But as noted above, there is a tendency among them to too great caution when it comes to turning over responsibilities to the younger men. Much of Plymouth Brethren growth has been by division, with the new leadership taking the initiative in this only way that is open to them. There would be absolutely phenomenal advances in their growth patterns if this large body of capable emerging leaders were channeled into a church-planting ministry. Other Churches have so structured their leadership patterns that the thought of an emerging leadership developing in ways other than through the established institutions is not even dreamed of. Consequently no tension develops, nor is the dynamic for growth potential, which is available to the other Churches, operative.

A corollary to this feature of church growth concerns the matter of church divisions or "splits." Most divisions are produced by leadership tensions expressed in personality antagonisms, even though ostensibly the motivating reason might be identified as theological. The plea of this paragraph is that there be a place for cordial divisions or multiplication of churches. The basic factor involved in a positive interpretation and harmonious reorientation of a divisive movement is forgiveness. Where there is an absence of that humility which accepts personal guilt and partial blame for a division of the continuing body, and an unforgiving attitude toward the new body, the division tends to become crystallized and later institutionalized into a new movement; and even more tragic, an absence of spiritual ties with the former body. When the dynamics of leadership tensions are clearly understood, rather than wait until a division erupts, provision will be made for the emerging leadership which wishes to express itself. It may also be observed that where there is no leadership tension of this type, either there is not sufficient leadership, the external leadership (missionary) is absolutely dominant, or the structures are so static that leadership can emerge only through prescribed and selective processes which protect the establishment. The basic problem is not the mere presence of leadership tensions, which will always exist in an expanding organization or movement, but the wise channeling of the new leadership. Such a direction of leadership dynamics into productive evangelistic ventures will produce an accelerated rate of church growth.

6. *Harnessing the Spirit of Nationalism for Church Growth*

This brings us to the sixth factor which influences church growth in Argentina. It concerns the degree to which the Churches have been able to hammer out a relationship which is cordial to, or at peace with, the spirit of nationalism. Nationalism is generally viewed as a foe to Christian mission. Many kinds of political nationalism have indeed been bent into a posture hostile to missions, and even to the national Churches. Furthermore, different areas of the world are subject to ideological overtones and pressures which at certain moments make it difficult or even impossible to harness for Christ's glory this incipient desire for national self-identity in the emerging Church. Communism, secularism and renascent oriental religions in many of the developing countries are openly hostile to Christianity and often turn nationalistic passions against the messengers of the Cross. My remarks are directed to those situations where political circumstances permit the channeling of this spirit in paths conducive to the greater glory of God. Argentina and most of the rest of Latin America provide such an opportunity. But even here unwise missionary planning and action can produce harmful reactions. The nationalism which contributes positively to church expansion might be designated as Christian nationalism. It is the legitimate expression of national self-identity in forms cordial to the essence of the Christian Gospel, even though at times it might include negative overtones of anti-missionary sentiment.

Perceptive analysts have pointed to this problem for a long time. Browning (1928:77) and Mackay (1935:186) lament the fact that the form of Christianity which has been taken to Latin America by the Protestant missionaries is far too Anglo-Saxon in temperament and expression. Their desire is for an expression of the Gospel more congenial to the Latin emotional and intellectual make-up. When a Church has been able to nationalize its understanding and expression of the Gospel in Latin forms and concepts, church structures and worship patterns more in keeping with the local culture and customs have resulted. Too often the process by which the church grows is so confining that it frustrates rapid growth. When growth is slow, or almost exclusively dependent on the multiplication of foreign missionaries and funds, the foreign missionary has too great an opportunity to denationalize the movement. Not only are the forms of church life and worship the object of this harmful denationalization, but it adversely affects the leadership patterns as well.

Related to this process of nationalization or indigenization is the perennial problem of mission-church relationships. The tensions which develop between the mission and the Church center around the question of foreignness: the foreignness of forms and the foreignness of leadership authority. Most North Americans will recognize how religion and nationalism are related in their own country in the numerous and intimate ties which exist between Protestant Christianity and national patriotism. The Christians in mission lands soon see the foreignness of the particular denominational form of Christianity which came to them and seek more indigenous expressions of the essential elements of their faith. If the emerging Church grows too slowly, these national aspirations and longings are absorbed, frustrated and denationalized by the overbearing mission organization. The degree to which this happens depends on how efficient and powerful the mission organization and training program are.

This principle provides a way of understanding and interpreting what happened in the Pentecostal movement in Argentina. Pentecostalism, which began in about 1900, reached Argentina and the rest of Latin America before it was a highly structured ecclesiastical organization. It possessed more dynamic than structure, more power than form, and more vitality than organization. The early Pentecostal missionaries were individuals impelled by a newly released dynamic. They were not part of a rigid and definite church or mission organizational structure. Church organization and mission policy were eclipsed by the new and fresh charismatic experience of the Holy Spirit. They sought to communicate this subjective experience to everyone. Their basic concern was not the introduction of an organizational structure or program. They passionately desired that everyone participate in their exhilarating and inhibition-breaking experience and cared little about denominational forms. This being the case, the Pentecostal Churches have been able to develop indigenous structures congenial to the Latin temperament. The resulting Christian nationalism has enabled Pentecostals to interpret themselves more readily and rapidly to the populace. The foreign missionary who works among them must bend to the Latin pattern, and not the church to the foreign pattern. Many criticize the Pentecostals for not reflecting more faithfully certain features of church life that have become traditional among Anglo-Saxons. Many of these criticisms might be fair, but our interest here is an attempt to understand the dynamic behind their phenomenal growth.

Other Churches in Argentina have also achieved a degree of Christian nationalism. The Plymouth Brethren missionaries generally have always enjoyed cordial relationships with their Argentine brethren. There has been no mission organization behind which the missionary could hide or seek protection when opposition arose or problems developed, or from which he could draw authority and power not personally his to speak out dogmatically on this or that issue. He could not enjoy such privileges merely because of his missionary ties. The Plymouth Brethren missionary served among the assemblies and their leaders on an individual and spiritual basis. His authority was spiritual and obeyed the spiritual dynamics of inter-personal relationships alone. Having no monolithic organization against which to react, tensions beyond the inter-personal level were at a minimum. The absence of tension polarized as mission-versus-church conflict provided the atmosphere for a mutual sharing and contribution to the nature of the developing Church. The Methodists, as well as many of the other highly structured Churches, have achieved a degree of nationalization through the training of capable men who have assumed the leadership. The end result appears similar, but the process has been different. In the latter case it is the nationalization of a foreign structure, whereas in the former (and also in the case of the Pentecostals) it is the national expression of a dynamic which comes from God, even though mediated by foreign missionaries. Granted, in the case of the Plymouth Brethren, the missionaries in large part brought the form of the structure with them, but it happened to be a cordial form and one which has proved to be appropriate to Argentina. The crucial question for our consideration is whether the dynamic or the structure is of greater importance.

7. Learning to Satisfy Pressing Natural Needs

The seventh factor which affects church growth has been referred to in Part I in discussing Pin's (1963:29ff.) presentation of the religious motivations of the people of Latin America. Pin points out that many nominal Catholics interpret their religious experiences as a virtually magic means by which natural needs are satisfied. Participation in religious activities (both legitimate and syncretistic) is determined by physical and emotional crises, which seemingly cannot be solved otherwise, far more than by genuine religious devotion. This is the extent and nature of the religious experience of the vast majority of Catholicism's nominal adherents. Pin feels that this drive to satisfy natural needs provides the Protestant Church with an open opportunity for expansion among Roman Catholics. Undoubtedly, his primary reference is to the observed appeal of much of Pentecostalism to these pressing natural needs demanding urgent resolution.

There can be no doubt that many desperate people have found release and salvation through this kind of contact with the Evangelical Church. They have come seeking health, financial aid, blessing in their business venture, restoration of the unfaithful husband or wife, or a cure of the alcoholic who neglects his family. This is particularly true of the Pentecostal Churches, who through their emphasis on divine healing and miraculous divine intervention have been the instruments of blessing and release to many. These pressing needs, coupled with the fact that much of popular Catholicism is based on the hope of gaining the favor of some powerful saint, have led many to seek assistance from the Evangelicals, who seem to be enjoying greater success. When word spreads through the neighborhood of the power of the Evangelical's God, many make the break and find genuine release. When it turns out to be only an opportunistic search or an exclusively emotional release, the people turn back to their former "gods." This in large part accounts for the unusually high percentage of leakage among the Pentecostal Churches. Where this interpretation of the Evangelical public image is being communicated, rapid growth patterns are evident. A tragically negative corollary to this method of evangelism is the grossly limited understanding of the average adherent who comes to embrace the faith of the Evangelicals with these imperfect motivations. The fact remains, however, that such motives have brought vast multitudes into the Pentecostal Churches and to a more limited extent into the other Churches also.

8. Responding in a Religious Vacuum

The degree and effectiveness of Roman Catholic pastoral care has affected the growth of Evangelical Churches in Argentina. This factor is understood both when comparing Argentina with other Latin American nations and when comparing different areas within Argentina itself. Internationally, Argentina stands high in the favorable ratio of clergy to inhabitant. There are 4,300 Catholics per priest as compared with 12,300 Catholics per priest in Guatemala (Alonso 1964:213). The annual growth rate of the Evangelical Church in Guatemala is 11 per cent as compared with 5 per cent in Argentina. A similar relationship between the number of priests per Catholic as compared to the growth rate of the Evangelical Churches can be demonstrated for a number of Latin American countries. This is particularly true of Brazil. Chile, however, stands in sharp contrast to this general observation. There are 3,100 Catholics per priest in Chile, considerably less than the ratio in Argentina, yet the growth rate of the Evangelical Church in Chile stands higher than that in Argentina. The continuing dynamic of the Pentecostal movement in Chile is partial explanation of this difference. This exception calls for further investigation.

The situation in Brazil is one priest per 6,400 Catholics. The annual growth rate of the Evangelical Church in that country is 8 per cent. Robert Ricard (Mörner 1965:28,29) advances the theory that it was the shortage of priests of the Mendicant Orders after the expulsion of the Jesuits from Brazil in 1759 that produced the subsequent weakness of the Catholic Church in that country. He maintains that it was these priests of the Mendicant Orders that saved the day in the rest of Latin America. The Jesuits, latecomers to the American colonies, had to settle for the peripheral areas of Spanish and Portuguese interest in Latin America. The priests of the Mendicant Orders had already firmly entrenched themselves where the gold and the power were concentrated. Their influence in the Viceroyalty of Perú is largely the reason that Evangelical progress has been slower there, where the Church did not suffer as greatly with the expulsion of the disciples of Loyola. It is not accidental, then, that the Evangelical Churches have grown so rapidly in Brazil. The Catholics themselves consider the Church weak there.

Generally, the Evangelical Church has grown more rapidly in the countries outside the Viceroyalty of Perú than in the countries which comprised this early colonial political division. This viceroyalty included the present countries of Venezuela, Colombia, Ecuador, Perú, Bolivia, Paraguay, Uruguay and Argentina. Argentina and Uruguay are not included in this area in our observations since these two countries fell under a completely different set of influences beginning even before independence with the establishment of the Viceroyalty of La Plata in 1776 and the unusually heavy currents of immigration beginning a century later. Brazil and Chile were excluded from this political division during colonial times. The Evangelical Churches in the countries of Central America and Mexico, all outside the Viceroyalty of Perú, have also experienced a more accelerated growth rate.

In the postwar years we have begun to see a change in this trend as the Churches begin to break the pattern of resistance and stagnation. In the early 1960's, although the countries which were part of the early Viceroyalty of Perú (excepting Argentina and Uruguay) contained 22 per cent of the total population of South America, the communicant members of the Evangelical Church in that same area numbered only 3.6 per cent of the total communicants in South America. This figure is up from 1.4 per cent in 1911, but down since 1938 from 6.5 per cent. This recent drop is largely due to the Pentecostal surge in Brazil, Chile and Argentina since World War II. This fact of strong Spanish and Roman Catholic influence in this area and consequent slow Evangelical church growth is reflected in the general pattern of later entry by Evangelical missions into these countries, the absence of a strong Pentecostal breakthrough and the reduced number of Anglo-Saxon immigrants into the area as compared to Chile, Argentina (especially in areas outside the six northwestern provinces) and Brazil. Pentecostal membership in this area, according to DuPlessis (1958:201), represents only 1.8 per cent of the total in South America. The area has not been neglected by missions, especially in recent years. In 1938 the percentage of missionaries in Latin America who occupied these countries stood at 31 per cent, and rose to 39.4 per cent in 1962. Slow growth in this area is most probably due to the strong Roman Catholic influence.

Another aspect of this observation is the fact that the area within Argentina which fell under the stronger dominance of Perú, namely the six northwestern provinces, represents the area within Argentina of least church growth (3.6 per cent of the communicants as

compared to 11.8 per cent of the total Argentine population). It is
also the area of least Pentecostal penetration, with only 1.5 per cent
of the total for Argentina. The fact that Bolivia and both Colombia
and Venezuela are seeing a break in this static growth pattern should
be sufficient indication to others working in these countries, or areas,
that an increasing responsiveness is developing. This is one of the
areas of future great church growth in Latin America. A major factor
involved in church growth in this entire area is an understanding of
the Indian. This area is largely equal to the greatest extension of the
Inca Empire, from Colombia in the North down into what is
present-day Argentina. In this area the Roman Catholic Church has
also achieved little more than a syncretistic adaptation of some of
the exterior forms of Christianity on the part of the Indians.
The heart of the Indian still remains to be won for Christ.

With this international perspective in mind, within Argentina
itself a similar correlation is observed. In the newly formed urban
areas which absorb the migrating masses from the interior, Evangelical Churches are finding their areas of most rapid growth. These are
also the areas where the Roman Catholic parishes are slow to form
and where the percentage of practicing Catholics is down to a low
2.3 per cent. The rapid growth of Evangelical churches in these
newly burgeoning shanty towns around the cities is evidence of this
factor. The Roman Catholic Church, which in the past was too
deeply entrenched in traditional approaches to pastoral care, has
become aware of this fact and is attempting to respond with
methods not wholly unlike those which have proved successful for
the Evangelicals.

9. Making Peace with the Masses

Another important factor affecting church growth is the degree
to which both the church leadership and the missionary staff are
able to make peace with the masses. A congenial adjustment on the
part of all concerned with the proclamation of the Gospel in
Argentina to this most responsive segment of society will be
evidenced in healthy expansion of the Church. By far the greatest
percentage of converts throughout Latin America is coming from
this displaced, disillusioned and dissatisfied element of humanity.
Yet the primary thrust of the majority of the older denominations is
directed toward the rising middle classes. Prestige-starved missionaries and churches seek to shore up their image by winning converts

from the classes when in reality the majority of the converts come from among the masses. When church leaders come to live at peace with this fact and through determined effort seek to win the masses, radical changes in growth rates will be immediately evident.

This is a problem of both the foreign missionary staff and the indigenous church leadership. Both are affected by this prejudice, although for different reasons. For the missionary, the determining factor is his cultural dislocation within and cultural distance from the host culture, as well as the urgent necessity to preserve his image as a successful missionary for the supporting constituency in his country of origin. Located in a culture not his own, he is prone to mistakenly identify on the basis of material accouterments and educational achievement with that element in society which is not responsive to the Gospel. Here the cultural distance, at least of externals, is less and the tensions diminish. He automatically directs his principal evangelistic thrust to this element and senses the deepest and most gratifying emotional satisfaction when one or two become Christians. One such convert is worth one hundred peons of the lower masses in the propaganda organs of the mission. The lightning visits of mission executives can reinforce this view, while the masses for whom Christ died are overlooked and neglected as the chief source of church growth. The modern missionary's passion to eradicate the false image of a sleeping and underdeveloped Latin America, prevalent in the minds of church people in North America and Europe, oversimplifies and takes deputation pictures of new sky-scrapers and growing factories. He misses the teeming masses crushed by poverty and disease which live in the same cities, but enjoy almost none of its privileges. Evangelical films produced in Latin America which overemphasize the opulence and urbanity of certain segments of society also contribute to this tendency to ignore the masses. These newcomers to the underdeveloped "outer city" of Latin America are the present opportunity for effective evangelism.

This problem of the missing of the masses also afflicts the Churches of Latin America. Although some of the mistaken missionary sentiment and orientation has almost certainly rubbed off on the Churches, there are also other reasons peculiar to the Latin American congregations. Second and third generation Christians, through the evident results of their new life in Christ, have achieved a social status which separates them from these masses. Ironically enough, the majority were converted when they formed a part of these same masses. Of course, those who have recently achieved some little social status sense the greatest threat through identification with this lower strata of society. In these cases, social position has become far more dominant in church life than propagation. This is particularly true of the older, established denominations, since the younger growing Churches are largely concentrating on the masses, with spectacular results, and are themselves composed of this element of society. The old arguments that certain denominations are ideally suited to minister to specific segments within society will have to die if we desire to see vigorous church growth.

The issue at stake here is not sociological or anthropological. Rather, basic Christian principles have been neglected and even violated (James 2:1-9), and we are reaping the consequences in stagnant churches. The degree to which this tension of identification can be resolved in genuine Christian love and evangelistic passion by all concerned will determine in large part the rate of growth we can expect in the next two decades. Revolutionary pressures continue to mount, and their principal weight falls heavily and mercilessly on this element. They clamor for a new sense of community and a new set of values. Only Christ can provide full and authentic satisfaction of their legitimate needs. The opportunity for effective evangelism among these masses will not diminish but continue to increase in the coming years. Churches alert to this expanding opportunity will see spectacular results from their Spirit-guided evangelism.

10. Fitting Ministerial Training to the Cultural Milieu

A final factor influencing church growth is the nature and emphasis of the education offered to the candidates for the ministry. Any program of ministerial training which does not adequately and appropriately fit the needs of the very special set of circumstances which prevail in a growing church can do irreparable damage. Great effort must be exerted by all concerned to prevent this leaven from infecting the young Church. Once it has begun to work, all resources must be marshaled to set in motion a training program which will release and channel the power and dynamic of the emerging Church. The degree to which such a program is operative among a set of churches will in large part, greater than generally imagined, determine the rate of growth among those churches.

The characteristics which constitute the growing Church are radically different from those operative in the established and stable

Churches. By far the majority of the people in any great movement into the Christian faith are simple people of limited educational background and an unsophisticated orientation and outlook on life. This is amply demonstrated by the type of people who are moving into a meaningful Christian experience through the multiplying Pentecostal Churches of Latin America. In such circumstances tradition-bound missions and missionaries, whose views of the ministry and ministerial training are limited to those standards employed in their stable, nongrowing, sending Churches, find it almost impossible to be flexible enough to adapt to appropriate patterns and practices. They find the more readily adaptable Churches and missions reaping a harvest which they, too, could enjoy. Such were the tragic circumstances on the North American frontier during the nineteenth century, according to Latourette:

> Zealous though the Congregational, Presbyterian and Epis-copal missionaries were, they did not succeed in attracting as large constituencies on the frontier as did the Methodists, Baptists, Christians, and Disciples of Christ. They stressed an educated ministry, and men with that kind of preparation did not know how to appeal to the rank and file. Their congregations were gathered chiefly from the minority who had some formal education and a degree of culture (1961:24).

Frontier conditions prevail in Latin America today as far as the growth of Evangelical Christianity is concerned, and men with a frontier mentality remain almost totally unmoved toward Christian decision by the sophisticated intellectual approach of too highly or improperly educated pastors.

The experience of educational leaders related to the older denominations and the World Council of Churches in attempting to aid in the improvement of the educational level of Chilean Pentecostal Churches is illustrative. The cordial fraternal relationship growing out of the reception of Pentecostal Churches into the WCC at New Delhi led to this educational assistance program. After several years of mutual exposure, it was realized that an education along traditional lines, if successful according to the standards of the proponents, would strip these Churches of their dynamic. It was recognized that apprenticeship training as practiced by these Churches was far more adequate to the need of these growing churches than traditional educational approaches (Lalive d'Epinay

1967). Any future attempt at assisting these Churches with a
program of higher education must build on these observations or run
the risk of frustrating church growth.

A program designed to train the pastoral leadership of growing
churches must avoid the common and facile mistake of unthought-
fully importing the present level and emphases of educational
developments in North America and Europe. This is equally true of
those organizations which wish to break the pattern of stagnation
and begin a process of growth. This kind of missionary dominance is
the most insidious and harmful to the emerging Church and the most
frequently perpetrated by the national church leadership. It should
be patently evident to all concerned that these emphases are not
achieving spectacular growth among the Churches which practice
them in the Northern Hemisphere. This alone should lead missionary
and national church leadership into specific research to discover
what is being done to educate pastors by those Churches which
continue to experience church growth. The pressures of finances and
expertise introduced into this educational picture by international
theological education assistance groups must be bent and harnessed
for programs which will produce the desired growth.

A program which generously provides for adult on-the-job-train-
ing, thus allowing for late vocations, is needed. The provision of
ample opportunity in the form of growing responsibilities for
emerging church leadership is also indicated. This will provide
growth and practical training simultaneously as new churches are
begun and the youth press to serve Christ and discover their gift in
His Church. Careful attention must be given to avoid the cooling off
processes which are set in motion by the cultural dislocation of the
ministerial candidate. Mission-dominated educational programs are
especially prone to produce this unfortunate consequence of
successful education, but infatuation with exotic theological con-
troversies is equally damaging. Granted, orientation to today's
theological debate is essential to segments of the more highly
educated clergy, but we question whether this is necessary for those
who stand on the frontier of church growth. A pastor wrongly
educated finds it difficult to relate meaningfully to the large
majority of those coming to Christ today. Provision in the
educational program must be made for broad and increasingly
responsible lay participation in the pastoral functions of the
churches. Specific mechanisms must be designed for the most

successful from among these laymen to give full time to the ministry even if full educational requirements are not met. A strong emphasis on night education (common throughout Latin America) can greatly increase the possibilities of broad lay education. When these and other techniques are imaginatively applied, educational programs will be forthcoming which are congenial to the needs of growing churches.

CHAPTER 18

What Should Missions and Churches Do Now?

A. REVEALING DISCOVERIES

Among the pleasant fruits of serious research into the underlying dynamics and dimensions of church growth are the many revealing discoveries which come to light. Some are happy, especially when they confirm what we had already believed to be productive mission policy. Others, although not so welcome at first discovery because of the disquieting emotional reactions they sometimes produce, are however the more important, for they have a particularly relevant bearing on the question of how we can more successfully and effectively accomplish the task to which Christ has commissioned His Church. Often they call for changes in our methods of winning men to faith and obedience in Christ that seem too difficult. But these too difficult changes often are the key that opens the door to greater spiritual blessings and accelerated church growth.

Therefore, these discoveries—both pleasant and disquieting—must be carefully taken into account by the churchmen and missionaries presently active in Argentina. Their significance in helping to discover the Spirit-guided ways of greater church growth must not be overlooked. In the face of the disturbing fact that Argentina is not achieving a rate of growth commensurate with today's potential in Latin America, we must find and adopt those methods and attitudes which can change the *status quo*. Because a far more rapid rate of growth of the Evangelical community is realistically possible and probable, a sympathetic and sincere attempt must be made by

232

every mission organization and Church to find God's way to accomplish the evangelization of Argentina's millions.

Our investigations have brought to light several helpful revelations about the growth of the Evangelical Churches in Argentina. For example, it is precisely those Churches about which the world Christian community knows the least that have shown and continue to maintain the more accelerated growth rates. In some cases these growth rates have been more than ten times the rate of the established missions and Churches. This has produced the little recognized fact that in terms of sheer numbers the Argentine Church preserves an essentially Conservative Evangelical character. Their divided fellowship, however, stands as an obstacle to these Churches assuming a more significant and influential role of Evangelical leadership among the River Plate countries.

An encouraging disclosure for both Churches and missions in Argentina is the fact that there have been spectacular breaks in the *status quo*. Prolonged patterns of stagnation have gradually yielded before the persevering implementation of new approaches. Imagination and experimentation, guided by genuine spiritual principles, have led to radical breaks in the growth patterns of several Churches. Where missionary and church leadership in Argentina have learned to bring their methods and attitudes into harmony with sound church growth principles, there has been growth. Probably the most damaging influences here are those attitudes which stifle growth. The ingrown, defensive posture of many of the Churches militates against their searching among sister congregations for ways to halt the process of cooling off to a static state that threatens them.

B. HOW CAN FULL POTENTIAL BE REALIZED?

Against this background of discoveries stands the fact that the Argentine Evangelical Church in general is not achieving the rate of growth commensurate with current potential and responsiveness. The rate continues to be higher than the annual rate of population increase, but it is slipping ominously. The significant discovery of this study is that it is the new emerging Pentecostals who are holding up the rate with their unusually healthy growth. This is no comfort to the established denominations and missions. This fact of Pentecostal growth against the slower rate of the other Churches indicates that the Evangelical Church in Argentina, following antiquated policies, does not seem to be able to take advantage of the potential which exists.

Furthermore, a comparison of Argentina with other countries in Latin America where very similar conditions exist would indicate that a far higher rate of growth should be considered normal for Argentina. In some countries the rate stands at more than double that of Argentina. Although Argentina's rate of 5 per cent per year has generally been considered good in church growth studies of Asia and Africa, it should not be accepted as normal for today's optimum conditions of responsiveness prevailing in Latin America. Any tendency to justify the present rate of growth as normal or "all we can expect under our very special conditions" is sheer rationalization. Such attitudes are not in harmony with what the Spirit desires for the Churches.

The first step toward breaking this pattern of settling for less than the best is the exposure and resolute elimination of the detractors from healthy church growth. Here we must be mercilessly honest with ourselves and the policies which formerly guided us during long periods of drought. There are five such detractors which must be boldly attacked and removed.

1. Drive for Excellence

The irresistible and inherent drive for excellence has three traditional expressions. First, the drive for *material excellence* as expressed in improved physical facilities and an increasingly elaborate program. Although all good in themselves, they stifle the emerging spiritual life and consciousness of the young Church when they become the goal or means of church growth. They are legitimately the results of growth, but only in a very minor sense are they the direct cause of growth.

Next is the drive for *spiritual excellence* which seeks to prematurely superimpose the characteristics of a mature Church upon a people just becoming Evangelical Christians. Even after their loyalties to old "gods" have changed and the people seek salvation in Christ, many of the fruits of righteousness might be slow in expressing themselves. We must make every effort to improve their understanding and experience of their new Christian faith. On the other hand, we cannot refuse at first contact those who come with mixed motives. Perhaps the parable of the wheat and the tares has meaning here. This will undoubtedly mean that there will be greater leakage (return to the world), but the increased intake will initiate new days of church growth.

Coupled with this drive is that which insists on *cultural, social* or even *racial excellence.* This irresistible drive of many Anglo-Saxon missionaries has led them into highly unresponsive segments of the population in search of converts in the hope of establishing a "respectable" Church. This attitude tragically misses the segments of greatest growth potential. Great growth has the beneficent side effect of later spilling over into other social classes, resulting in the long run in more converts from both classes. This is the story of the primitive Church, and is confirmed by the weight and wisdom of Toynbee's observation that the religion of the proletariat is adopted by the classes, instead of the reverse.

2. Distraction of Contemporary Issues

The second detractor which must be exposed and eliminated is the competitive preoccupation with contemporary political and ecclesiastical issues. These passionate concerns of the international Church are not conducive to evangelism and church growth. They are luxuries of the established non-growing Churches far too expensive for those who wish to be involved in vigorous extension of the Gospel of Christ.

3. Unwillingness to Innovate

The tenacious resistance to innovation with regard to methods and attitudes must be removed if we are to see stagnant patterns of growth broken. "We've always done it this way" is commonly heard from those who achieve the least growth. There is the inveterate drag of vested interests which are jealously protected and protracted by favorable budgetary appropriations. These golden calves of *status quo* and traditional programs must be recognized, resolutely ground up to fine powder and scattered on the River Plate if we wish to see God's blessings in Argentina.

4. Complacent Introversion

Another detracting posture which has many missionaries rationalizing that their Church is doing all right is the attitude of complacent introversion. Missionaries and church leaders holding this attitude are virtually incapable of admitting that the successes of others might contain lessons they should learn. They have a built-in aversion to, and unwillingness to learn from, the experience of Churches of different denominational identification. This is especially true of the established Churches' attitudes toward the Pentecostal Churches which are enjoying such healthy growth. Certainly we can be dispassionate enough to review their methods and attitudes while continuing to reserve judgment on many of their doctrines and emphases. None, even if they were enjoying relatively good growth, can afford to maintain themselves aloof from a sympathetic and systematic study of those situations where greater growth is happening.

5. Paternalistic Wolf in Modern Sheep's Clothing

The final detractor we would like to spell out is the old-fashioned paternalistic attitude. Modern-day expressions of this attitude have become highly sophisticated. It is the same old wolf masquerading in the sheep's clothing of modernized concepts of organization and thought control through token participation. This attitude springs from a desire to control the Church too closely and too long. Generally, people holding different shades of this view believe in what we might call "progressive" growth. Such growth is said to be produced through carefully programed organizational decisions and archaic concepts of devolution. We need to develop cordial feelings and attitudes toward movements which expand so rapidly that they absorb and control the parent organization. This is what happened to the Assembly of God mission effort in Brazil which today numbers over a million members. The mission still makes its contributions, but the main thrust of the movement is unmistakably Brazilian, not only in leadership, but even more important, in forms.

C. WHAT MUST EACH CHURCH DO NOW?

1. Honest Reevaluation

Once these distracting influences have been exposed and eliminated, each Church can begin the constructive task of devising methods and attitudes conducive to church growth. The first task which must be undertaken with determination is perhaps the most difficult. It is the honest reevaluation of the situation within her own denomination with regard to growth. The basis of such an investigation is the experience of other Churches which are achieving greater growth than she. The denominational profiles can serve as a beginning of this investigation, but deeper digging will be needed to get at all the facts which can be helpful. A careful, objective and dispassionate analysis of the nature of growth or non-growth in the denomination is absolutely necessary. The specific causes and reasons which have produced the present stage of development must be identified and defined as being either harmful or helpful to church growth. This can be a very painful process, but a penetrating inward look is the key to new beginnings. Time spent wisely in this venture will be amply rewarded and will serve as the basis of new patterns of growth.

2. Identification of Growth

The second task is the sympathetic identification of growth wherever it occurs and the clear understanding of its causes. Here we must be careful to distinguish between essential causes and accidental influences. Some attribute the growth of others to the most incidental factors. Hyper-emotionalism is frequently identified as the chief cause for Pentecostal growth. Or too much weight is given to British influence in the growth of the Plymouth Brethren. Although these elements were certainly influential, such simplified judgments are superficial. We will have to do some tenacious digging to get at the real causes. For example, probably one of the main reasons for Pentecostal growth is that their churches are located where the growth is happening. They are alert to responsiveness and deploy their forces accordingly. The factors developed in this book along with the profiles can aid in this discovery of where growth is happening. Probably one of the best ways to identify it is to take a long look to see what the church across town is doing to achieve its growth. Here we might have built-in prejudices because of the members they have taken from our church and, consequently, are blinded to the positive things these negative experiences could teach us. A sympathetic look, however, will identify far more keys to growth that we can adopt than those we will find we have to reject.

3. Development of New Methods and Attitudes

After an honest evaluation has been completed and the growth of other Churches has been identified and understood, we are ready to turn to a positive task. The best resources in manpower and organization must be mobilized to develop and implement new methods and attitudes capable of breaking the pattern of stagnation or slow growth and opening the entire Church to productive evangelism. The bases of a new approach and outlook on the work have been developed in Chapter XVII. The factors affecting church growth in Argentina must be applied to the situation prevailing in each Church. There must be a determined effort to eliminate attitudes and methods which, although adequate in another era, are not suitable to today's radically changing conditions and the unusual opportunities which they represent. Furthermore, new methods must be accompanied and supported by budgetary adjustments conducive to church growth. The fact that evangelism often has suffered from a shortage of funds in the past should help mission administrators see the need to bend all expenditures to the central task of evangelism.

4. Heading for a Breakthrough

When new approaches to the task of stimulating church growth have been devised, further and extremely difficult work still lies ahead. A breakthrough in traditional patterns of stagnation and slow growth may not be readily forthcoming. Because of the highly complicated nature of the combination of factors applicable to each specific situation and within each church, first efforts to apply new methods might meet with only limited results. A good deal of experimentation is called for until approaches adequate to the prevailing conditions and opportunities for growth are discovered. This difficult process should not discourage anyone. The attitude of faith of many of the newer Churches appearing in Latin America in the last half century has led them into many avenues of experimentation. Some of them have proved highly productive while others have produced only very limited results, and yet others have been almost total failures. When productive methods are discovered either by observation of other Churches or through experimentation they must be pressed into broad service. That vigorous growth is possible has been demonstrated by the breakthroughs experienced by several Churches in Argentina. Stagnation need not be normal, but imaginative and tenacious determination to secure a breakthrough is called for.

D. FURTHER RESEARCH NEEDED

The efforts to understand the Argentine church growth picture presented in this book are at best only preliminary. This has been the beginning of a continuing task which must now turn its attention to specific areas of further research. The Church Growth Research in Latin America team has conducted similar investigations on a continent-wide scale, but we still desperately need answers for most of the Latin American countries. This further investigation will get us deeper into the roots of church growth dynamics manifested in Argentina. These future observations of what is happening in Argentina will lead us into increasingly productive avenues of evangelism and church planting. What are some of the areas demanding further research which have been brought to light by this investigation?

1. Understanding Certain Churches

The first area for research is the clearer understanding of the internal dimensions of several denominations. Among these is the need for a more penetrating in-depth analysis of Pentecostalism. Our study has not touched the specific situation of the vast majority of the Pentecostal Churches. This rewarding task remains to be done, but it requires tedious and expensive field work at the grass-roots level. The true situation in the Lutheran Churches remains at best clouded. The predominantly ethnic character of these Churches presents the church growth investigator with a totally new set of factors. How men become active Christians within these Churches comprised largely of immigrants follows a completely different pattern. This is equally true of the processes leading to the abandonment of their faith, which frequently is thought of almost exclusively in terms of ethnic identity. A clearer picture of the various acculturative influences contributing to this abandonment is needed. The understanding of what lies behind ethnic Christianity in Argentina should be of keen interest to all Lutherans. Furthermore, a fuller insight into the causes of Plymouth Brethren growth is needed. This largest Evangelical Church in Argentina can provide us with further valuable keys to growth in that country.

2. Nature of Religious Convictions

In addition to these denominational studies, research must be conducted into the nature and degree of religious convictions in the different segments of the Evangelical community. Helpful insights would be received from a closer understanding of the average

Evangelical Christian's grasp of his own faith. An analysis of his previous religious experience and the reasons why he became an Evangelical Christian would shed light on the formation of future methods of evangelism. The discovery of what compels nominal Catholics to become Evangelical Christians would be a part of this study. Furthermore, we need to understand the attitudes of Roman Catholics toward the Evangelicals. The attitudes of the average class-conscious middle- and upper-class Argentine are somewhat understood, but we must capture the image that the average person carries.

3. Responsive Segments Identified

Throughout the study it has been observed that growth occurs where there is potential for growth. In other words, church growth is not accidental. Concerted effort on a broad scale must discover where these specific pockets of responsiveness are and identify them for rapid occupation. This will be a continuous task, but extremely valuable to church growth.

E. CONCLUSION

The contemporary golden opportunities for the generous expansion of the Evangelical Church in Argentina remain largely undiscovered and unexploited by many of the Churches. The discoveries of this survey and the discouraging or encouraging experiences of several of the Churches active in Argentina amply demonstrate this fact. Some continue in their patterns of stagnation and non-growth, while their sister congregations enjoy accelerated rates of church growth. Much like the *conquistadores,* some know where the "gold" lies buried and how to dig for it while others continue monotonously in their relatively unproductive ways. Certain segments of Argentina's population represent a growing potential for productive evangelism and church planting. No part of the Evangelical Church in Argentina need be satisfied with its present performance when accelerated patterns of growth can be normal. The opportunities are, in fact, so bright in some areas and among some sections of the population that we ought to see a "gold rush" of the Churches from low to high yield fields. This has been our burden, and a generous response of the Churches will be the reward of all.

Notes

Chapter 1

[1] Luzbetak (1963:244-248) provides us with an interesting discussion from a Catholic point of view of the causes and control of syncretism. Shepherd's (1966) treatment is from an Evangelical perspective.

[2] Pin's observations and hypotheses about religious motivations in Latin America are available in English in a volume co-authored with Francois Houtart, entitled *The Church and the Latin American Revolution*, New York, Sheed and Ward, 1965. The observations they make about Catholicism in the midst of these revolutionary times are accurate and exceedingly helpful for a clear understanding of what is happening on the religious scene in Latin America today.

Chapter 2

[1] The concept of *basic personality* was developed by Ralph Linton and Abram Kardiner. For a fuller treatment of its meaning see pp. 55-58.

Chapter 4

[1] Pendle's (1961:58, 59) excellent account and bibliographic material about this settlement, which preserved its religious distinctives in the face of an inhospitable atmosphere, should be consulted by those who wish to study this matter further.

Chapter 7

[1] An excellent treatment of the racial complexion of northern Argentina during colonial and post-colonial times is the article by Carlos Reyes (1958).

2 A description of these isolated villages is contained in the monograph *Santa Victoria e Iruya*, published by the Dirección de Estadística e Investigaciones Económicas of the Province of Salta in 1965.

Chapter 17

1 Arnold Strickon's (Heath 1965:324-341) article on "Class and Kinship in Argentina" develops the nature of these ties among the people of a typical *pampa* town. The insight provided in this article contributes greatly to the missionary's understanding of these relationships.

2 Of special interest here are the reasons for the cooling-off of a religious movement which have been developed by Nida (1960:150-155).

Bibliography

ACENELLI, Delfor R.
  1954 *Yo Fui Testigo,* Buenos Aires, Libreria Alianza.
AITKEN, James J.
  1966 "South American Division," *Review and Herald,* June 22, pp. 8-10.
  1967 Letter to author.
ALONSO, Isidoro
  1964 *La Iglesia en América Latina,* Friburgo, Suiza, F.E.R.E.S.
ANDERSON, Justice C.
  1968 Letter to author.
ASAMBLEAS DE DIOS
  1966a *Estadística—Asambleas Afiliadas Año 1966,* Xerox copy of type-written manuscript.
  1966b *Totales Estadísticos Año 1966,* Xerox copy of typewritten manuscript.
ASSEMBLIES OF GOD
  1962 *Argentina,* Springfield, Missouri, Foreign Missions Department.
BALL, Henry C.
  1950 "The Seed is Growing," *The Pentecostal Evangel,* June 3, p. 6.
BARCLAY, Wade Crawford
  1957 *History of Methodist Missions,* III, New York, The Board of Missions of the Methodist Church.
BEACH, Harlan P., BURTON, St. John
  1916 *World Statistics of Christian Missions,* New York, Committee on Reference and Counsel of the Foreign Missions Conference of North America.
BEACH, Harlan P., FAHS, Charles H.
  1925 *World Missionary Atlas,* New York, Institute of Social and Religious Research.

244   MAN, MILIEU, AND MISSION IN ARGENTINA

BEDFORD, Allen Benjamin
      1957 "A Critique of Argentine Mission Work in the Light of Funda-
            mentals Laid Down by Christ and Applied by the Apostles." An
            unpublished Master of Theology thesis, Southwestern Theolog-
            ical Seminary, Ft. Worth, Texas.
BIBLE SOCIETY RECORD
      1967 "The Tavern That Became a Church," 112, 1:13.
BINGLE, E. J., GRUBB, Kenneth G.
      1957 *World Christian Handbook—1957.* London, World Dominion
            Press.
BLOCH-HOELL, Nils
      1964 *The Pentecostal Movement.* Oslo, Universitetsforlaget.
BRITISH AND FOREIGN BIBLE SOCIETY
      1825 *The Twenty-first Report.* London.
BROWN, Hubert W.
      1901 *Latin America.* New York, Fleming H. Revell Company.
BROWN, Paul E.
      1953 "Satan's Power Broken," *The Pentecostal Evangel,* 2053:7.
BROWNING, Webster E.
      1928 *The River Plate Republics.* London, World Dominion Press.
BRUCE, James
      1953 *Those Perplexing Argentines.* New York, Longmans, Green and
            Company.
BUCKWALTER, Albert
      1955 "Building the Church Among the Toba Indians," *The Mennonite
            Quarterly Review,* 29, 4:263-275.
      1967 Letter to author.
CAMPBELL, Norman
      1966 "A Church for Mar de Plata," *The Pentecostal Evangel,* 2729:6,
            7.
CANCLINI, Arnoldo, ed.
      n.d. *Los Bautistas en Marcha,* Buenos Aires, Junta Bautista de Publi-
            caciones.
CANCLINI, Santiago
      1948 *Escritos de Pablo Besson.* Buenos Aires, Junta Bautista de Publi-
            caciones.
      1958 "Argentine Baptist Convention," in Norman Wade Cox, ed.,
            Encyclopedia of Southern Baptists. Nashville, Broadman, I:59,
            60.
CARROLL, Daniel Marion
      1960 "The Development of Religious Education in the Baptist Work
            of Argentina 1909-1959." An unpublished Doctor of Religious
            Education dissertation, Southwestern Baptist Theological Semi-
            nary, Forth Worth, Texas.
CASTRO, Emilio
      1963 "Christian Response to the Latin American Revolution," *Chris-
            tianity and Crisis,* 23, 15:160-163.
CHILDS, Howard L.
      1955 "The Constitutions of the Latin American Republics," *Consul-*

tation on Religious Liberty in Latin America, Part II, Committee on Cooperation in Latin America.

CHRISTIAN AND MISSIONARY ALLIANCE

Minutes of the General Council (1959, 1960, 1961, 1963, 1966) and *Annual Report* (1958, 1959, 1960, 1961, 1962, 1965).

1964 *Missionary Atlas.* Harrisburg, Pennsylvania, Christian Publications, Inc.

CHRISTIAN CENTURY

1954 "But What About Hicks?" 71, 27:814-815.

CHURCH GROWTH RESEARCH IN LATIN AMERICA

Files, Pasadena, California.

CHURCH OF THE NAZARENE

1965 *World Mission Field Statistics.* Kansas City, Missouri.

CLARK, Francis E., CLARK, Harriet A.

1909 *The Gospel in Latin Lands.* New York, Macmillan.

CLARK, R. B.

1938 *Under the Southern Cross.* Harrisburg, Pennsylvania, Christian Publications.

CLIFFORD, T. Alejandro

1954 *Bajo la Cruz del Sur.* Córdoba, Argentina, Ediciones Amanecer.

1967 Letter to author.

1968 Letter to author.

CLISSOLD, Stephen

1965 *Latin America.* London, Hutchinson.

CONN, Charles W.

1959 *Where the Saints Have Trod.* Cleveland, Tennessee, Pathway Press.

CONSERVATIVE BAPTIST FOREIGN MISSION SOCIETY

1966 *Annual Field Report, Argentina–1966.*

CONSIDINE, John Joseph, ed.

1964 *The Church and the New Latin America.* Notre Dame, Indiana, Fides.

1966 *The Religious Dimensions in the New Latin America.* Notre Dame, Indiana, Fides.

CONVENCION EVANGELICA BAUTISTA

1965 *LVII Asamblea Anual* (1964-1965), Actas e Informes.

1966 *LVIII Asamblea Anual* (1965-1966), Informes.

CONVERSE, Hyla Stuntz

1961 *Raise a Signal.* New York, Friendship Press.

COXILL, H. Wakelin, GRUBB, Kenneth G., eds.

1962 *World Christian Handbook–1962.* London, World Dominion Press.

1967 *World Christian Handbook–1968.* London, Lutterworth Press.

CULPEPPER, Hugo

1958 "Missions in Argentina," Norman Wade Cox, ed., *Encyclopedia of Southern Baptists.* Nashville, Broadman, I:59.

DAMBORIENA, Prudencio

1962 *El Protestantismo en América Latina.* Friburgo, Suiza, F.E.R.E.S.

DANIELS, Margarette
    1916 *Makers of South America.* New York, Missionary Education
         Movement.
D'ANTONIO, William D., PIKE, Frederick
    1964 *Religion, Revolution and Reform.* New York, Frederick A.
         Praeger.
DARINO, Agustín F., SNYDER, Mario O.
    1966 "Argentine Church Plans Ahead," *Gospel Herald,* 59, 39:
         880-881.
DAVIS, J. Merle
    1943 *The Evangelical Church in the River Plate Republics.* New York,
         International Missionary Council.
DEHAINAUT, Raymond K.
    1967 "The Crisis in the Argentine University Reform Movement,"
         Motive, 27, 4:40-43.
DENNIS, James S., BEACH, Harlan P., FAHS, Charles H.
    1911 *World Atlas of Christian Missions.* New York, Student Volunteer
         Movement for Foreign Missions.
DERBY, Marian
    1960 "The Mission to Latin American Countries," *The Christian Mis-
         sion Today.* New York, Abingdon Press, pp. 142-153.
    1967 Letter to author.
DERBY, Marian, ELLIS, James F.
    1961 *Latin American Lands in Focus.* New York, Board of Missions of
         the Methodist Church.
DE SANTA ANA, Julio
    1963 "Argentina and Uruguay at the Crossroads," *Christianity and
         Crisis,* 23, 5:224-228.
DICKMANN, Enrique
    1946 *Poblacion e Imigracion.* Buenos Aires, Editorial Losada, S.A.
DIRECCION DE ESTADISTICA E INVESTIGACIONES ECONOMICAS
    1965 *Santa Victoria e Iruya.* Salta, Argentina, Provincia de Salta.
DISCIPLES OF CHRIST
    1938 *Survey of Service.* St. Louis, Christian Board of Publications.

         The Christian Churches, Yearbook (1916, 1920, 1925, 1930,
         1935, 1940, 1945, 1950, 1955, 1960, 1965). Indianapolis, In-
         diana, International Convention of Christian Churches.
DUBOIS, Cora
    1960 *The People of Alor.* Cambridge, Mass., Harvard University Press.
DUPLESSIS, David J.
    1958 "Twentieth-Century Pentecostal Movements," *International Re-
         view of Missions,* 47:193-201.
ECHOES OF SERVICE
              (1900, 1901, 1910, 1915, 1920, 1921, 1924, 1925, 1930, 1931,
              1934, 1935, 1940, 1941, 1960).
EMMERSON, Kenneth H.
    1957 "Divine Dividends in Argentina," *Review and Herald,* December
         5, pp. 16-17.

ENNS, Arno W.
   1961 "Comparison of Field Surveys of 1956 and 1961." Unpublished table of Conservative Baptist Statistics for 1956 and 1961.
   1966 "Over the Argentine Wall," *Impact,* 23, 8:4, 5, 15.
ERICSSON, Augusto
   1967 Letter to author.
ESTANDARTE EVANGÉLICO
   1966 "Cuarenta Años Cumple la Librería 'La Aurora,' " 84, 5:73.
ESTRADA, Santiago
   1963 *Nuestras Relaciones con la Iglesia: Hacia un Concordato entre la Sede Apostólica y el Estado Argentino,* Buenos Aires, Ediciones Theoria.
FILLOL, Tomás Roberto
   1961 *Social Factors in Economic Development–The Argentine Case.* M.I.T. Press, Cambridge, Mass.
FLAGG, William M.
   1968 Letter to author.
FORSBERG, Gösta
   1967 Letter to author.
FUERBRINGER, L., ed.
   1925 *Men and Missions.* St. Louis, Mo., Concordia Publishing House.
LA GACETA
   1964 Tucumán, Argentina, 52, 18.997:1.
GARBER, J. D.
   1966 "Vision in Argentina," *Gospel Herald,* 59, 18:420.
GEHMAN, Henry S.
   1958 "Observations and Impressions," *The Princeton Seminary Bulletin,* 51, 4:35-43.
GLOVER, Robert Hall, KANE, J. Herbert
   1960 *The Progress of World-Wide Missions.* New York, Harper & Brothers.
GOSLIN, Tomás S.
   1956 *Los Evangélicos en la América Latina.* Buenos Aires, Editorial La Aurora.
GREENMAN, Robert
   1967 Letter to author.
GRUBB, Kenneth G., BINGLE, E. J.
   1949 *World Christian Handbook–1949.* London, World Dominion Press.
   1952 *World Christian Handbook–1952.* London, World Dominion Press.
HARGRAVE, Vessie D.
   1967 Letter to author.
HARLOW, R. E., SMART, John
   1964 *Who Is My Neighbor?* New York, Fields.
HEATH, Dwight B., ADAMS, Richard N., eds.
   1965 *Contemporary Cultures and Societies of Latin America.* New York, Random House.

HERRING, Hubert
        1961 *A History of Latin America.* New York, Alfred A. Knopf.
HERSHEY, T. K.
        1961 *I'd Do It Again.* Elkhart, Ind., Mennonite Board of Missions and
              Charities.
HISPANIC AMERICAN HISTORICAL REVIEW
        1954 Duke University Press, 34, 4:482.
HODGES, Melvin
        1954 "Buenos Aires Challenge," *The Pentecostal Evangel,* 2105:6.
        1955 "A Step Forward in Buenos Aires," *The Pentecostal Evangel,*
              2122:9.
        1967 Letter to author.
HODGES, Serna M.
        1956 *Look on the Fields.* Springfield, Mo., Gospel Publishing House.
HOUTART, Francois, PIN, Emile
        1965 *The Church and the Latin American Revolution.* New York,
              Sheed & Ward.
IGLESIA METODISTA ARGENTINA
        1960 *Actas Oficiales de la 68* (Sexagésima octava) *Reunión de la
              Conferencia Anual de la Argentina.* Buenos Aires, Imprenta
              Metodista.
ILLICH, Ivan
        1967 "The Seamy Side of Charity," *America,* 116, 3:88-91.
INGENIEROS, José
        1918 *Sociología Argentina.* Buenos Aires, J. Rosso.
IRVINE, Eastman E., ed.
        1948 *World Almanac and Book of Facts for 1948.* New York, New
              York World-Telegram.
KARDINER, Abram
        1939 *The Individual and His Society.* New York, Columbia University
              Press.
        1945a "The Concept of Basic Personality Structure as an Operational
              Tool in the Social Sciences," Ralph Linton, ed., *The Science of
              Man in the World Crisis.* New York, Columbia University Press.
        1945b *The Psychological Frontiers of Society.* New York, Columbia
              University Press.
KENNEDY, JOHN J.
        1958 *Catholicism, Nationalism and Democracy in Argentina.* Notre
              Dame, Indiana, University of Notre Dame Press.
KESSLER, Jean Baptiste August
        1967 *A Study of the Older Protestant Missions and Churches in Perú
              and Chile.* Goes, Oosterbaan & le Cointre, N.V.
KING, Louis L.
        1967 Letter to author.
KLUCKHOHN, Florence Rockwood
        1954 "Dominant and Variant Value Orientations," in Kluckhohn,
              Murray and Schneider, eds., *Personality in Nature, Society and
              Culture.* New York, Alfred A. Knopf.

KRATZ, James D.
    n.d.   *Christian Education and the Toba Church.* Unpublished manu-
            script.
    1966   "Argentine Conference," *Gospel Herald,* 59, 12:287-288.
    1967   Letter to author.
LALIVE D'EPINAY, Christian
    1967   "The Training of Pastors and Theological Education—The Case
            of Chile," *International Review of Missions,* 56, 222:186-192.
LATOURETTE, Kenneth Scott
    1961   *Christianity in a Revolutionary Age,* Vol. III (The Nineteenth
            Century Outside Europe). New York, Harper & Brothers.
LEAR, Gilberto M. J.
    n.d.   *The Argentine Republic.* London, Pickering Inglis.
    1951   *Un Explorador Valiente.* Lanús, Argentina, Librería Editorial
            Cristiana.
LENKER, J. N.
    1896   *Lutherans in All Lands.* Milwaukee, Wisconsin, Lutherans in All
            Lands Company.
LIGGETT, Thomas J.
    1967   Letter to author.
LINTON, Ralph
    1945   *The Cultural Background of Personality.* New York, Appleton-
            Century-Crofts.
LOEWEN, Jacob, BUCKWALTER, Albert, KRATZ, James
    1965   "Shamanism, Illness, and Power in Toba Church Life," *Practical
            Anthropology,* 12, 6:250-280.
LONG, Luman H., ed.
    1966   *World Almanac—1967.* New York, Newspaper Enterprises Asso-
            ciation.
LOPEZ, Floreal
    1967   "Church Grows in Argentina," *Missions,* 31, 11:14.
LUTHERAN CHURCH IN AMERICA
    n.d.   *LCA World Missions 1965-66.* New York, Board of World Mis-
            sions, Lutheran Church in America.
    n.d.   *Argentina.* New York, Board of World Missions, Lutheran
            Church in America.
LUTHERAN CHURCH—MISSOURI SYNOD
    n.d.   *Argentina and Its Mission Outreach Countries.* St. Louis, Mo.,
            Concordia Publishing House.
    n.d.   *Our Missions in Argentina.* St. Louis, Mo., Evangelical Lutheran
            Synod of Missouri, Ohio and Other States.

            Statistical Yearbook (1905, 1910, 1920, 1925, 1930, 1935,
            1940, 1945, 1950, 1955, 1960, 1965) *of the Evangelical Luther-
            an Synod of Missouri, Ohio and Other States.* St. Louis, Mo.,
            Concordia Publishing House.
LUZBETAK, Louis J.
    1963   *The Church and Cultures.* Techny, Illinois, Divine Word Pub-
            lishers.

250 MAN, MILIEU, AND MISSION IN ARGENTINA

MACKAY, John A.

1935 *That Other America.* New York, Friendship Press.

1965 "Latin America and Revolution," *Christian Century,* 82, 46:1409-1412 and 82, 47:1439-1443.

MAFUD, Julio

1959 *El Desarraigo Argentino, Clave Argentina para un Estudio Social Americano.* Buenos Aires, Editorial Americalee.

1965 *Psicología de la Viveza Criolla.* Buenos Aires, Editorial Americalee, S.R.L.

MARGRETT, Anna Sowell

1951 *Under the Southern Cross.* Nashville, Broadman Press.

MATHER, Cotton

1901 *Diary of Cotton Mather.* New York, Frederick Unger Publishing Co.

MCGAVRAN, Donald Anderson

1955 *Bridges of God.* New York, Friendship Press.

1959 *How Churches Grow.* London, World Dominion Press.

MCGAVRAN, Donald A., ed.

1965 *Church Growth and the Christian Mission.* New York, Harper & Row.

MEANS, Frank K.

1960 *Across the Bridge.* Nashville, Convention Press.

MECHAM, J. Lloyd

1966 *Church and State in Latin America.* Chapel Hill, University of North Carolina Press.

MENNONITE BOARD OF MISSIONS AND CHARITIES, eds.

1958 *The Living Church in Action.* (The 52nd Annual Meeting) Elkhart, Ind., Mennonite Board of Missions and Charities.

1964 *Stewards of the Gospel—1964.* Scottdale, Pa., Mennonite Publishing House.

MERRITT, Hilton

1967 Typescript of telephone interview with the Rev. Tommy Hicks. May 22, 1967.

METHODIST CHURCH

n.d. *Partnership in Missions – 1967.* New York, Board of Missions of the Methodist Church.

MILLER, Edward R.

1964 *Thy God Reigneth.* Fontana, California, World Missionary and Prayer Fellowship.

MISSIONARY HERALD

1824 "South America," 20, 12:374-376.

MISSIONARY RESEARCH LIBRARY

1966 *North American Protestant Foreign Mission Agencies.* New York, Missionary Research Library.

MONTGOMERY, J. Dexter

1956 *Disciples of Christ in Argentina.* St. Louis, Mo., Bethany Press.

MONTI, Daniel P.

1967 "Centenario de la Organización del Culto en Castellano en el Río de la Plata," *El Estandarte Evangélico,* 85, 3:5-9.

MÖRNER, Magnus
    1965 *The Expulsion of the Jesuits.* New York, Alfred A. Knopf.
NELSON, Wilton M.
    1966 "Breve Historia de la Iglesia en América Latina," *Pensamiento Cristiano,* 13, 50:97-106.
NEWSWEEK
    1966 "Argentina, Books vs. Boots," September 5, 1966, p. 49.
NICHOL, John Thomas
    1966 *Pentecostalism.* New York, Harper & Row.
NIDA, Eugene A.
    1959 "The Role of Cultural Anthropology in Christian Missions," *Practical Anthropology,* 6, 3:110-116.
    1960 *Message and Mission.* New York, Harper & Row.
    1961a "Christo-Paganism," *Practical Anthropology,* 8, 11:1-15.
    1961b "The Indigenous Churches in Latin America," *Practical Anthropology,* 8, 3:97-105.
    1961c "Communication of the Gospel to Latin Americans," *Practical Anthropology,* 8, 4:145-156.
NUESCH, Daniel
    1967 Letter to author.

OLSEN, M. Ellsworth
    1926 *A History of the Origin and Progress of Seventh-Day Adventists.* Washington, D.C., Review and Herald Publishing Association.
O'MARA, Richard
    1966 "The Church in Argentina," *Commonweal,* 84, 22:612-614.

PAMPA BREEZES
    1967a "Cosmos Leaders of Latin America Meet in Argentina," 36:4.
    1967b " 'Avanzadas," A Pattern of Growth," 36:5.
PARKER, Joseph I.
    1938 *Interpretative Statistical Survey of the World Mission of the Christian Church.* New York, International Missionary Council.
PAYNE, Will, WILSON, Charles T. W.
    1904 *Missionary Pioneering in Bolivia, with Some Account of Work in Argentina.* London, Echoes of Service.
PENDLE, George
    1961 *Argentina.* London, Oxford University Press.
    1963a *Argentina.* 3rd ed., London, Oxford University Press.
    1963b *A History of Latin America.* Baltimore, Penguin Books.
PIKE, Frederick B., ed.
    1964 *The Conflict Between Church and State in Latin America.* New York, Alfred A. Knopf.
PIN, Emile
    1963 *Elementos para una Sociología del Catolicismo Latino-americano.* Friburgo, Suiza, F.E.R.E.S.
POTENZE, Jaime
    1966 "The Shadow of Peron," *Commonweal,* 83, 22:662, 663.
POWELL, David
    1967 Letter to author.

POWELL, Reginald
        1967   Letter to author.
PRIMERA PLANA
        1966   "Iglesia Argentina: El Exodo de Curas," 4, 177:40-45.
RAMOS, Samuel
        1963   *Profile of Man and Culture in Mexico.* New York, McGraw-Hill.
RAY, T. B., ed.
        1910   *Southern Baptist Foreign Missions.* Nashville, Sunday School
               Board, Southern Baptist Convention.
READ, William R.
        1965   *New Patterns of Church Growth in Brazil.* Grand Rapids, William
               B. Eerdmans.
REYBURN, William D.
        1959   *The Toba Indians of the Argentine Chaco: An Interpretative
               Report.* Elkhart, Indiana, Mennonite Board of Missions and
               Charities.
REYES, Carlos
        1958   "El Indio, El Negro y El Gringo en Martín Fierro," *Revista del
               Instituto de Antropología.* Universidad Nacional de Tucumán,
               Argentina, 9, 1:59-99.
ROBERTS, W. Dayton
        1963   "Pentecost South of the Border," *Christianity Today,* 7, 21:32.
RYAN, Edwin
        1932   *The Church in the South American Republics.* New York, Bruce
               Publishing Company.
RYCROFT, W. Stanley
        1958   *Religion and Faith in Latin America.* Philadelphia, Westminster
               Press.
RYCROFT, W. Stanley, CLEMMER, Myrtle M.
        1961   *A Statistical Study of Latin America.* New York, United Presby-
               terian Church in the U.S.A.
        1963   *A Study of Urbanization in Latin America.* New York, United
               Presbyterian Church in the U.S.A.
SABANES, Carlos M.
        1966   "Urbanization in Latin America," *International Review of Mis-
               sions,* 55, 219:307-312.
SARAVIA, José Manuel
        1959   *Argentina 1959, Un Estudio Sociológico.* Buenos Aires, Edi-
               ciones del Atlántico.
SCHISLER, Jack
        1967   Interview.
SCOBIE, James R.
        1964   *Argentina, A City and a Nation.* New York, Oxford University
               Press.
SCOPES, Wilfred, ed.
        1962   *The Christian Ministry in Latin America and the Caribbean.*
               Geneva, World Council of Churches.
SEVENTH-DAY ADVENTISTS
               Statistical Report of the Seventh-Day Adventists (1905, 1910,

1915, 1920, 1925, 1930, 1935, 1940, 1945, 1950, 1955, 1960, 1965). Takoma Park, Washington, D. C., General Conference of Seventh-Day Adventists.

1956 *The Story of Our Church.* Mountain View, California, Pacific Press Publishing Association.

1966 *Encyclopedia of Seventh-Day Adventists,* Vol. 1. Takoma Park, Washington, D. C., Review & Herald Publishing Association.

1967 *Seventh-Day Adventist Yearbook–1967,* Washington, D.C., General Conference of the Seventh-Day Adventists.

SHANK, J. W., *et al.*

1943 *The Gospel under the Southern Cross.* Scottdale, Pa., Mennonite Publishing House.

SHAULL, Richard

1963 "The New Revolutionary Mood in Latin America," *Christianity and Crisis,* 23, 5:44-48.

SHEPHERD, Jack F.

1966 "Missions and Syncretism," *Study Papers, Congress on the Church's Worldwide Mission,* April 9-16, 1966, Wheaton, Ill.

SOUTHERN BAPTIST CONVENTION

1948 *Mark Time, Retreat or Advance?* Richmond, Virginia, Foreign Mission Board, Southern Baptist Convention.

1966 *The Field is the World.* Richmond, Virginia, Foreign Mission Board, Southern Baptist Convention.

1967 Letter to author.

SPALDING, Arthur Whitefield

1962 *Origin and History of Seventh-Day Adventists.* Washington, D.C., Review and Herald Publishing Association.

SPOONER, Stephen G.

1967 Letter to author.

STEWARD, Julian H., FARON, Louis C.

1959 *Native Peoples of South America.* New York, McGraw Hill.

STOKES, Louie W.

1950 "Work in Argentina," *The Pentecostal Evangel,* January 7, p. 11.

1954 "We Must Hold These Converts," *The Pentecostal Evangel,* 2109:7.

1955 "Crowds Throng New Center," *The Pentecostal Evangel,* July 3, p. 7.

1958 "Busy Days," *The Pentecostal Evangel,* 2287:14.

1965 "The City of Good Airs," *The Pentecostal Evangel,* 2652:9.

1967 Letter to author.

STUNTZ, Homer C.

1916 *South American Neighbors.* New York, Methodist Book Concern.

SVENSKA KYRKAN

1967 "The Swedish Church Work in Argentina." Typewritten manuscript.

TAMAGNO, Roberto

1963 *Sarmiento, Los Liberales y el Imperialismo Inglés.* Buenos Aires, A. Pena Lillo.

TATLOCK, Lloyd
    1967 Letter to author.
TAYLOR, Carl C.
    1948 *Rural Life in Argentina.* Baton Rouge, La., Louisiana State University Press.
TAYLOR, Jaime R.
    1967 Letter to author.
THOMSON, James
    1827 *Letters on the Moral and Religious State of South America.* London, Nisbet.
    1847 "South America No. VII," *Evangelical Christendom,* I:387-389.
TIBESAR, Antonini
    1966 "The Shortage of Priests in Latin America," *The Americas, 22,* 4:413-420.
TIME
    1966 "Argentina, Trouble from the Pulpits," 88, 9:28.
TOYNBEE, Arnold J.
    1962 *America and the World Revolution.* New York, Oxford University Press.
UNITED CHRISTIAN MISSIONARY SOCIETY
    1965 *Handbook of the United Christian Missionary Society.* Indianapolis, United Christian Missionary Society.
U.S. NEWS AND WORLD REPORT
    1966 "Why the Military Took Over in Argentina," 61, 2:59, 60.
VOTH, Myron C.
    1967 Letter to author.
WEBER, Lewis S.
    1945 *Argentina From Within.* Scottdale, Pa., Mennonite Publishing House.
WENGER, A. Grace
    1961 *God Builds the Church in Latin America.* Scottdale, Pa., Herald Press.
WHITAKER, Arthur P., ed.
    1942 *Latin America and the Enlightenment.* New York, D. Appleton-Century.
WHITAKER, Arthur P.
    1964 *Argentina.* Englewood Cliffs, New Jersey, Prentice-Hall.
WHYTE, William F., HOLMBERG, Allan R.
    1956 "Human Problems of U.S. Enterprise in Latin America," *Human Organizations,* 15, 3:1-40.
WINEHOUSE, Irwin
    1959 *The Assemblies of God.* New York, Vantage.
WONDERLY, William
    1961 "Cities of Latin America, Challenge to the Church," *Latin American Evangelist,* Sept.-Oct., pp. 3-5.
WORLD CALL
    1925 "Congress on Christian Work in South America," 7, 2:30.
YODER, Charles F.
    1930 *The Argentine Mission Field.* Ashland, Ohio, Brethren Publishing Company.

Index

Alberdi, Juan Bautista, 26, 37, 43
American Bible Society, 73
Andress, Paul, 111
Anglican Church, 25, 45, 66, 72, 176
anthropology, 56f., 128
Argentine Baptist Convention; see
  Convención Evangélica Bautista
Ariel, 45, 47
Armenian Brethren, 176
Armenian Congregationalists, 73, 176
Armenian Evangelical Church, 176
Arrastia, Cecilio, 154
Asamblea Cristiana, 83
Asamblea Cristiana Cultural, 83
Asambleas Bíblicas, 176
Assemblies of God, 76-87, 180, 188,
  236
Assemblies of God—Canada, 83

Baptist General Conference, 105, 176
Baptists, 70, 73, 78, 159, 165, 229
Baptists, Conservative, 96-105, 120,
  215
Baptists, Southern, 88, 139, 166-174,
  177, 179f., 190, 212
Barbieri, Sante Uberto, 140
basic personality, 15, 38, 43, 54-66
Besson, Pablo, 159, 166ff., 171, 174
Bolivia, Bolivian, 13, 40, 72, 97ff.,
  105, 149, 225f.
Brazil, 36, 59, 72, 92, 97, 115f., 127,
  134, 184f., 192, 224f., 236

Brethren Church (Ashland, Ohio),
  176
Brethren Church (Winona Lake,
  Ind.), 176
Brigham, John, 72
British and Foreign Bible Society, 24,
  70f., 166
British and Foreign School Society,
  70, 166
Browning, Webster E., 199ff., 220
Bruner, Juan Pedro, 167
Buenos Aires, 25, 31, 41, 47f., 70,
  72, 76f., 81, 87f., 93, 96, 111,
  115, 123ff., 127, 134, 141, 145,
  147ff., 160, 166ff., 170, 212
Buteler, Alfonso M., 29

Catamarca, 96, 105
caudillo, 26, 28, 38f., 43, 46, 48, 50,
  62
Cervantes, Miguel, 37f.
Chaco, 73, 82, 96, 103, 125, 141,
  151, 207
Chile, 31, 33, 36, 49, 59, 64, 72,
  168, 171, 184f., 192, 224f.,
Chiriguano, 97f., 105; *see also* Guar-
  ani
Christian and Missionary Alliance,
  75, 78, 88-95, 96, 106, 180, 201
Christian community, 183ff.
Christian Missions in Many Lands,
  145, 147

christo-paganism, 21
Church of England; see Anglican Church
Church of God (Anderson, Ind.), 176
Church of God (Cleveland, Tenn.), 54, 58, 82f.
Church of God Prophecy, 83
Church of Scotland; see Presbyterian
Church of the Nazarene, 176
Cisneros, Cardinal Jiménez de, 20
Clifford, Jaime, 145, 154
Colegio Ward, 107, 110f., 137, 139f.
Colombia, 31, 225f.
communicant membership, 175ff.
community, 34f., 42f., 62, 210ff.
Concilio Evangélico de Iglesias, 176
Congregational Christian Board, 176
"conservative evangelical," 191f., 194, 196, 214, 233
Convención Evangélica Bautista, 172f., 177
cooperation, 106f., 112f., 137, 139f., 153
Córdoba, 51, 115, 125, 147f., 150, 154, 171
Corrientes, 92, 96
Creighton, David, 70
cultural milieu, 14f., 54f., 228

Davis, Merle J., 83, 89, 179, 199, 203f.
Dempster, John, 72
Disciples of Christ, 106-113, 137, 180, 203, 229
DuBois, Cora, 58

Easdale, Thomas, 97
Ecuador, 31, 225
education, 108ff., 116, 139, 143, 160
Emmanuel Holiness Church, 83
English Pentecostals, 83
Entre Ríos, 88, 158f., 160, 168
Europeanism, 44ff.
Evangelical Foreign Missions Association, 189f., 204
Evangelical Union of South America, 97, 177
Ewen, J. H. L., 145

Facultad Evangélica de Teología, 107, 111, 137, 142f., 200
Federales, 48
Federation of Evangelical Churches, 96, 107, 188f.
fellowship, 35, 211, 212
Fernández, Maximinio, 168
Fillol, Tomás Roberto, 56, 60, 62, 122, 209f.
forgiveness, 61, 66, 203, 208ff., 212, 219
formalism, 62f.
Four Square Gospel, 83
Francescon, Louis, 76
Frei, Eduardo, 50
functional substitute, 155f.

Gardiner, Allan, 72f., 207
Gattinoni, Juan E., 140
gaucho, 22, 39-44, 48, 124
Gehman, Henry S., 120
Graham, Billy, 79, 154
Greenman, Robert, 97
Gregory VII, 21
Guaraní, 23, 97; see also Chiriguano
guilt, 61, 66, 208f.
Guinness, Grattan, 145
Güiraldes, Ricardo, 44

Hart, Joseph L., 166
Hauge, Hans Nielson, 121
Hernández, José, 39, 44
Hershey, T. K., 123
Hicks, Theodore, 77ff., 90, 92, 188, 206f.
Holy Spirit, 36, 71, 85, 89, 102, 206ff., 214, 221, 228, 232, 234

idealism, 38, 61f.
Iglesia Evangélica Pentecostal, 83
Iglesia Reformada, 177
Iglesia Unida Evangélica; see United Evangelical Church
Illich, Ivan, 31
immigrants, 27, 35, 40ff., 73, 99, 114f., 147ff., 159
Indian, 39f., 72, 128, 209, 226
individualism, 38, 61f.
Ingram, J. H., 82

International Foreign Missions Association, 189f., 204
Irigoyen, Hipólito, 47
Irish Baptists, 177
Italian, 40f., 82, 107f., 147

Jesuits, 20, 23, 26, 224
John XXIII, 29, 202
Jujuy, 96ff., 101, 147ff., 150

Kardiner, Abram, 56f.
Kluckhohn, Florence R., 56f., 60, 194

Lagar, John R., 82, 128
La Pampa, 93
La Plata, 88
La Rioja, 96, 105
Larrain Errazuriz, Manuel, 30
Las Casas, Bartolomé de, 21
laymen, 94f., 104, 156, 164, 171, 214ff.
leadership, 63, 86, 208, 216ff.
Lear, Gilbert, M. J., 154, 207
Linton, John, 97
Linton, Ralph, 56f.
literary contribution, 43ff.
Little, George, 97
Loyola, Ignatius, 20, 23
Lutheran Church—Missouri, 73, 114-122, 180, 194
Lutheran Church, 27, 73, 114, 119ff., 159, 176f., 239

Mackay, John A., 37, 220
Mafud, Julio, 41ff., 58, 60, 210, 216
Martín Fierro, 32, 39, 44
Martínez, Pedro, 128, 207
masses, 41, 65, 90, 99, 111, 200, 203, 211f., 226ff.
Mataco, 73
Mather, Cotton, 69
Matórraz, Cristóbal, 151, 207
Mazzucco, Marcos, 82
McGavran, Donald A., 211
Mendoza, 29, 147, 168, 170
Mennonite Church, 73, 78, 105, 122-135, 180, 188f.
mestizo, 22, 40, 98f.

Methodist Church, 71f., 74, 78, 107, 110, 136-144, 171, 179ff., 202, 213f., 222, 229
Mexico, 33, 36, 59, 225
Míguez Bonino, José, 142
Miller, Edward, 119
Milne, Andrew, 73
ministerial training, 87, 102, 104, 121, 126f., 134f., 154, 173, 199ff., 218, 228ff.
mission-church relationship, 89, 111, 133, 136f., 156f., 163, 172, 192f., 201, 221f., 236
Mitre, Bartolomé, 48, 74
moralism, 60f., 208f.
Moravians, 69
Morris, William, 141, 207
Movimiento Cristiano y Misionero, 79, 83
Müller, George, 145

national consciousness, 46ff.
nationalism, 47, 63f., 116, 201, 220ff.
natural needs, 33, 222f.
New Testament Missionary Union, 177
Norske Pinsevenners Ytremisjon, 83

Onganía, Juan Carlos, 30
opportunities, 24f., 33, 35, 40, 71

Paraguay, 40, 92f., 97, 127, 134, 141, 168, 171, 225
Patagonia, 40, 72, 75, 79, 170
Payne, William, 75, 145ff., 149, 154, 207
Pentecostal Churches, 15, 25, 33, 54, 64, 77-87, 110, 176f., 179, 181, 184, 189, 191f., 194, 203, 214, 216, 218, 221ff., 226, 229, 236f., 239
Penzotti, Francisco, 74, 106
people movement, 128, 151, 188, 207
Perón, Juan Domingo, 27f., 34, 47, 50f., 77f., 163, 170
Perú, 74, 224f.
Pin, Emile, 32-35

Plymouth Brethren, 75, 77f., 103, 108, 139, 145-157, 171, 179ff., 188, 190, 203, 206, 212, 214f., 219, 222, 237, 239
Pravin, Theophilus, 72
Presbyterian, 71f., 137, 176; see also Church of Scotland
priests, shortage of, 31, 35, 224
proletariat, 50ff.; see masses

Quechua, 98
Quixote, 37f.

Ramos, Samuel, 46, 56, 58
Reformed Church (Dutch), 73, 177
Reformed Church (French), 177
religious liberty, 27f., 72, 74, 148, 167, 170
religious motivations, 32ff., 222f.
religious temperament, 36, 159, 164f., 194ff., 213f., 220
Reyburn, William, 128
Riffel, Jorge, 158
Rivadavia, Bernardino, 26, 46, 70, 72
Roca, Julio, 74
Rodó, Enrique, 45, 47
Rojas, Ricardo, 45
Roman Catholicism, 17-36, 49, 61, 65f., 69ff., 78, 110, 150, 202, 208f., 211, 213, 223ff., 239f.
Rosario, 139, 143, 146ff., 168, 171
Rosas, Juan Manuel de, 26, 46, 74

Salta, 96ff., 147, 149
Salvation Army, 75, 177, 191f.
San Martín, 82
Santiago del Estero, 105, 149f.
Saravia, José Manuel, 58, 60-65, 208, 217
Sarmiento, Domingo F., 43, 45f., 48, 74
Seventh Day Adventists, 75, 158-165, 180, 184, 191, 194, 204, 215, 218
Sewell, Samuel, 69
Shank, J. W., 123
Simons, Menno, 123
Sixtus IV, 25
Slavic Gospel Mission, 177

Smith, Oswald J., 154
Snead, A. C., 89
social change, 205
social involvement, 181, 201f., 205
social revolution, 29f., 49-54
South American Missionary Society, 177
Sowell, Sidney M., 166f.
Spain, 20, 23, 25f., 37
Spooner, George, 146
Stockwell, B. Foster, 137, 207
Stokes, Louis, 77, 79
Straubinger, John, 32
Svenska Fria Missionen, 83

theological dilution, 139, 181
"third force," 25, 179, 181
Thomson, James, 24, 70ff., 166
Thomson, John F., 74, 207
Toba, 73, 82f., 105, 125, 127ff., 134, 141, 188, 207
Torre, Charles, 145f., 154
Toynbee, Arnold J., 50, 52f.
Tucumán, 32, 70, 96f., 99, 103, 147f., 161, 170, 218

Union Seminary; see Facultad Evangélica de Teología
Unitarios, 48
United Evangelical Church, 83, 141, 129, 188, 191
urbanization, 31, 73, 92, 127, 140f., 171, 225
Uruguay, 31, 73, 92, 127, 140f., 171, 225

Varetto, J. C., 170, 173f., 207
Vatican Council II, 29f., 34, 36, 202
Venezuela, 225f.
Vergara, Ignacio, S. J., 15

Waldensians, 27, 73, 137, 177, 203
Waldo, Peter, 73
Welsh Protestants, 27, 40, 73, 75, 140, 166
Westphal, F. H., 159
White, Ellen G., 159, 161
Woods, Alice C., 76f.
World Council of Churches, 189ff., 204, 229